The Merriman Chronicles

Book Nine

The Canadian Mission

Copyright Information

The Merriman Chronicles - Book 9

The Canadian Mission

Copyright © 2025 by Robin Burnage

With the exception of certain well known historical figures, the characters in this book have no relation or resemblance to any person living or dead.

All rights reserved. This book and all "The Merriman Chronicles" are works of fiction. No part of this book may be reproduced or used in any manner without written permission of the copyright owner except for the use of quotations in a book review.

First edition August 2025

Book cover painting of HMS *Mercury* and USS *President*

by Colin M Baxter – Marine Artist

ISBN: 9798284885383 (paperback)

ISBN: 9798284885574 (hardcover)

www.merriman-chronicles.com

Books in the series

A Certain Threat

The Threat in the West Indies

The French Invasion

The Threat in the East

The Threat in the Baltic

The Threat in the Americas

The Threat in the Adriatic

The Threat in the Atlantic

The Canadian Mission

Related content

The Fateful Voyage

Notes on history and fiction

This latest novel in The Merriman Chronicles is set at the very start of the War of 1812—a conflict that pitted Britain against the young United States. Often viewed as a by-product of the wider Napoleonic Wars, it was fuelled by trade restrictions imposed by Britain and France in their struggle to undermine each other's economies, and exacerbated by slow communications, maritime tensions such as impressment, and divided American politics.

As with earlier volumes, the story draws on real events of the time, real people and ships, weaving them into a narrative intended to bring the age to life with drama, tension, and action. Writers of historical fiction often embellish situations, creating characters and episodes that blend with recorded history to explore the people and the period. This, and all the Merriman novels are no different. While many of the events are grounded in fact, others have been reimagined or adapted to serve the arc of the story. In keeping with the legacy of Roger Burnage, we've embraced what he fondly called "artistic verisimilitude"—a blend of authenticity and invention not intended to mislead, but to inform and entertain.

We hope this new chapter in the Merriman saga pays respectful tribute to the real people and events that inspired it. Every effort has been made to avoid glaring historical inaccuracies or distortions that might be construed as misrepresenting the truth or diminishing the importance of those involved. At the same time, we have sought to honour the tone and vision of the original author—preserving both the historical integrity of the period and the evolving legacy of the Merriman family.

Robin Burnage

Prologue

In darkness, they crossed from the Michigan Territory into Upper Canada. Hokolesqua knew these lands but not as well as Tecumseh, who seemed familiar with every road and track. The chieftain led the way north in silence. Some of the ten men with him had fought in the great battle and several carried wounds. Those who had arrived after the clash – like Tecumseh and Hokolesqua – might have escaped physical harm but they were equally preoccupied by recent events.

'He is angry,' said Agushawas, coming up alongside Hokolesqua on the narrow path. Agushawas was of the Odowa tribe. He had fought the American troops and was known to be an excellent shot with both musket and bow.

'What did you expect?' snapped Hokolesqua, doing his best to keep his voice down. 'Before we left, he told his brother not to be drawn into battle. Tenskawata ignored his advice. Now hundreds are dead, and Prophetstown is a pile of ash.'

He could still smell the smoke on his clothes. It was only three days since he had returned alongside Tecumseh to find the ruined settlement that had promised so much for the native peoples. What had begun as a small encampment outside the town had eventually housed several thousand from numerous tribes. Now they were scattered, traipsing back to forest refuges and their old grounds.

'Tenskawata is the prophet,' countered Agushawas. 'It was he who foresaw that we could expel the Children of the Evil Spirit. He believes that this first failure will one day lead to success.'

'We *all* hope for that. And perhaps in time it will come to pass. But it is a question of being realistic. His…rush of blood will set the confederacy back years.'

Agushawas was quiet for a moment. They walked on through the black trees, only the three-quarter moon above them lighting the way.

'He had no choice. The American Harrison brought a thousand soldiers. He was bound to attack us.'

'But Tenskawata struck first! Was he certain that Harrison was there to make war? And what did he tell you all? That he had cast spells to make our warriors invulnerable to bullets! How did that work out, Agushawas?'

Hokolesqua shook his head in disbelief. He thought of his young cousin, a relative of both Tenskawata and Tecumseh. Barely sixteen years old: shot between the eyes by an American marksman.

Hokolesqua had always valued Tecumseh's brother's ability to rally the tribes but the man's unshakable faith in his visions and magic had made him an unreliable ally. Now Tecumseh's worst fears had come true. Usually so energised and voluble, the leader had barely said a word since Prophetstown. They had halted only for rest and to reclaim the strongbox from its hiding place.

Agushawas again collected his thoughts before replying. 'I'll grant you that attacking first was a mistake. But the battle could have gone differently. We killed many of them.'

'Now was not the time. We must gather more tribes, more strength.'

'Tecumseh has been trying that for years. What of the Wyandot? The Menominee? They did not heed him.'

'And the fifteen other tribes that did?' answered Hokolesqua. 'He is our best hope.'

'I hope you are right,' said Agushawas. 'I have always trusted in both brothers. That is why I am here.'

Two days later, they reached Moraviantown. There was no permanent British fort, only a small detachment commanded by a captain who Tecumseh had dealt with before. The tribesmen arrived around midday and were directed to a house where the captain was currently billeted. He was being hosted by a German couple who refused to even allow the new arrivals to wait by the door.

As they stood in the street, many townsfolk gazed at them curiously. The air was thick with woodsmoke and the smells of cooking. At the far end of the street, a repeated metallic clanging sounded from a blacksmith. A passing fur trapper offered a cordial good morning to Tecumseh; he was well known among all peoples on both sides of the border.

Tall and straight-backed, Tecumseh's black hair reached down past his shoulders. As usual, he wore a soft red hat with a single eagle feather along with buckskin breeches, tunic and jacket.

The captain – a man named Taylor – was still buttoning his red coat when he emerged from his billet. Hokolesqua recalled that he and Tecumseh had first met when Taylor held a lesser rank. Several years earlier, he had been charged with escorting Tecumseh to a meeting with the British chief in Upper Canada: a man named Simcoe.

Taylor cast a curious eye at the new arrivals before offering his hand to their leader.

'Chief Tecumseh, I am glad to see you alive. Word arrived this morning of the battle. I did warn your people that Harrison was not to be trifled with.'

Tecumseh clearly did not want to reopen that particular wound.

'Is there somewhere private where we can speak?'

'Certainly. A moment.'

Taylor turned and spoke to his host, who remained in the doorway. After a brief conversation, the German shrugged and closed the door, his wife already hectoring him.

Captain Taylor waved away another redcoat who was hurrying down the street and led the tribesmen into a barn beside the house. Towards the rear were four horses in stalls; at the front was large work table. The tribesmen had two ponies with them, one carrying the strongbox, which had been roped to a saddle. Tecumseh asked Hokolesqua and another man to bring it over.

Taylor stood opposite Tecumseh, on the other side of the table.

'Your losses?'

'Fifty dead. As many more wounded.'

At that, Taylor frowned. 'Word from Detroit is that the Americans lost two hundred. Are you sure your brother wasn't victorious?'

'Far from it. Prophetstown is lost. The Americans wish to banish us from all the lands they have claimed. There can be no turning back now.'

'You said that before,' countered Taylor. 'After the Treaty of Fort Wayne.'

Instead of replying, Tecumseh pushed back the bolt that secured the strongbox and opened it. He delved into the straw used to protect the contents and retrieved a long package wrapped in hide. This he laid carefully beside the box. Opening the hide, he revealed a long wampum belt made of lines of hollow bead shells mounted on string. This one was coloured white in the middle and black at both ends.

'Is that what I think it is?' asked Captain Taylor.

Tecumseh nodded. 'After what you call the Seven Years War, this was presented by your chiefs to ours. A symbol of our alliance.'

Hokolesqua was not surprised by the exact clarity of what Tecumseh then said. He knew the chief would have memorised his words for this occasion and others to come.

'Captain Taylor, I ask you to convey myself, my party and this belt to Lieutenant-Governor Prevost, Captain-General and Governor-in-Chief of Upper and Lower Canada; and Commander of all His Majesty's Forces. Five decades after it was given, I return this belt as a symbol of the friendship and loyalty of the Fifteen Tribes. As chief of that confederacy, I now seek a new, permanent and binding alliance with Great Britain.'

Chapter One

The Calm Before the Storm

April rains had soaked Shelby Manor for much of the previous night and day. Taking the opportunity to get some fresh air, Captain Sir James Abel Merriman left his wife and children to their games of whist and pharaoh and embarked upon a walk around the grounds. Lady Arthur's gamekeeper described a three-mile route to the southern edge of the estate and back, which he followed at some speed. He passed cattle, sheep, even a noisy peacock.

Not for the first time in his life, Merriman felt tremendous gratitude to his wife. Helen – and indeed the children – had done an excellent job of keeping him occupied since they'd arrived in Hampshire. He had tried not to dwell on the upcoming court martial, spending only the requisite time with his legal counsel and reviewing his notes on the loss of HMS *Thunder* during the battle with the French warship *Hercule* the previous year.

Despite the loss, Merriman had taken *Hercule;* then he and his crew had sailed her back to England. It had been a terribly difficult journey, burdened as they were by hundreds of French captives. It wasn't until they'd reached the Portuguese coast that he'd been able to offload some of them and bring on much-needed provisions. The weather had then closed in nastily and it wasn't until the first day of October that the great French ship docked in Plymouth, drawing a crowd of onlookers.

The court martial was entirely expected; virtually guaranteed given the loss of an immensely valuable (and recently refitted) ship-of-the-line. Merriman was anxious to get it over and done with and was immensely frustrated that it had been so delayed. Until it was completed, he was suspended as an officer of the Navy. The delay was partly due to the demands of war upon the Admiralty, as well as a shortage of the lawyers and fellow officers who would decide his fate. But now the time had at last arrived, and the trial was to begin the following day. At dawn, he would take a carriage and travel the eight miles from Shelby Manor to Portsmouth.

The widowed Lady Arthur was an old friend of Sir Laurence Grahame, Merriman's long-time ally and compatriot. He lived close by and it was he who'd arranged their stay at the beautiful estate. Merriman was very grateful to him too. Had he stayed in Portsmouth itself, he would have been inundated by support from fellow Navy men past and present, which would bring its own kind of pressure. The captain knew from the letters he'd received that most felt he would escape sanction but it was difficult to be sure.

Court martials could be unpredictable and elements of his conduct during the battle had been far from conventional. Only two years earlier, the controversial court martial of Admiral, Lord Gambier at the Battle of the Basque Roads had exposed bias, rivalry and division amongst senior commanders of the Admiralty. It had also demonstrated how different officers could perceive naval engagements in different ways. Merriman knew only that he would be judged by five fellow captains: in the morning he would discover their names.

He walked on across the rather beautiful parkland at one side of Shelby Manor, spotting the pale green leaves of field maples and hornbeams. On the last stretch of his work, he passed some hawthorns and an early display of their small white blooms. He and Helen had already been on several walks and his wife had been enraptured by the gardens, astonished that Lady Arthur employed no less than a dozen men to maintain them. Even so, they all longed for their home at Burton Manor. Merriman hoped they would be there soon, because then Helen,

Robert and Mary-Anne could resume normal life. He would be free from the cloud that had hung over him since his return.

Shelby Manor was so large that he couldn't remember exactly which door on the eastern side of the huge structure he had left through. As he stood there, one of the staff exited and hurried towards him. All the male house servants wore smart black attire and the gleam on their buttons and shoes was the equal of any marine.

'Captain Sir James?'

'Just captain is fine, thank you.'

'Very well, sir. I was bringing this to the east wing when I saw you outside. Apparently, there was some delay with the post.'

The servant – whose name Merriman could not recall – handed him a letter. Thanking him, Merriman opened it and smiled when he realised the identity of the sender. Sitting down on a nearby bench, he began to read, smiling again at the small, neat writing he had reviewed on many a logbook.

Alfred Shrigley, the naval officer he had known since Shrigley's days as a midshipman, now captained his own vessel. Following their last voyage – and due largely to Merriman's influence and patronage – Shrigley had been promoted to the rank of commander. In Merriman's mind, this was long overdue and, in truth, Shrigley's determination to stay as his first lieutenant had held him back. With the war with France now in its ninth year, the Admiralty had more need for accomplished officers than ever.

Once they had returned to England and Shrigley had been reunited with his wife and newborn son, Merriman had waited a few weeks, then visited them at their home in the Hampshire village of Droxford. Shrigley had been desperately worried about his precious wife throughout their perilous voyage and Merriman and Helen had been thrilled to find a scene of domestic bliss. However, unless he planned to let his career stagnate, it was essential that Shrigley petition for his own command, or risk appearing to lack ambition.

It appeared that his moment had come. After a nervous few weeks, Shrigley had been awarded his first commission and now Merriman could read the details. Commander Shrigley had taken charge of the Speedy class brig-sloop *Romulus,* in the port of Plymouth. He was writing in the days before the ship's departure: part of a convoy protecting merchantmen bound for Halifax, Nova Scotia. Rising tensions with the United States over various issues made war there more likely and the threat remained from French raiders on this side of the Atlantic.

Shrigley pronounced himself excited but nervous at his first assignment. Had there been time to write back, Merriman would have told him that he had no doubt he would succeed. If pressed, he might not have placed Shrigley in the bracket of "natural sailor" but the man had learned so much and now possessed a wealth of experience and knowledge. Perhaps a tad quiet and reserved for a captain, Shrigley would find his way; of that Merriman was sure. As he knew all too well, the great cabin could be the loneliest of places. Yet loyal, earnest, hardworking lieutenants like Shrigley had made his job easier. He hoped his friend would enjoy such support.

*

Lady Arthur did not dine with the Merrimans that night because she was not feeling well. Now in her eightieth year, she had been widowed a decade earlier and presided over the great house and sprawling estate ever since. She had no children and it seemed to the guests that the staff were her family. The housekeeper, Mrs Trescothick, assured them that their hostess was suffering only with a mild headache.

Once again, the staff had prepared a fine meal. First came vegetable soup and, while they ate, young Mary-Anne began talking about how much larger the staff at Shelby Manor was than their few employees at Burton. Merriman and Helen had never told the children that he was executor (and indeed beneficiary) of the enormous inheritance of Lord Stevenage, his deceased mentor and friend. It wasn't sufficient to purchase a property on the scale of Shelby Manor but could have funded an impressive estate. However, Merriman and Helen saw no need to use the money for themselves; he had done well from a captain's wage and prize money over the years, while they had both inherited from their parents.

Due to various legal challenges from a distant relative in Ireland, Merriman's lawyers had still been unable to free up the Stevenage money, which he had earmarked for the Marine Society Fund, who did excellent work assisting up and coming sailors from poorer backgrounds. Indeed, Alfred Shrigley had been a recipient twenty years earlier.

Once Mary-Anne had finished speaking, young Robert for once talked about something other than his intention to join the navy. During Merriman's time away, he had fallen in with another boy whose father was a first lieutenant and the two had decided that they would become midshipmen at the earliest opportunity. Needless to say, the long-suffering Helen was rather dismayed by this idea. Merriman felt a mixture of pride and concern; the latter being largely based on consideration for his wife.

As Robert continued to natter on about the estate's many animals, Merriman at last realised what was going on: Helen had told them not to talk about the court martial, perhaps even suggested that they distract their father with other subjects. No doubt if he had spent more time at home and less at sea, he would have realised their game sooner. It was sweet of them.

After Mary-Anne pronounced that the vegetable soup was the best she'd ever tasted, the servants removed their bowls and began to serve the main course: braised beef. Offered yet more of a superb claret, Merriman was reminded by his wife that he'd already drunk two large glasses. He refused a third, knowing the importance of keeping a clear head the following day. He always tried not to get drunk in front of his wife and children and sometimes wondered what Helen would make of some of the excessive imbibing that occasionally occurred aboard ship.

'There was a letter for you,' she said as they began to tuck into their beef. 'Came late.'

'Yes indeed. Shrigley.' Merriman felt himself smile. 'He departs imminently from Plymouth. Part of a convoy bound for Canada. Little brig-sloop. The *Romulus*. A well-deserved first command.'

Robert's eyes widened with enthusiasm. 'His own sloop! Lucky Shrigley.'

'At least he's not headed straight into action,' said Helen.

'I wouldn't be so sure,' replied Merriman. 'There have been some French raids on the approaches of late. Then there's the Americans.'

'I heard the grooms talking about America,' said Robert before spearing a lump of beef with his fork. 'They've thrown their lot in with Boney, haven't they, father?'

'It's a little more complicated than that,' replied Merriman. 'Some American merchantmen wish to trade with the French but that's not the only reason for poor relations. The Americans are always expanding their territory – much like we have, I suppose – and they have their eyes on Canada.'

'They know we're busy with the French,' said Robert. 'Taking advantage, the sneaky swine.'

'Possibly. Not all Americans are against us.'

'The rebellious spirit is found across the world,' said Helen. 'Some argue that the French are responsible but the Americans sought their own path first. It is often the way. Why, we did it here against the Romans.'

'Boudicca!' announced Mary-Jane. 'A woman warrior! Imagine that.'

'Fighting is for men,' contended Robert.

'Boudicca rode a chariot and slaughtered the Romans, Robbie. You've read the history books same as I have.'

Merriman noted that Helen added nothing more. Presumably one child coveting a military career was enough for the moment.

He finished his beef, then leaned back in his chair, feeling quite full and glad that his nerves hadn't affected his appetite. 'The Americans have their factions, their parties, as do we. In naval circles, it is impressment that has caused the most consternation.'

'We only take back our English sailors from American ships though,' stated Robert.

'Why are English sailors on American ships in the first place?' added Mary-Anne.

Helen sighed. Merriman smiled at her; he didn't mind answering these questions and at least they weren't discussing the court martial.

'Some go across the Atlantic and take positions on American ships because the pay is better. Then there are some men whose nationality is hard to establish. To be honest, when we captains need hands, we tend not to ask too many questions and ignore answers we don't like. And the Navy needs every last man we can find to sail our ships.'

'Well, I think they've got quite a nerve,' exclaimed Robert. 'Most of them are British too – if you go back far enough.'

'Not sure that's quite how they see it,' replied his father.

'And aren't there lots of French in Canada?' added Helen.

'There are,' said Merriman as the servants cleared their dinner plates.

'What's for pudding?' asked Robert.

'Plum duff, young sir,' answered one of the maids with a smile.

'Ooh, yum!' exclaimed Robert.

Before it could be served, however, one of the footmen hurried in. 'Sorry to disturb your dinner, captain, but there's a visitor for you. Sir Laurence Grahame.'

Though the temperature was rising after the rain, April in the draughty manor house was quite chilly. The staff had prepared a drawing room for the guests' use and a pleasant warmth emanated from the fireplace as Merriman and Sir Laurence entered. Grahame had been to visit the family and Lady Arthur on the day of their arrival and so Merriman was rather intrigued by his reappearance. Intrigued and concerned; in his experience, an unexpected visit from the Treasury man rarely boded well.

The old friends sat opposite each other before the fire, Sir Laurence folding his slender frame into an armchair. Merriman wasn't sure of his exact age but his hawkish face seemed to grow more lined every time he saw him.

'By God, I have had enough of rattling carriages and muddy roads.'

'You are supposed to have retired, Sir Laurence. And you mentioned another trip to London? Weren't you supposed to be spending more time in your garden?'

Grahame brushed something off one of his jacket buttons and shook his head. 'Somehow, I cannot drag myself free of my former profession. It's a quiet day when I receive less than ten pieces of correspondence.'

Sir Laurence had been one of the Treasury's best-connected, most able, and most *ruthless* agents for virtually the entirety of the war. It was no surprise to Merriman that all his hundreds of acquaintances spread across every part of government and the military continued to seek his advice.

'Much talk of America at dinner,' he said. 'Anything new?'

'The augurs are not good. Apparently, some earthquake in Ohio had got the God-fearing types believing that the end times are near. President Madison seems to be falling for French tricks, imagining there's more to be made through commerce with them then us. War remains possible…then again, it has for many years.'

'Shrigley has departed for Canada,' said Merriman. 'Convoy.'

Sir Laurence nodded and gazed at the flames for a time. 'How are you faring, James?'

'As good as can be, I suppose. Thank you again for arranging this. Lady Arthur has been exceptionally kind.'

'I was exceptionally kind to her husband,' said Grahame with a knowing look.

'Frankly, I just want to get on with it,' continued Merriman. 'Have my say.'

'Of course. And I still believe that you will be justly treated. However, I have travelled this evening to make you aware of an additional complication.'

'I see.' No matter how many times Merriman heard momentous news from Sir Laurence, he could rarely predict what it might be.

'I mentioned the post I receive on a daily basis. Even more arrives at my old desk at the Treasury. My replacement passes on anything directed to me. Much of it is anonymous. Tip offs, hints, suggestions. It generally regards intelligence, espionage, corruption and so on. Some is useful, some is designed simply to damage a foe, some is probably disinformation that emanates from Paris. This week I received one such anonymous message. A short message – rather vague. Untraceable. It suggested that you and I pay special attention to the members of the court martial panel. It suggested that we should be wary of…interference.'

Merriman let his eyes close, recalling his earlier thoughts about the Gambier case. 'That's all we know?'

'As I said, very short and very vague. But I am appreciative of our mysterious ally. Forewarned is forearmed. Please give some thought to anyone who might have an axe to grind against you.'

'I can think of plenty…but most are French.'

'I am telling you because I cannot attend the court martial without arousing suspicion. You must observe your five peers, see if you can identify which of them might have it in for you. For my part, once we have the five names, I will engage what resources I still possess to discover more.'

'Court martials seldom last more than two weeks. Especially not in the current circumstances.'

'Time is of the essence then. I will send a man down to Portsmouth to keep me apprised. He will not make himself known to you unless it becomes necessary.'

'Very well. Thank you, Sir Laurence.'

'I am sorry not to bring better news, James. Let us trust that good will prevail. We have endured far worse, have we not?'

Chapter Two

The Court Martial

HMS *Gladiator* had never left port. Launched thirty years earlier, she had been originally used as a convalescent ship. Despite her uneventful career, the fifth-rater had also been a flagship and enjoyed a share of prize money. Due to her static history, she was often used for court martials. The current commander was a Captain Thomas Dutton and it was one of his officers, a Lieutenant Poole, who welcomed Merriman aboard.

Proceedings were to begin at ten o'clock. As the accused, Merriman was not to enter until the judge-advocate, the officers of the panel and the witnesses were present. His stomach hollow with nerves, Merriman had paced the dock for a time with his legal counsel, an experienced man named Debbage. Out in the harbour, a frigate had just raised its anchor and the captain felt a pang of envy for whoever was in command.

'Fine day,' said Poole as he personally conveyed Merriman below. He was quite right; the sun had been shining all morning and it felt more like June than April.

'Unusual duty you have here,' said Merriman, removing his hat as they passed a pair of marines.

'Certainly,' said Poole. 'Hardly the most glorious but I've noted that most officers appreciate court martials being conducted aboard ship. I've heard some say they felt it brought them luck.'

'I suppose that rather depends on the outcome.'

Poole halted outside the great cabin and responded with a thin smile. 'I'll leave you in the hands of Provost-marshal Charles, captain.'

'Thank you.'

Waiting outside the great cabin, Charles was a tall, moustachioed fellow who nodded politely. 'Captain Merriman, the court is ready. If you please.'

The provost-marshal gestured to the doorway. Merriman adjusted his collar, which for some reason seemed unusually tight. Hat in hand, he strode into the middle of the cabin and halted at the spot indicated by Charles. In front of him, at the rear of the cabin, were two tables, both covered with green felt. The table to the left was occupied by the five members of the panel, imposing in their blue and gold. The other, to his right, was occupied by the judge-advocate: a civilian who was nonetheless an expert in naval law. He was assisted by two clerks. The president of the court occupied a table on the right side of the cabin, along with the recorder and other administrators. To the left were the witnesses; some familiar faces from HMS *Thunder*: Lieutenants Essex and Jones plus Bosun Brockle.

As commander of the *Gladiator*, Captain Dutton also acted as president of the court. It was he that stood and began the session, identifying Merriman and the charges against him. It was at this point that Merriman surrendered his sword, a traditional process that symbolised his suspension from duty. When Provost-marshal Charles took it from him, Merriman comforted himself with the thought that he possessed several others.

Dutton then explained the reason for the delay. Though Plymouth was an exceptionally busy port, most captains were involved in wartime operations or preparing for departure; after all, their reputations were earned while afloat, not in courtrooms. As Dutton spoke, Merriman stood with hands clasped behind him, doing his utmost to appear calm and dispassionate. He had been through this process before – most men of his age and rank had – and he understood it well. Yet he couldn't help feeling aggrieved that, after all he'd done and sacrificed for his country, he was being made to feel like a criminal. Forcing these thoughts aside, he inspected the panel.

Two of the men he had met. Captain Edgar Fellowes had been part of the fleet despatched to the Adriatic three years earlier. Captain James Crabbe was only a year or two older than Merriman and the pair had run into each other on and off since the first days of the war. Crabbe hailed from Bristol and the pair had dined together with their wives half a dozen times, though not recently. Merriman had every reason to think he would be sympathetic.

Captain Dutton then introduced the judge-advocate, who was named Popham. He appeared very aged; frail of frame and with a frown etched on his face. His two clerks were at least three decades younger and were busily placing papers in front of their superior.

Dutton then moved onto the panel and Merriman learned more about the other three who would decide his fate. One was a Vice Admiral Percy, who was considerably older than the other four. Merriman knew the name but nothing else. The last pair were two captains named Wyborne and Gillespie. Merriman considered the intelligence offered by Sir Laurence Grahame and wondered if and when it would become apparent that one or more members of the panel might be prejudiced against him.

Merriman was first to give his oath on the Bible, followed by the panel-members and the judge-advocate. Dutton then read out the usual "letter of complaint":

'On the 9th of June, in the year of our Lord eighteen hundred and eleven, during a naval engagement with the French vessel, *Hercule*, approximately one hundred miles north-west of the Orange River on the west coast of Africa, Captain Sir James Merriman presided over the loss of His Majesty's Ship *Thunder*. This court martial seeks to establish the degree to which Captain Merriman is responsible for that loss, in which case he may be found guilty of reckless conduct. Under naval law, any person found to have, by design or negligence, caused any ship of His Majesty to be lost, may suffer imprisonment or any such punishment subsequently decided by the court.'

Captain Dutton then surprised all present by announcing that – on direct orders from The Admiralty – the court-martial would be concluded within just three days, citing again the limited availability of the officers as the reason. Apparently, Captains Fellowes and Wyborne were due to leave port within a week. Merriman had been told by Debbage to expect a duration of between five and ten days. He was glad it would only be three; as long as all was done fairly.

With the commencement of the court martial, the witnesses were dismissed before they were to be questioned independently. Careful to avoid the gaze of his faithful officers and friends, Merriman withdrew to the small table close to the door where he and his counsel were stationed. While Dutton spoke to Judge Popham, Debbage turned to the side, covering his mouth with his hand.

'How many of the panel do you know, captain?'

'Two.'

Debbage nodded at this, then began arranging his papers. The lawyer had been recommended to Merriman by two trusted friends in Portsmouth. He was only twenty-nine years but seemed a bright and diligent character. Merriman had spent two whole days at Debbage's office in the city, going over the battle with *Hercule* and likely points of contention. The lawyer had successfully defended three other captains who had lost their ships but remarked early on that this was an unusual case: Merriman had simultaneously captured a ship-of-the-line while losing his own.

The first witness was Lieutenant Jones, Merriman's second officer aboard *Thunder*. Merriman had known him for some years and the man had proved himself again to be competent and trustworthy during the long journey south along the African coast before the confrontation with their French nemesis. Five years older than Alfred Shrigley, Jones often proudly stated that second lieutenant was the limit of his ambition after two decades at sea. Known to all for his excellent violin-playing, he was a kind fellow who did not relish combat like some but could be relied upon in a crisis. As he stood facing the rear of the cabin, Merriman noticed for the first time that

Jones' brown hair was thinning at the crown. As his cross-examination would take some time, a table and chair were provided by the two subordinates of the provost-marshal.

As the senior officer of the panel, Vice-Admiral Percy led the way, inviting Jones to summarise the journey of the *Thunder* before focusing on the concluding battle. Like those he faced, Jones had his notes with him, though he referred to them only to clarify dates. He was asked briefly about his previous service with Merriman and the refitting of the *Thunder* as well as his fellow officers.

From Portsmouth, the ship had sailed south, only halting when it reached a certain spot on the Portuguese coast. Merriman found himself growing nervous at this point, unsure what Jones might say and unaware of what the panel already knew.

'For the benefit of the court,' said Vice-Admiral Percy, 'please explain this diversion and describe what occurred.'

'A small town called Sao Jacinto. The captain was supposed to meet an agent by the name of Charles Moreau. I believe he was in possession of important information regarding the war in the Peninsula. The captain did not share that information with us, nor did we ask. He went ashore with our captain of marines, Cary, as well as two marines and a Portuguese crewman. The captain and his party left before dawn and returned in late morning, accompanied by Mr. Moreau.'

Hearing this, Captain Fellowes made his first contribution. 'I am aware that Captain Merriman has a reputation for taking matters into his own hands but did it not seem odd to you, that he went ashore personally – placing himself at risk?'

Merriman did not particularly begrudge Fellowes' question. It was an entirely reasonable point.

'Sir, as I recall, First Lieutenant Shrigley offered to go in his place. I was not party to the captain's explanation of why he went himself. However, as you say, the captain is not averse to taking command on land as well as sea. Also, this was clearly a sensitive matter and I gather he has known Charles Moreau for many years.'

Percy frowned. 'And what do we know about this Moreau character?'

At this, the elderly Judge Popham was spurred into action by one of his clerks.

'The Treasury was not initially very forthcoming on this matter. Neither were they keen to supply information regarding Moreau. They did confirm, however, that Sir Laurence Grahame, who is now retired, personally requested that Merriman fetch the agent from Portuguese soil.'

Popham picked up a piece of paper. 'We have this morning, in response to my request, received this brief statement from Sir Samuel Ogilvy of the Treasury. "In making the request to Captain Merriman, Sir Laurence was acting independently. However, the Treasury can confirm that the information obtained from the agent Charles Moreau was of the utmost importance and passed immediately to the Army Intelligence Department."'

Popham nodded to another page brandished by one of his clerks. The younger man read it.

'Sir Samuel also included a copy of a letter from one Colonel Rose, formerly of Lord Wellesley's staff, thanking the Treasury and the Navy for the information, which was indeed very significant and useful.'

Vice-Admiral Percy addressed the other members of the panel. 'I've known Samuel Ogilvy for many years. We can take his word as gospel.'

Possibly with the need for haste in mind, Percy immediately pressed Lieutenant Jones to continue his account. Jones then explained how the *Thunder* sought a ship heading north so that Moreau (and his information) could be swiftly conveyed back to England. Captain Fellowes asked if the Admiralty had known that several days were lost for this Treasury mission. Jones could of course not comment and the judge said that they had no information regarding that point.

Merriman was beginning to wish Captain Fellowes was a little less curious. Though the diversion to Portugal had been successful, it did demonstrate some degree of disobedience; his original orders had called for the capture or destruction of the *Hercule* with all due haste.

Jones went on to describe how they soon found a friendly vessel heading north and, with Moreau offloaded, continued south. Passing the Cape Verde Islands, *Thunder* had encountered a vessel named *Arrow* of the West African Squadron and assisted a Captain Lukin with capturing a slave ship.

After a few more questions from the panel, Jones continued, iterating how *Thunder* had given valuable powder and shot to the commander of a besieged Fort James: an isolated British facility on the perilous Gold Coast. Though Jones made it clear that the commander had been desperate for help, the members of the panel questioned why the ship had been repeatedly distracted from its main mission. Jones answered that there was a good case for every intervention but Captain Gillespie countered that every lost hour or day endangered the crucial shipping that *Thunder* had been tasked to protect by defeating the *Hercule*. Jones explained that they had at every turn sought intelligence regarding the location of their enemy.

Merriman realised that an impression was building of some questionable decision-making but he reassured himself with the knowledge that he could defend every choice. He was after all, dealing with men who had commanded ships themselves: they knew the difficulty of such decisions and that no man got every one right.

Lieutenant Jones then described the harrowing few days in which the *Thunder* had been embayed after assisting a British vessel being pursued by pirates. The brief clash had been followed by a gale that had pushed the ship into a bay from which there was no easy escape. Only by putting out her anchors and using her boats had *Thunder* avoided disaster. The loyal Jones was full of praise for Merriman; so much so that Judge Popham reminded him not to offer an opinion unless asked.

The members of their panel continued their questioning. Captain Wyborne in particular voiced the view that joining battle so close to the coast with an onshore wind had been questionable. Captain Crabbe came to Merriman's defence, arguing that – in directly protecting British shipping – he was doing what most captains would do.

As midday approached, Lieutenant Jones at last reached the events leading up to the battle with *Hercule*; how *Thunder* initially pursued the French vessel down the African coast before losing her in darkness. At dawn the following day, the *Hercule* sailed straight for the *Thunder* with the sun at her stern. Jones explained how there was no particular wind advantage for either vessel. Here he was questioned by the panel and eventually had to admit that *Thunder* was slightly upwind and that Merriman could have manoeuvred to retain this advantage.

Despite the grave look on Debbage's face, Merriman was not overly concerned; he knew exactly why he had made that choice. His crew had pursued the *Hercule* and Captain Patrice Jourdan for weeks. They were well-drilled but tiring. Given the French captain's reputation for crafty tricks, Merriman thought he might not do much better than a straight clash in fair weather.

Jones then iterated how the British and French vessels had passed each other at one hundred and fifty yards and exchanged broadsides. Though some damage was done to *Hercule*, *Thunder* fared much worse, losing four guns and suffering over twenty casualties. The ships had then gone through the wind and exchanged fire once more. Again, the larger ship had sustained some damage but the *Thunder* lost more guns and more men.

Jones admitted that he had not been present to hear the captain's reasoning but swiftly understood that his plan was to close with the French ship because they would not prevail at range. Jones recalled the captain ordering Captain Cary to ready his marines and that the larboard batteries were loaded with canister shot, the guns to be adjusted for close-range fire. He also explained that the captain had many sailors armed with cutlasses, ready to support the marines in boarding the *Hercule*.

At this point, Judge Popham allowed the panel some questions. Vice-Admiral Percy again took the lead, asking if any of the officers had opposed the decision. Jones remarked that he heard none directly but was later made aware that Bosun Brockle had been reprimanded by Merriman for doing just that.

'How do you know this if you weren't present?' asked Crabbe.

'It was Brockle himself who told me, sir,' replied Jones. 'Some days after the battle, as we sailed north on *Hercule*. He had thought we should not resort to an attempted boarding so early. I believe Brockle was embarrassed that he had challenged the captain. He felt he should have had more trust in him.'

'And what did *you* think of the decision?' asked Captain Wyborne.

'I'll admit it was a surprise. Then again, we can usually rely on superior gunnery prevailing but that was not so in this case. The captain had evidently seen enough from the results of the first two passes.'

'These sailors with weapons who were to support the marines,' said Captain Gillespie, leaning back in his chair. 'Who were they precisely?'

'Men from the starboard gundecks, sir,' answered Jones. 'And some others too. Only those at the larboard guns were to remain at their posts in order to fire the canister shot.'

'The starboard side of the decks was empty then? By the time of contact and then boarding?'

'I couldn't say, precisely, but there wouldn't have been many sailors there.'

As there were no further questions, Judge Popham prompted Jones to continue.

'We turned in before either ship fired their third volley. Our bow struck them amidships at about forty-five degrees. The rigging was tangled quickly. It was quite obvious to me that the French were surprised. The marines were up to the gunwales in short order and got their hooks over. The larboard battery fired the langridge.'

As he spoke, Jones continued to consult his notes. 'The marines secured ladders and Captain Cary led the bulk of them onto the *Hercule*. There was a good deal of musket fire and the marines also threw grenades. Cary got several dozen men across within a minute or two, I believe.'

At this point, Captain Gillespie asked to intervene. 'You *believe*?'

'I was below with Lieutenant Essex. Following the third volley from the *Hercule*, we suffered considerable damage. Some powder had exploded, accounting for at least two guns. With the ships being so close, some guns on both sides could not be brought to bear but I knew a few more volleys might do serious harm. Leaving Essex in charge, I went on deck to inform the captain. He then decided to join the boarding party and ordered me to accompany him.'

Vice-Admiral Percy leaned forward onto the table and spoke up. 'Did the captain explain his reasoning at the time or afterward?'

'No, sir. I assume he realised we didn't have long. And I imagine he wanted to lead personally in order to encourage the men. I was ahead of the captain and I'm ashamed to admit that I fell from the ladder while crossing. I found myself in the water and had to swim around the bow. It took me some time to make my way around to the starboard side and I eventually climbed up the nets. My best guess is that perhaps ten minutes had passed by then. I am aware of at least two more volleys from the *Hercule* but, at some point, they ceased. I assume that the French crews were directed on deck to repel our boarders.'

Judge Popham spoke up. 'Perhaps it is time to focus on the crucial matter of the fire in and above the spirit room.'

'Yes, sir. Well, I can attest that it was well alight by then because I had to swim around it. Burning timbers were falling into the water from the starboard side. From what I heard, it had been started by a ball igniting the alcohol. There were also two more holes on the larboard side: one towards the bow, one on the beam. The captain put men in a boat as well as the crew in the spirit room. I should say it took another five minutes at least to extinguish the flames.'

Merriman found himself back aboard the ship, reliving the terrible moment when he realised *Thunder* couldn't be saved.

'The French surrendered at around half-past eleven,' continued Jones. 'I recall one of the midshipmen entering it in the logbook. The ships were then lashed together. I thought we had a chance and indeed the hole at the bow was repaired. However, soon after the surrender, we were hit by bad weather which made both vessels roll. All I spoke to agree that this is what did for the *Thunder*. The ingress of water was simply too much. By three o'clock she was listing badly.'

Captain Gillespie took his turn again. 'The hole from the spirit room fire was the largest of the three by some distance, correct, lieutenant?'

'It was, sir. More than ten feet, I believe.'

'As we know from your own testimony, initially at least, there would not have been many present on that side of the vessel. It's possible that the fire burned untended for some time, is it not?'

'I couldn't say, sir, as I don't know precisely when it was discovered.'

Vice-Admiral Percy asked if Jones thought the ship could have been saved if it hadn't been attached to the *Hercule*. Jones answered in the negative but Captain Fellows disagreed and a lengthy discussion ensued amongst the members of the panel.

By the time it concluded, Judge Popham had decided it was time to adjourn for luncheon. At the order of the president of the court, the provost-marshal entered the great cabin and Merriman was escorted outside.

Once back on the dock, he waited for Debbage. It was a great relief to be out in the fresh air and sunshine.

The lawyer stepped onto the dock and joined him. 'What do you think, captain?'

'Largely as expected, I suppose.' Merriman had not yet formed an opinion regarding who on the panel might possess malign intent. Only Crabbe had been entirely in his favour. It was, after all, the job of his fellow captains to interrogate the witnesses.

'I agree.'

The lawyer had already explained that the officers and judges would be provided with food aboard the *Gladiator*.

'I know a quiet hostelry nearby,' said Debbage, 'if you are in need of refreshment.'

'I am not. In fact, I shall take a walk.'

'Very well. I shall meet you back here at one o'clock.'

Merriman did not go far. He walked along the dock until he reached a slipway where a dozen sailors were unloading a boat. From the looks of it, they were bringing off bundles of blankets and sheets. In command was a squeaky-voiced midshipman who could not have been more than fifteen. The youth reminded Merriman of a young Shrigley and he thought of his former first officer, who would now be at sea, heading west. He wished he was with him.

Once all had returned to the great cabin, Jones concluded his account, describing how the crew continued past three o'clock on that fateful day to effect repairs and pump the bilges. Sailing Master Henderson had reported eight feet of water in the well and, shortly afterward, Bosun Brockle admitted defeat in the spirit room.

'It was then that Captain Merriman gathered myself and First Lieutenant Shrigley. Essex was busy elsewhere and Smythe we lost in the assault. The captain thought we might have had a chance with a calm sea and hours of daylight ahead. We had a tot of rum and he asked if we had any ideas for saving the ship. We did not. The crew were on deck and were then sent over to the *Hercule*. Shrigley and I searched the ship for stragglers but we could not access the lower decks. *Thunder* was listing heavily. I believe it was a quarter to four when the captain came aboard. We watched the old girl go down. Everyone was very low, of course. But I told the captain we'd stopped the *Hercule*, defeated Jourdan.'

'Steady, lieutenant,' advised Judge Popham, 'you've been told about simply stating the facts.'

'And we protected the merchantmen,' added Jones, showing a boldness not normally in keeping with his character. 'Thanks to Captain Merriman, we completed our mission.'

Chapter Three

An Unexpected Twist

The next morning, Merriman took breakfast with Helen and the children at Shelby Manor. He still didn't have much appetite but, at his wife's urging, he ate a little bread and ham with his coffee. Though there was no sign of Lady Arthur, she had come down after dinner the previous evening to offer Merriman some words of support. He and Helen again thanked her for her hospitality and Mary-Anne presented their host with a bouquet she'd made with the maids. Before departing for bed, Lady Arthur asked if there had been any more word from Sir Laurence. There had not, nor was there any morning post for Merriman.

'Who is telling their story today, Pa?' asked Mary-Anne.

'They're not telling a story!' insisted Robert. 'They are *giving evidence*. Isn't that right, Pa?'

'That's right. Well, Lieutenant Essex must finish his account and then Bosun Brockle and finally my character witness, Admiral Edwards.'

Essex, by nature a taciturn character, had been rather blunt and short with his descriptions, which had the result of slowing proceedings because he had to be pressed at every turn. Though Merriman mentioned nothing to Helen, he and Debbage were becoming concerned by the attitudes of both Captain Gillespie and Captain Fellowes. Fellowes had spent half an hour grilling Essex on Merriman's general decision-making while Gillespie seemed fixated on the choice to close with *Hercule* and board. Merriman could hardly blame him for that – it was the crux of the matter, after all – but he was alarmed that both men seemed be erring in one direction. Could one – or both – be conducting the "interference" that Grahame had mentioned? And if so, why?

Upon leaving Shelby Manor in a carriage borrowed from Lady Arthur and manned by her steward, he passed the mail-coach heading in the opposite direction. Hailing the driver, he was disappointed to find they had nothing for him. Merriman had no doubt that Grahame was pursuing the matter but – with the court martial to conclude within three days – he had no time to spare.

*

Once again last into the great cabin with Mr. Debbage, Merriman noted the five panel members deep in discussion as he took his place. While Crabbe still seemed supportive, Merriman again searched his memories for his brief time serving with Fellowes in the Adriatic. Was there something he'd missed? Some forgotten sleight or dispute? Even if there had been something, surely Fellowes wouldn't have held a grudge for so long? Seeing his five fellow officers talking to one other reminded him that – while each would form their own opinion – they were all open to influence. If two were against him, and they convinced a third to join them, he was in serious trouble.

The president of the court again got matters under way and Lieutenant Essex took up his account. The god-fearing northerner continued to give short, straightforward answers and seemed especially diligent in not offering opinion unless asked directly. At the conclusion of his narrative, however, he was asked by Vice-Admiral Percy if he had been surprised by Merriman's decision to force close action with the *Hercule*.

'I was surprised, sir, yes.'

'Why?'

'I have not seen such a manoeuvre or heard of it. I had assumed we would stand off and exchange volleys. It struck me that this was a tactic a smaller vessel, such as a frigate, might use.'

Hardly a surprise, thought Merriman. Essex was the least experienced of his four lieutenants aboard *Thunder*.

Captain Gillespie was next to ask a question. 'For the sake of clarity, you have previously stated that, before the French surrender, *Thunder* suffered at least four volleys from the *Hercule* at point-blank range.'

'Yes, sir.'

'And, in your opinion, those volleys caused the damage that ultimately resulted in the loss of the vessel?'

'Yes, sir.'

Gillespie simply nodded at that. 'No more questions for now.'

Before the next witness could be called, Debbage asked for a brief moment with his client, which Judge Popham allowed. Seeing Bosun Brockle waiting outside, Merriman studiously ignored him and followed Debbage to a shadowy storeroom.

'This Gillespie is like a dog with a bone,' whispered the lawyer. 'He has shown us more of his cards today. I think we must assume we have at least one opponent.'

'I agree. Mr. Debbage, I wanted to see how we fared yesterday but you should know that I have received some intelligence regarding the panel. It has been suggested by an anonymous source that we may face malign interference from one or more of them.'

Debbage visibly blanched. 'Well we have the first of them in Gillespie. And what of Fellowes, captain? Did anything spring to mind?'

'No. I've been unable to think of any reason for him to oppose me. It may be that he's simply trying to be thorough.'

'Possible but with Gillespie now appearing downright hostile, if Fellowes sides with him and one more can be persuaded…'

Merriman tapped a fist lightly against a nearby bulkhead though he felt more like smashing it to pieces. 'I'd expected some criticism but this is most unfair. How many merchantmen have cleared the Cape since I stopped Jourdan?'

Merriman felt a pang of guilt at that. It was hardly as if he'd achieved it alone. Many of his sailors had given their lives to defeat the French raider.

'Captain, frustration will not advance your cause. Let us not forget that, even before you offer your own defence, we still have another witness and Admiral Edwards to speak in your favour. I'll venture we'll have more cause for optimism by the end of the day. Come, we must return.'

Merriman had never seen Bosun Brockle look so smart. The thick-set sailor appeared to even have combed his hair and the buttons on his jacket sparkled. Beyond *Gladiator*'s great cabin, some other sailor – a bosun himself, perhaps – was bellowing instructions aboard a vessel in the harbour, his cries reaching the court as Brockle's account began.

As the third witness, he was not expected to recite the voyage in detail. Brockle was a working man and his replies were those of a practical, straightforward fellow. When the questioning began, a familiar pattern emerged. Wyborne and Percy questioned him in a generally neutral tone. Crabbe made no attempt to hide that he was well-disposed towards Merriman. Fellowes was interrogative. Gillespie held off and only intervened occasionally but, point by point, little by little, he continued to undermine Merriman's defence.

This culminated just after midday. Judge Popham had ordered that Brockle's testimony would be concluded before luncheon. Debbage confided to Merriman that he had seldom seen a judge hurry so, and this did little to lift his spirits. Neither captain nor lawyer were surprised that Gillespie weighed in after Brockle briefly described his aforementioned dispute with Merriman.

'As we have heard, bosun, you challenged the captain's decision to close with the *Hercule*.'

'I admit it, sir.'

'And what precisely was your objection?'

'I…I was concerned that an exchange of fire at that close range would…would not turn out well for us.'

'An entirely fair point. Had the captain listened, what would you have advised?'

'Sir, it's not my place to-'

'Well, you must have thought of something, Brockle, otherwise there would have been no challenge. What would you have done in the captain's place?'

'I would have kept our distance, sir. But in the days afterward, all this was discussed. I hadn't taken the marines into account. I'm just a sailor, after all-'

'Enough,' said Vice-Admiral Percy. 'Bosun, answer the captain's question.'

'I would have held off sir, trusted in our accuracy and rate of fire to inflict some damage on our foe. Our crews were quite capable and, as a rule, our gunnery will best a French ship over the piece.'

At this, the faithful Crabbe spoke up. 'And yet we have already established that *Thunder* suffered considerable damage on the first two passes. Was it not already clear that you were outmatched?'

'Perhaps, sir. I…I would have trusted in our guns to bloody his nose at least.'

'Make him think twice, you mean?' suggested Fellowes. 'Perhaps withdraw and strike again when in a more advantageous position?'

'There are always choices, sir,' said Brockle. 'But they're not mine to make and I reckon it's just as well.'

Returning after luncheon, the court was to hear from the retired Admiral David Edwards, who Merriman had known for nearly three decades. However, upon returning to the *Gladiator* after another walk, he found Debbage in a rather agitated state.

'A new witness,' said the lawyer as Merriman joined him at the table. 'I protested at the lack of notice of course but Popham has allowed it.'

'Who is it?' asked Merriman, assuming it would be another member of his crew.

'Some bloody American. Nathaniel Twist. Well-named. I didn't see this turn of events.'

'Ah,' said Merriman. 'I remember the name from the *Hercule*'s lists. Topman.'

'That's the fellow. I also tried to argue that he is both an enemy combatant and of insufficient rank but Vice-Admiral Percy wants to hear from him.'

'You think it will work against us?'

'Hard to know,' replied Debbage.

Upon the order of Judge Popham, the American sailor was ushered in by the provost-marshal's men. He carried with him the bitter odour of stale sweat and the judge and his clerks were close enough to visibly react to the smell. None of the sailing men did so.

At the urging of Vice-Admiral Percy, the American briefly recounted how he came to be aboard the *Hercule*. Born in Connecticut, he had plied his trade across the Atlantic on merchantmen for several years. Then, one of his many ships had been taken as a prize by the French navy. He had been impressed into service but soon found that he quite liked his wage and the prize-money that came his way. From a frigate, he graduated eventually to the *Hercule*.

Having spent eight years amongst the French, Twist had acquired a very mixed accent. He recounted a tale familiar to Merriman, who had spoken to the French officers during their long trip home. For many months, Captain Jourdan had merrily preyed upon British merchant shipping, accumulating huge amounts in prize money and causing immense damage to trade and the war effort. It was clear from Twist's tone that he wished they had been able to continue.

Describing the battle from his perspective, he expressed a surprise shared by his crewmates at the *Thunder*'s decision to close only minutes into the battle.

'Did not see that coming,' said the topman. 'Don't think the capitaine did either.'

'The manoeuvre did catch Jourdan and his officers off guard then?' said Captain Crabbe.

'It did, sir. Surprised us all. Captain Merriman must have known he'd get a bellyful from those twenty-eight pounders. I guess he reckoned it was worth it.'

'What part did you play in the battle?' asked Percy.

'Once the rigging was all snarled up, we were given swords – told to fight. Got to say though, those marines tore it up on the foredeck. Fine fighters, hand to hand. Didn't expect us to surrender so quick.'

'And what was the prevailing view after the battle?' asked the vice-admiral.

'Prevailing, sir?'

'What did the French officers think afterwards? That they could have won?'

'We would have won if it had been a fair fight,' said Twist.

'Explain yourself,' added Percy.

'Lot of the officers said it wasn't a fair fight between ships. Captain Merriman turned it into an infantry battle. Guess you could say that was pretty crafty. Word was he knew we didn't have the number of marines he did.'

Merriman felt that this reflected rather well on him. Twist's final words did not.

'If you ask me though, taking another ship ain't much of a victory if your own sinks to the bottom.'

The second day in court concluded with the testimony of Admiral David Edwards. He entered the great cabin with the assistance of his son. The provost-marshal had already put out a chair and it took some time for Admiral Edwards to descend. Once in place, he handed his stick to his son, who withdrew to the door. Now almost eighty, the admiral pressed down his snowy white hair and looked around the cabin, peering at individuals in turn. Seeing Merriman behind him, he nodded before turning back to the panel.

The admiral took his oath, then was asked by Vice-Admiral Percy to describe how he knew Merriman. Edwards explained the youthful Merriman had initially come aboard his vessel as a midshipman. Subsequently, again under Edwards' orders, Merriman had conveyed Sir Laurence Grahame to Bombay to protect British shipping and learn what they could about the activities of Tipu Sahib, ruler of Mysore and ally of the French.

When asked how Merriman had fared, the retired admiral answered with some enthusiasm. 'A capital job on both occasions! And of course I have followed the captain's career ever since. A fine career it has been, at that. Many an enemy and prize taken, many a scheme defeated.'

Fellowes said, 'Indeed, it seems that Captain Merriman has been occupied with tasks for the Treasury as often as he has followed orders from the Admiralty.'

'And what of it, young sir? There are a fair few in the Navy would do well not to insult our colleagues in Leadenhall Street. Division helps only the enemy, you know!'

Before another question could be answered, Edwards pointed a finger at the panel. 'Now, I don't want you to think these were all matters of intrigue and espionage. Let us talk of seamanship. Before charging Captain Merriman with a mission, I wrote to several former compatriots. All agreed that he was an excellent captain; a fine navigator, a courageous fighter and a natural leader of men.'

Merriman appreciated the sentiment, though the admiral's words did sound rather over-rehearsed.

The character witness statement was not supposed to last long and so Vice-Admiral Percy brought it to a close by thanking the admiral, who had travelled all the way from Cornwall.

Before he could stand and leave however, Captain Gillespie politely asked if he could ask another question.

'Please,' said Edwards, stick already on hand.

'Admiral, it is correct to state, is it not, that you haven't personally seen Captain Merriman conduct himself aboard a ship for more than twenty years?'

Merriman forced himself not to react but noted the grimace on his lawyer's face.

'Well, I suppose that is correct,' said Edwards. 'Still, a courageous fighter and leader of men!'

After reviewing the day's events with Debbage, Merriman returned to Shelby Manor, spending most of the journey gazing out at a sky of white and grey cloud, his spirits low. Debbage had attempted to raise them but did acknowledge that the crafty Gillespie had landed yet more blows. Debbage confided that he had been carrying out some research and learned that the captain was currently without commission. In fact, he had not actually commanded a vessel for two years, since the loss of his ship during a storm off the Welsh coast. He too had been cleared of misconduct but, given the urgent need for commanders, it was odd that he remained out in the cold. Debbage had not unearthed the reason for this but asserted that it might mean Gillespie was in need of money.

They agreed that Fellowes still seemed quite critical but Debbage had heard from former subordinates that he was by nature harsh and exacting. The lawyer had also reviewed Vice-Admiral Percy's decisions in the two-dozen court martial panels he'd attended. He concluded that Percy was thorough but fair and he reassured Merriman that the senior man on the panel would not rob the Admiralty of a captain with his estimable record.

As for Admiral Andrews, Debbage admitted to Merriman that he'd been wrong in advising him to ask the highest-ranking officer he knew to provide the character reference. They both agreed that they should have chosen someone younger, who had seen action alongside Merriman in recent years. But, as Merriman had pointed out, most of them were currently at sea.

He cursed quietly to himself as the carriage trundled up the drive to Shelby Manor. At least when in command, he could do something to determine his own fate. Even though he would have an opportunity to speak himself the following day, it all felt utterly out of his hands.

Sensing his dour mood, Helen let the children greet him and then took him for a walk. Merriman wasn't entirely open about what had occurred but she could tell he was gravely concerned about the outcome.

'I know there have been miscarriages of justice – even some outright corruption – but I refuse to believe that you will not be cleared, James.'

'I hope you're right, my love.'

'Robert is hiding it well but he is angry that they're putting you through this. So am I.'

'I wonder if it might be enough to dissuade him from the naval life?'

'I doubt that.'

'I am sorry.'

Helen stopped and turned towards him. They were not far from a dozen cattle, grazing by a meandering stream.

'What are you sorry for, James?'

'Well, if I wasn't a naval man, the thought might never have entered his head.'

Helen sighed and made an adjustment to her hair, which was tied back. 'If not the navy, it might be the army. If he wanted to be a doctor or a chaplain, he might just as easily end up in danger. It is his misfortune – all of ours – to live during a war that shows no sign of ending. And even if it does, there is always another.'

'By God, I have had enough of sitting in silence in that bloody great cabin,' muttered Merriman, 'in that bloody ship that never bloody moves.'

They continued walking and Helen changed the subject. 'I had a letter from cousin Hettie. Apparently, there is all manner of uproar at court.'

'That's no surprise. The role of regent is a thankless task.'

'They call the king's son "Prinny".'

Merriman shook his head as they turned back toward the house and passed one of Shelby Manor's two mazes.

'The man is simply not suited to power. The indecision, the adultery. One would have thought that nothing could be worse than a *mad* king.'

'Hettie thinks it was grief that pushed the king over the edge. The death of Princess Amelia.'

'There is hardly much point in your average captain of soldiers or sailors doing his job when those at the top are inadequate. The Tories and Whigs aren't much better.'

'You must play with the children after dinner, James. It will lighten your mood.'

'Yes, I must. Perhaps you and Mary-Jane will sing something?'

'Of course.' Helen squeezed his hand as they left the maze behind and approached the house.

Husband and wife were sitting on a bench, removing their muddy boots, when another of the footmen approached.

'A letter for you, Captain Merriman. It was delivered to the gate by a rider who did not give his name and rode off instantly.'

'Grahame, most likely,' said Merriman. 'At least he's doing something.'

In fact, the letter was not from Sir Laurence. Opening it, Merriman read the single sentence on a small sheet, etched in blue ink and capital letters.

IN THE MATTER OF THE MONEY, DO WHAT IS RIGHT AND ALL SHALL BE WELL.

Merriman leaned back against the wall. 'Now it becomes clear.'

'The Lord Stevenage money?'

Merriman nodded. 'The Irishman. Cathal Graves. His familial connection to Lord Stevenage is weak at best, yet year after year he has put up legal obstacles. Remember Christmas time? He went so far as to send my lawyer a letter authorising the transfer of funds directly to his bank in London. The mountebank expected me to simply sign it. No doubt he now expects me to do so – in return, he will call off Captain Gillespie.'

Helen was still gazing at the letter. She was not a lady given to anger but Merriman saw that she was grinding her teeth. Helen then slapped the bench they were sitting on with some force. 'This is a disgrace! A scandal! We must inform the Admiralty at once, the Treasury too. The court martial must be stopped.'

Merriman thought for a while before replying.

'This was well-timed. At the point of maximum pressure. Graves has been clever. What evidence is there that he is involved? A single sentence delivered by an unknown hand. And the man has never even been seen in London – in England, for all we know. In any case, I will not give in to this threat. Never.'

'James, what if it's not just this man Gillespie? What if others have been bribed by Graves? We must at least contact Sir Laurence.'

Helen called out to the footman waiting at the end of the corridor. 'You there. We need a messenger. Your best rider, your best horse.'

Midnight came and passed. Merriman had ordered Helen to bed but she of course refused and sat with him in the kitchen. This was the room closest to the rear door, where the messenger would return. Most of the staff were abed but the steward and the housekeeper stayed with them, supplying husband and wife with tea.

'It is most unlike him not to contact me,' said Merriman. 'He is not a young man. Perhaps something has befallen him and he is in no position to help.'

'Then you must go to the Admiralty tomorrow, James. To the president of the court, at least. Show him the letter.'

'What does it prove, Helen? Only that an old foe of mine is taking advantage of this situation. I can hardly cast aspersions upon Gillespie due to harsh questioning.'

Twice they'd imagined the sound of rapid hooves but, on this occasion, it turned out they were correct. The messenger was one of the grooms and he lurched into the kitchen panting, his face slick with sweat. He took an envelope from a satchel and passed it to Merriman.

'Thank you.'

Hurrying over to the nearest lantern, he was relieved to see the familiar handwriting of Sir Laurence Grahame. The retired spymaster had, however, written only a few lines.

James,

I know of the plot. Action is being taken tonight. If it is successful, all will go well tomorrow.

Your friend, Laurence.

Chapter Four

Spies and Thugs

On the morning of the third and final day of his trial, Merriman was invited by the president of the court to give his testimony. Arriving in Portsmouth just after dawn, he met Debbage at his offices and – as agreed – they reviewed the statement prepared weeks earlier. In response to the way the trial had unfolded, they adjusted certain passages, allowing Merriman to make his best possible defence. After Debbage reminded him to deliver his statement dispassionately, Merriman told him of the previous evening's events.

Though Debbage had not dealt with the Lord Stevenage inheritance, he and Merriman had discussed it. The lawyer shared Helen's concerns about a wider conspiracy but agreed with Merriman that there was insufficient evidence to present to the Admiralty. When they reached *Gladiator*, Merriman assured his counsel that Sir Laurence was not one to be easily bested in the darker arts but he found himself gripped by nerves as he stood to begin his statement.

It was an overcast day and, though six lanterns were alight, the rear of the great cabin was crisscrossed by shadows. The five men in blue and gold who would judge Merriman all gazed at him from the gloom. His eyes paused momentarily on Captain Gillespie but he could deduce nothing from his expression.

His statement ran to eight pages. As instructed by Judge Popham, questions were to be addressed only upon its conclusion. Merriman read as smoothly and steadily as he could, though only when he stumbled over a few words did he realise how nervous he truly was. It seemed to him that he had been speaking for at least half an hour when he finally reached his conclusion.

'In summary, then, I do not claim to have made perfect choices during the voyage, nor do I believe that to be possible. In the matter of closing quickly with *Hercule*, I saw no other workable choice. At the point the decision was made, I had established both that her gunnery was superior to ours and that our marine contingent was almost certainly superior to theirs. I took this course of action while fully aware that my own vessel might sustain significant damage. As has been noted, we overcame the enemy less than fifteen minutes after boarding the vessel: a considerable achievement for Captain Cary, his marines and every other man who fought. I gave the order in the full knowledge that, in aiming to capture the *Hercule*, I put my crew and vessel at great risk. Am I responsible for the loss of the *Thunder*? Yes. Was it due to design or neglect? No. Am I responsible for the defeat of Captain Jourdan and the capture of *Hercule*? Yes.'

This last line was the creation of Debbage. Merriman found it rather hyperbolic but he agreed with emphasising the fact that his orders had been fulfilled, despite the loss of his vessel.

Vice-Admiral Percy was asked by Captain Dutton to begin the questioning.

'Thank you for your account, Captain Merriman. Having attended many court martials, I can say it was thorough and precise. The only issue you did not adequately address was that of the starboard side. As Captain Gillespie iterated yesterday, the lack of crewmen there may have allowed the fire to develop and worsen. Do you accept that allocating all those sailors to the boarding party might have been a mistake; and contributed to the fire?'

'That is possible, sir, yes.'

Merriman sensed that it would be counter-productive to deny any culpability.

Captain Crabbe had no questions. Captain Wyborne asked him to expand on some points regarding what he knew of Captain Patrice Jourdan, while Captain Fellowes asked only for clarification regarding Bosun Brockle's protest; namely that no other senior man had followed suit.

At last, attention turned to Captain Gillespie.

When he spoke, Merriman felt his shoulders sag and relief run through him.

A grim look on his face, Gillespie simply said, 'No questions from me.'

With that, the president of the court arose once more and ordered that the court be cleared while the panel deliberated upon their verdict. Escorted out by the provost-marshal, Merriman and Debbage crossed the wooden walkway onto the docks.

'Well done, captain. Reading the signs, I would say there is reason to feel optimistic.'

'Please, Mr. Debbage, do not tempt fate.'

'Quite right. Shall we take a walk? Though much will have already been debated and decided, the panels feel obliged to give at least the appearance of a final reckoning. I've not known them conclude in under an hour.'

'Yes. I would like to keep moving.'

The captain and his counsel walked along the dock, past some marching marines and a trio of fishermen being roughly escorted out of the dockyard by another provost-marshal and his deputies. Debbage made some half-hearted attempts to distract his client with conversation but Merriman could not summon any enthusiasm. He wanted only to return to *Gladiator* for a final time and leave the ship with his suspension over and his name cleared.

According to Debbage, forty minutes had passed when they returned to the ship. Merriman noted the green weed on the vessel's hull; it seemed to him a waste and a great shame that a ship built for war should never ride the waves of the open sea.

The mast-less deck of the *Gladiator* was empty and so the pair traipsed onward, Merriman carrying his hat and wishing he had a drink to ease his parched throat. They were barely past the bow when a shout went up. Turning, they saw Provost-marshal Charles waving at them.

'Captain, your presence is required in the court.'

Down into the great cabin once more. Though Gillespie had given away nothing before, his disappointment was now clear. He had pushed his chair away from the table and sat alone, head cocked at an angle indicative of defeat.

Asked to stand before the court for a final time, Merriman listened as Captain Dutton announced that the panel had reached its decision and that it had been ratified by each man signing the appropriate papers.

'In the matter of the loss of His Majesty's Ship *Thunder*, on the 9th of June, in the year of our Lord eighteen hundred and eleven, during a naval engagement with the French vessel, Hercule; having heard the evidence brought forward, it is the finding of this court that Captain Sir James Abel Merriman is not guilty of reckless conduct, by design or negligence, and is most highly deserving of every praise his country and this court may give. This court does therefore most honourably acquit Captain Merriman.'

With a slightly warmer tone, the president of the court gestured to the doorway. 'Captain Merriman, you are free to leave. Provost-marshal, you will please return the captain's sword.'

Once back on the dock, Merriman put on his hat, already enjoying the feeling of the sword hanging over his hip.

'Ha, yes, indeed!' exclaimed Debbage, clapping his hands. 'You'll be standing proud on the deck of a new command in no time, captain.'

Merriman had just wiped his face, ashamed to feel his eyes wet with tears.

'Quite a relief,' he said, wishing Helen were present so that he could embrace her. 'Thank you, Debbage.'

'Not at all. Back to my office? We keep some brandy there for such occasions.'

'Perhaps. I must get word to Helen.'

'Of course.'

'Captain? Captain Merriman, sir?'

Approaching from the street that ran between two of the dockyard's many workshops was a familiar figure. A tad more bulky than when Merriman last seen him, Midshipman Silas Eades was advancing at a run. He was not wearing the blue jacket and hat that signified his profession but was clad in grey trousers and coat.

'Eades? What in the blazes are you doing here?'

'The decision, sir?'

'Not guilty,' said Debbage proudly. 'The captain is a free man.'

Eades' grave expression instantly became a broad grin. 'What news. What wonderful news!' Eades stepped forward and shook Merriman's hand with some gusto. 'Sir, can you please come with me? I've been sent to collect you. It's not far.'

'Collect me? What's not far?'

'It's easier if I just show you, sir, which is what I was requested to do. The inn is no more than ten minutes' walk.'

*

Given this mysterious invitation, Mr. Debbage elected to return to his office, parting from Merriman with a hearty handshake. The excitable Eades assailed the captain with a series of questions but Merriman only half-listened, instead absorbing the reality that he really was free; that all the strains of recent days, weeks and months were truly behind him.

'And what about you, young man?' said Merriman eventually. 'I assumed you'd have found a position weeks ago. The navy needs up and comers, you know.'

'I didn't want to accept a post until the court-martial was decided, sir. I haven't even looked at the lists. And I'm not alone in that.'

They reached a rather middling tavern named The Seven Stars. Close as it was to the dockyard, Merriman noted several old salts nursing tankards of ale as Eades led him through to the back room. With a knowing smirk, the midshipman opened the door for him.

The first face Merriman saw was Bosun Brockle. 'Were you cleared, captain?'

Merriman nodded and smiled and a great cheer went up. Eyes moving right to left, he took in Sailing Master Tom Henderson and another midshipman, Clarence Adkins. As all three came forward to shake his hand, Merriman realised that there was another man seated behind them. He was by the unlit hearth, his fine cape and elegant shoes incongruous in the rough tavern. Sir Laurence Grahame's hawk-like face had already broken into a grin.

When all the jubilation and congratulations had died down, Bosun Brockle came close, his broad face anguished.

'So sorry that I spoke of our…disagreement, sir. But having taken my oath on the Bible-'

'It doesn't matter, Brockle. And, for the record, if I didn't listen to my bosun I wouldn't consider myself much of a captain. Who knows – maybe you were right.'

'Not a chance. What are you drinking, sir? Got to be rum, hasn't it?'

'I would say so, yes.'

After he'd sat down and briefed his friends and colleagues on the final day of the hearing, Merriman demanded an explanation. As Brockle returned with a bottle and began pouring their tots, Sir Laurence delivered it.

'I would say we have not discovered all that I would wish, though we have been able to achieve the required result. At the conclusion of the first day of the court martial, I had some operatives follow the members of the panel. I didn't have the numbers I would like and in fact these first pursuits revealed nothing of interest. However, on the second evening, Captain Gillespie was tracked to a lawyer's office in Southsea. My men asked around and learned that the senior man there is named Gallagher.'

'Let me guess,' said Merriman. 'An Irishman?'

'Quite so. And, given what you told me of your legal troubles, there was a single obvious conclusion to be made. From there, we moved from surveillance to action. Mr. Gallagher worked late that night, not departing until nine o'clock for a nearby guesthouse. When he answered his door, my operatives accosted him, dragged him to the nearest window and hung him from the sill by his legs.'

Merriman's eyes widened at this and he took a long slug of rum.

'Apparently, he made quite a noise,' added Grahame. 'He was told in no uncertain terms that – if he wished to see another day on Earth – that Captain Gillespie was to be deterred from his current course. It would appear that message was sent and understood.'

Having noted the reaction of his former crewmen during this tale, Merriman had made his own conclusions. 'Well, Sir Laurence, even in retirement, it seems you have been able to round up some very capable spies and thugs to do some dirty work.'

'Willing participants, every one.'

'By God,' said Merriman, shocked by all the scheming that had unfolded on his behalf. 'How fortunate I am to have compatriots who would take such risks. To you all.'

The captain raised his glass. The others matched him and they all drank.

'I must concede that I am feeling quite drained,' said Sir Laurence. 'I really am getting too old for such escapades.'

'If I may, captain,' offered Tom Henderson. 'Hope it won't be too long before your next commission and that you'll take us with you if you can. Might be wise for us to get out of town for a while, if you know what I mean!'

Though implored by Henderson, Brockle and the midshipmen to stay for a meal and a longer celebration, Merriman knew he had to get back to Shelby Manor and impart the good news. After four or five rums, Sir Laurence was fading fast and so they gave their farewells. Merriman took the time to again thank each man in person before departing. He promised that any incoming commission would result in an offer of employment for all four of them.

Sir Laurence had a carriage waiting at a nearby stables and the pair were soon out of Portsmouth and heading for the manor.

'If I am too old for intrigues, I am certainly too old for tavern rum,' said Sir Laurence, gazing out at the passing countryside.

'And I am out of practice,' said Merriman.

'Something will be along soon, I'm sure of it.'

'Sir Laurence, my thanks again.'

'Think nothing of it, old friend. No fair judge could say that I didn't owe you a favour or two. What now then James? Back to Cheshire, I suppose?'

'I should think so. Though Helen's kept them hard at their studies, we must get Robert and Mary-Jane back in school. I could consult the lists but I must admit I've no great desire to seek a commission just yet.'

'Something tells me you will not have to wait long.'

Chapter Five

The Convoy

It had been agreed by the captains that the convoy would initially take a southern route. No path was without risk but it was known that French privateers were patrolling the shipping lanes off Ireland. The thirteen vessels – ten merchantmen, three escort ships – would therefore shape a course to clear the English Channel close to Land's End, then head south-west towards the Azores to take advantage of the gentle westerly trades.

The convoy assembled off Plymouth as planned, in the early hours of 24th April. Taking advantage of the slack tide and good morning light, they passed Drake's Island at seven bells of the morning watch. This left them a good five hours to make progress towards The Lizard, assisted by the south-west tidal race. All went as planned and, by sunset, they had covered more than fifty miles.

Commander Alfred Shrigley was relieved by the uneventful first day and slept surprisingly well during his first night at sea as captain of HMS *Romulus*. Waking at dawn, he lay in his cot for a time.

First, he thought of what he was leaving behind in Hampshire: his brave but frail wife, Amelia, and his sixth-month-old son, Frederick, who'd been named after his grandfather. Upon Shrigley's return, during his first visit to his local church in Droxford, he had thanked the Lord for (at the third time of trying) a successful pregnancy and birth. Though Frederick had suffered with various ailments in his first few weeks, he was now doing well and had been babbling his first words just before Shrigley's departure. Leaving them had been horrible but this was a trial set before the majority of naval officers and his father had endured the same. The pride of Amelia and the rest of his family and small circle of friends at his first commission had eased that pain.

Second, he thought of Captain Merriman. Shrigley had barely spent a day aboard a ship without the man he had met aged just fourteen. It was no exaggeration to say that Sir James had been like a second father to him; a point made by Frederick Shrigley himself, who admitted to being "damned grateful for it". Not only had he set sail without Merriman, he had left during his mentor's court martial and would likely not learn of the result for months. Shrigley could not believe it possible that so great a captain would be found guilty but he also knew that court-martials could be unpredictable.

The new captain was also aboard ship without out any of the familiar faces – officers *and* men – that he had sailed with for several years aboard *Thunder*. *Romulus* had been in the Mediterranean for some time and the only man he had served with was the surgeon, John Webster. Knowing him to be an excellent and forward-thinking physician, Shrigley had written to him immediately upon hearing of his commission. It was some comfort to have the conscientious Welshman aboard; and some small connection to *Thunder*.

As he lay there, hearing the sounds of the crew moving around as dawn broke, Shrigley glanced to his left, and the empty space of the great cabin. Though not on the same scale as *Thunder*'s, to him it seemed huge and he did not much like being there alone. It did not feel like his, nor could he imagine a time when it would. Ultimately, he did not feel that he yet deserved it. Regardless of how this mission and his career unfolded – or indeed the opinions of others – he would have to prove himself worthy of his commission.

In their last conversation, Merriman had told him to keep things simple: "One thing at a time, Alfred. A sharp eye on officers and crew. Take care of the details and the rest will take care of itself."

The first detail of the day was to dress himself. He had been up on his feet for barely a minute when his servant, Trelawney, knocked, then entered. A man of forty with the strongest Cornish accent Shrigley had ever heard, Trelawney was a dour character who communicated mainly with sighs, grimaces and grunts.

'You'll be wanting some breakfast, I suppose?'

'I do.' Though he seemed to have a permanent knot in his stomach, Shrigley knew he had to eat. 'Leave it in the cabin, I'll go up on deck first.'

Though he was entitled to task Trelawney with a multitude of jobs, Shrigley was so used to looking after his own gear in the confines of the officers' cabin that he didn't have much work for him. Once out of his nightshirt and into breeches and dress shirt, he took his jacket, socks and shoes with him into the cabin. His desk was mounted in the middle but he possessed no other furniture except for a bookshelf given to him by Amelia's family before departure.

As he sat at the desk and put on his socks and shoes, the cabin felt larger than ever. He had always marvelled at how different these places seemed when filled with officers at dinner. Shrigley had only held one dinner while preparing the ship and it had not gone well. Naturally reserved, he had mainly listened to his officers and senior men talk amongst themselves, and most of that talk concerned their previous captain – Elias Stone.

Having commanded *Romulus* for six years, Stone had been dismissed only a month earlier; found guilty in a court martial held in Plymouth of erroneously claiming prize money. Both Stone and his purser were now residing in Dartmoor prison.

Stone's misfortune provided his successor with an opportunity; Shrigley had been awarded his new commission, naming him Commander Alfred Shrigley, master of the brig-sloop HMS Romulus. This was sent from the Admiralty to the office of the senior commander at the port, Vice-Admiral Shelley.

Shelley had assured him that Stone was guilty. He had also explained, however, that some of Stone's officers and crew had defended him, claiming that their captain was a man of honour. Shrigley had vowed to make no mention of Stone, if he could avoid it. Yet he could tell that this sense of injustice had not left the ship. He faced an uphill struggle.

One thing at a time...

Launched in 1782, *Romulus* was a brig-sloop of the Speedy class. One hundred feet long, twenty-six across at her widest, she had a complement of ninety-eight. Her armament comprised fourteen twenty-eight-pound carronades and two six-pounders (longs) mounted on the forecastle.

The second lieutenant, Ives, was on duty, standing close to the helmsman. He was a sturdy-looking fellow with a thick head of wavy brown hair and sideburns that almost reached his jawline.

'Morning, Captain,'

'Morning Lieutenant Ives.' Shrigley was trying to use the officers' titles as often as he could. So far, Ives had been more amenable than the first lieutenant, Glanville.

'If you please.'

'Sir, the wind is still from the north, steady around fifteen knots. We are headed south-west at four and a half knots. The *Suffolk* is approximately a mile ahead of us. Around twenty minutes ago, we reduced sail in order not to come up too close on her. Lookouts report that spacing remains fair and that *Iona* and *Robin* are in sight, as is *HMS Galway*.'

Some of the ten merchantmen were carrying crucial supplies of muskets, cannon, powder and shot for the army in Canada. Others carried military supplies or provisions but also regular trade goods. The twin threat of war with America and French raiders had convinced the Admiralty that such protection was necessary. For this task, they had allocated the *Romulus*, plus two heavier frigates of the Leda class, each with thirty-eight guns and a crew of almost three hundred. *Galway* was commanded by an experienced captain named Thorpe, *Zeus* by a Captain Halliwell.

'Very good. All well with the middle watch?'

'All well, sir.'

Shrigley looked out at the water. Made dark by low grey cloud, the waters of the Atlantic offered a long, lazy swell. Other than the ships ahead, the only things visible on the surface were a few yellow-necked gannets bobbing nearby, apparently at ease above the immense depths and below endless skies. The captain walked past the helm and towards the bow, past idlers and topmen who tipped their hats. There was, however, not a greeting offered, and Shrigley felt almost as if surrounded by hostiles as he approached the bow.

He at least received a 'good morning', from the bosun, Diggs, who was making a show of inspecting a block.

'Morning, Diggs. You're up early.'

'Couldn't sleep, captain.'

'The matter of our departure still bothering you?'

'No. I suppose we'll just have to live with that.'

Shrigley had expected this issue to cause trouble. Despite the protests of some of the merchant captains, they had departed on a Friday, which was considered unlucky by sailors. He knew there would be mutterings but would have expected a petty officer to be rather more rational.

'It was the snorers kept me awake, captain,' explained Diggs. 'Given the chance, I'd throttle the lot of them.'

He made a matching gesture with his hands and, for the first time, Shrigley noticed that he was missing the top half of two fingers.

Diggs held the hand up. 'Done by a block just like that one. Proper jammed in it was. Hurt so much, I begged 'em to knock me out. Surgeon took one look and lopped them off. Luckily, I was already a bosun, which mostly involves shouting at layabouts.'

'I see. There invariably seems to be some fellow who snores – even in the officers' cabin.'

'But not in the *great* cabin, eh, sir?'

'That is one notable advantage. Looks set for another fair day, wouldn't you say?'

'I would, sir, yes.'

'Gunnery practice today, I think.'

Though he'd been assured by Glanville and Ives that the gun crews were well-drilled, Shrigley hadn't had time to see them in action and he knew that *Romulus* had been in dock since the arrest of Captain Stone.

'As you wish, captain.'

'I shall notify the lieutenants,' said Shrigley.

'Excuse me, sir.' Seeing a deficiency in the fore topgallant, Diggs issued some orders to the sailors nearby. Shrigley withdrew, passing yet more silent crewmen before hearing some sniggering. Five men gathered near the mainmast seemed unable to contain their amusement. Shrigley reddened, fearing that his clothing was stained or that he had something upon his face.

'What in the blazes are you laughing at?' he demanded.

The men separated, allowing him to see a small pair of feet. Walking to his left, he realised that the small feet belonged to the small figure lying against the mast: the youngest of the ship's two midshipman, fourteen-year-old Edgar Haskell.

'We didn't have the heart to wake him up, sir,' said one of the sailors with a smirk. 'What a sweet little angel.'

Though he felt like kicking the lad – and indeed the sailors – Shrigley approached and tapped Haskell's shoe with his own.

'Haskell.'

The boy was sound asleep, head lolled back.

'Haskell!'

Waking with a start, he shot to his feet with such speed that his hat fell off, causing more hilarity from the crew.

Haskell glanced around in confusion for a moment before recovering his hat and wringing his hands anxiously. 'My apologies, sir. I…I don't know how that happened.'

Sleeping on duty was a serious offence, though Shrigley remembered struggling himself at that age.

'You will report to my cabin at once.'

'Yes, sir.'

As the youngster traipsed off, two of the sailors were still gripped by hilarity.

'Names?'

'Butler, sir.'

'Kearney, captain.' The two crewmen put a knuckle to their foreheads.

Shrigley left it at that, knowing that simply taking the names would cause the crewmen anxiety as they awaited a punishment he was not planning to give. By the time he reached the hatch, the piper had done his work and he could hear the sound of the first watch assembling and hammocks being stowed away.

He was almost back in his cabin when he heard the high, unmistakably Welsh voice of John Webster.

'Good morning, Captain Shrigley.'

'Mr. Webster, feeling better?'

The surgeon was commencing only his second sea voyage and had struggled with sickness for the first day, prompting some jibes from the lieutenants, who wondered if he'd be well enough to treat anyone.

'Better today, thank you, captain. Already dealt with an abscess and a back strain.'

'Good. Would you take breakfast with me?'

'My thanks for the invitation but actually I have a question for you. I've had this fellow Greaves in the sick bay since yesterday evening.'

'Yes?'

'The problem is that there doesn't actually seem to be anything wrong with him. He claims to have a severe headache but I've observed him being quite voluble with my assistant and another visitor.'

'I'd suggest discharging him at once then.'

'Yes, I would, but Lieutenant Glanville suggested that I should "go easy on him". Apparently, he's considered some kind of hero or mascot for the *Romulus*.'

'How odd. I shall speak to Glanville about it. Anything else?'

'Now that I have a bit more energy, I shall have a proper look at the decks: see what we can do about ventilation and damp.'

'Very good.'

Both were eternal challenges at sea but Mr. Webster had studied under a noted physician named Turnbull and had some novel ideas about preserving the health of sailors. Captain Merriman had very much approved of this modern thinking and therefore Shrigley approved of it too.

As the two parted, Shrigley belatedly realised that young Haskell was lurking in the shadows outside the great cabin.

'Follow me,' he said, entering to find Trelawney still putting out his breakfast. It seemed to him that the dour servant was remarkably slow.

Shrigley put his hat on the table and turned to the fourteen-year-old. His face was very boyish; freckled and smooth-skinned.

'Well, that was not good, young man.'

'I am sorry, Captain Shrigley. I tried dunking my head in water, striking myself, asked cook for some coffee. I just…couldn't stay awake.'

'It is most serious. Sailors are flogged for such dereliction.'

No doubt most of those on deck would by now know of this infraction and it would be all round the ship once breakfast was concluded.

'Ensure you are getting adequate rest when not on duty, Haskell. Other than that, I have no advice, for this is your responsibility and yours alone. I will of course make a note of this infraction and consider the most appropriate sanction.'

'Yes, captain.'

'Dismissed.'

Once the midshipman had left, Shrigley surveyed his breakfast: bread, smoked ham and a hunk of cheddar. Shrigley first drank some coffee, another habit he'd picked up from Merriman, thought he didn't take it as strong. Before he could take a bite of food, there was a knock on the door.

'Come.'

In strode First Lieutenant Glanville. Average in height and built, the man was undeniably even-featured and handsome, with unusually white teeth. Shrigley gathered from his bearing and manner that he came from money.

'Morning, captain.'

'Morning, lieutenant.'

'I just wanted to come and explain the situation with Greaves.'

'Please do.'

'It is a queer one, I'll grant you. Greaves was with Captain Stone for all his time on *Romulus* and his previous vessel. There are so many tales, most of which I saw myself: Greaves was on lookout, spotted an enemy ship before anyone else; he had a dream about an American merchantman, we took her – prize money you wouldn't believe; his gun crew blasted the mainmast of a French third-rater."

Glanville flashed those sparkling teeth. 'I'll admit it seems far-fetched but the man is a living good luck charm. Captain Stone believed it. No doubt it seems like nonsense to you but I think there's some truth to it and so do most of the crew.'

Shrigley was not overly surprised. There was no category of men more superstitious than sailors and they invariably ascribed any development to good or ill fortune.

'The headaches,' continued Glanville, 'relate to the most incredible story of all. We had taken a French brig and some nasty swine took a potshot at the captain from the rigging. Greaves stepped in front of the captain a moment before and it was he who was hit. Top of his head. Surgeon got the bullet out and he was up and about a week later. Four years ago. But the headaches come and go.'

'Incredible indeed,' said Shrigley. 'And I can see why you might be inclined to give this sailor preferable treatment. But it is Mr. Webster who will decide who is fit for duty. Not you or I.'

'The man is a hero. And he is seen as-'

'I understand what you've said, lieutenant. Thank you.'

'Of course.' Glanville cleared his throat and then pointed at the empty bookshelf. 'Not much of a reader, captain?'

'When there's time.'

'What do you prefer?'

'Geography has always interested me. Exploration too.'

'I myself enjoy the poets. Had no choice at Charterhouse and I suppose they inculcated an interest within me. Where were you educated, captain?'

Shrigley had already experienced a taste of this at dinner. Glanville was very fond of talking about himself; *what* he knew, *who* he knew.

'Nowhere of note.'

Shrigley was beginning to tire of this fellow, with his excess of pride and his constant reference to his disgraced captain, who he still seemed to view as some kind of military saint.

'Lieutenant, we will conduct gunnery practice today. Two o'clock.'

'Any reason not to conduct it at the usual time, captain?'

'Enemies could be sighted at any time, could they not?'

'They could.'

'You may notify Ives but no one else. It should be a surprise to petty officers and men.'

'Very well, sir.'

'If there's nothing else…' said Shrigley.

Glanville took the hint and turned away. Though he couldn't see it, the captain felt sure that the man had rolled his eyes.

After breakfast, he began a list of things to do before the gunnery practice. Chief among them was a proper briefing with his lieutenant of marines, Cathcote, who commanded the sixteen soldiers aboard.

Before Shrigley could make any more progress with his list, there was another knock on his door.

'Yes?'

It was young Haskell back again. 'Sir, the mercury is dropping quickly. Looks like some bad weather coming.'

Chapter Six

The One-Legged Admiral

'What's it like, father?'

Robert had just looked up from the array of toy soldiers laid out on the dinner table. Merriman was sitting opposite him, reading *The Times*. He was halfway through an article concerning the ongoing effects of the Orders in Council of 1807. These decrees had been originally designed to restrict French trade but, over time, had soured British relations with neutral countries, including the United States. The Tory opposition was blaming them for the economic depression and rioting afflicting Britain.

'What's *what* like?'

Robert nodded towards the infantry and cavalry deployed before him: British, French, Russian. After a week back at school, he was making the most of his Sunday afternoon.

'Battle. Whenever I ask, you change the subject or find something else to do.'

'Do I?'

On reflection, Merriman knew that was exactly what he'd done. But he supposed Robert was approaching the age where he might be able to deal with something approaching an honest answer.

'Well.' Merriman put down his newspaper. Robert put down the two soldiers in his hands and leaned onto the table. They were alone in the house: Helen and Mary-Anne were out in the garden.

'I can say for certain that it is not something any man looks forward to.'

'What about Lieutenant Smythe on *Thunder*? You said he loved to fight.'

'Perhaps he was an exception. And he was very good at it too. If one had to fight alone, it would be so difficult as to almost feel impossible. But when you are with your compatriots, officers and men, there is such a feeling of camaraderie that…perhaps it takes the edge off the fear.'

'It's like being a soldier – but on a ship.'

'I suppose it is. As a captain, one must trust in the marines. They are the real experts. The true soldiers.'

Robert glanced down at his toys. 'You see men die.'

'Yes.'

'Father, have you…'

'Robert, I have told you something of what it is like. But it is not wise to talk too much of these things at your age. I did not with my father. You are still a child. Though it may not seem like it to you, there is more to life than sailing and soldiers and war. You know, much of life in the navy is quite dull.'

'One last question, father.'

'Very well but be aware you make not get an answer.'

'Are you happy when you see dead Frenchies? Or sad?'

'Not *happy* exactly, though I'll take victory over defeat any day. No, not happy, because they are all God's sons. I have known a good few Frenchmen, mostly officers, and some were quite pleasant.'

Robert nodded at this but Merriman could see in his eyes that he was still preoccupied by what they'd earlier discussed. He knew he had said too much.

He stood. 'Come on. Let's go and see if we can help in the garden.'

Advance notice of an imminent arrival came the next morning. The name of Vice-Admiral Sir Cuthbert Pertwee was well known. He had served with distinction at the Battle of the Nile and, since coming ashore, had commanded various departments before acting directly on behalf of the Admiralty. Due to his lack of mobility, he was permanently stationed in Liverpool and generally conducted his affairs by correspondence.

Pertwee arrived in the middle of the morning, accompanied by a young lieutenant, who helped him down from his carriage. The vice-admiral walked with a stick and made rather slow progress on his wooden leg. Though many assumed he had lost it in action, Merriman knew that it was in fact the result of a particularly vicious ulcer.

Pertwee wiped sweat from his brow as he approached the doorway. Merriman welcomed him inside and was introduced to Lieutenant Dunn, who Pertwee described as his "assistant". The host swiftly conducted his guests to Burton Manor's largest sitting room.

'Some cold cider, perhaps, admiral?'

'Fine idea, Merriman. Very fine.'

Merriman called out to the housekeeper for the cider and three glasses. Helen had taken the children out for a ride, purposefully to avoid the admiral's visit. Finding the sitting room a little stuffy, Merriman pushed two windows further open before taking a seat.

'Recovered from the court martial, Merriman?'

'Yes, thank you sir,' he answered, taking a seat opposite Pertwee. Lieutenant Dunn sat to one side, hat upon his lap.

'Faced a couple myself,' said Pertwee, laying his stick against his chair. 'Always felt you can't really call yourself a captain if you haven't lost at least *one* ship!'

Pertwee guffawed at that. Merriman and Dunn each forced a chuckle.

Then, with a grimace, Pertwee rubbed his thigh above the wooden leg. 'Reason I came to see you in person – partly to reassure you that the Admiralty still holds you in good regard. Also, we're aware that there may be grounds to examine the conduct of one member of the panel. Rest assured it is being looked into.'

Hearing that, Merriman wondered if Grahame had been at work again.

'However, we are mainly here to discuss a commission.'

'Sir.'

'You've been keeping abreast with the American situation?'

'I have.'

'Came under my purview of late,' said Pertwee. 'Been talking to the generals. Fact of the matter is that, if the Americans strike north into Upper Canada, we simply don't have the numbers to resist. Never have. Dependent on the Indians, like it or not.'

Merriman wondered if the commission might be an escort duty, like Shrigley's. Protecting troops ships perhaps? He would do it if asked but considered such missions highly burdensome. It was one thing to defend ships full of provisions or equipment, another to protect those full of men, each one not only a soul but a vital part of the war effort.

'Heard of Tecumseh?'

'No, sir. What language is that?'

'Not sure I know myself. Dunn here is the expert on all this.'

Dunn leaned forward. 'Captain, you will be aware that we have maintained alliances with the tribes of Upper Canada for many decades. Frankly, it has always been a "marriage of convenience". The Americans seem intent on civilising the tribes and forcing them to sell land. In the last few decades, that has pushed those on or around the border in our direction. We have always offered them more autonomy – largely because they provide a barrier between our possessions and the new republic.'

'Rather ironic,' observed Admiral Pertwee. 'On land we are the ones offering freedom of trade and movement; at sea, the Americans believe they are doing the same.'

'The reality of our situation is stark,' continued Dunn. 'The entirety of His Majesty's Forces in Canada can be swiftly described: The 8th, 41st, 49th and 100th Regiments; the 10th Royal Veteran Battalion and four companies of the Royal Artillery, 1st Battalion. Around five thousand six hundred men in total. There are other scattered Canadian units, local militias and so on but you can see the problem. Without our native allies, any concerted American invasion will inevitably meet with success.'

'The Yankees are terrified of them, apparently!' said Pertwee with relish. 'And I can't say I blame them.'

Neither did Merriman. He had heard a few tales of Indian warriors. All combat was brutal but any man could understand the profound fear of scalping and torture.

At that moment, the housekeeper arrived with the cold cider. As she departed, Pertwee downed half a glass and declared it, 'delicious'.

'Tecumseh is without doubt one of the most important native chiefs in the Americas,' continued Lieutenant Dunn. 'His name means "shooting star" in their language and he has long attracted a good deal of attention. He is of the Shawnee tribe. His father died fighting the Americans and he has fought them many times himself. In recent years, he allied with his brother, who is considered a prophet, to form a huge confederacy of tribes. They formed a settlement known as Prophetstown.'

Merriman raised a finger. 'I recall the name. Was it not destroyed by the Americans?'

'It was,' confirmed Dunn. 'Burned to the ground last November. It seems this defeat persuaded Tecumseh that there can never be peace with the Americans. No doubt he is aware that relations between ourselves and the Yankees are also deteriorating. After the battle, we received word that he is seeking a new alliance with us. However, given the history of betrayals and changing loyalties in that part of the world, he insists on the king's signature.'

Merriman still wasn't sure where a sea-captain might fit into all this but he remained intrigued.

Pertwee rubbed the top of his walking stick with his thumb before continuing. 'Apparently, Tecumseh was aware of the king's ill-health but insisted that the signature of the prince regent would not be sufficient. Fortunately, this was obtained during a…better period for His Majesty. The signed agreement is now ready to be despatched to Canada. It will be delivered in secret by an agent of the Treasury.'

'Ah,' said Merriman. 'Letter and agent will need to be conveyed across the Atlantic.'

'With the utmost haste,' said Pertwee. 'We are most fortunate with the season, for conditions are rather more clement than they were only weeks ago. A frigate, HMS *Mercury,* has been specially adapted for this task. She will travel with a skeleton crew, minimal supplies and armament. She was to be commanded by Captain Brakewell.'

'Thomas Brakewell?'

Merriman had met the man perhaps twice or three times, introduced at some social occasion in London.

'The same,' confirmed Pertwee. 'He was at home, settling a few issues on his estate before departure. He had gone into Nottingham on business and got caught up in some unrest. Attacked by a group of thugs who broke his arm. These accursed Luddites.'

'By God.'

'Well, Merriman. Will you take Brakewell's place?'

The captain felt a surge of excitement. This was a mission of the utmost importance and, above all, it confirmed that he retained the confidence of the Admiralty, the Treasury and the Crown.

'There are other candidates,' said Admiral Pertwee. 'But you are our first choice. It will take you a while to get down to Plymouth so you will have to leave immediately and by then *Mercury* should be ready to depart. I will need your answer now.'

Merriman asked for an hour. He hurried out to the stable and asked his groom if he knew which way Helen and the children had gone. Their first stop was apparently to be a windmill some ten miles away. As the groom saddled a swift mare for him, Merriman considered walking back into Burton Manor and simply telling Admiral Pertwee that he would gladly captain the *Mercury.*

He knew his wife would make no overt attempt to dissuade him, nor did she expect him to ask her permission. Yet they had been here so many times before. He had lost count of the occasions on which he'd departed at a moment's notice, invariably on some dangerous assignment. It was no different to what many an Englishmen had done for the past decade in households up and down the land. But Helen had been such a support during his recent dark times. Merriman felt that he owed it to her; to at least inform her of the facts before he accepted the commission.

The windmill at Mickle Trafford was a well-known local beauty spot. He gave his mount, Rosy, half a mile to warm herself then urged her into a gallop. Fortunately, there'd been no rain for a few days and these were bridleways he'd ridden since childhood. With no more than twenty minutes in the saddle, he caught up with Helen, Robert and Mary-Jane, who had stopped to admire a meadow teeming with flowers.

Robert was with the horses, sitting on a wooden fence.

'Hello, Pa!'

'Hello, Robbie.'

Merriman hailed Helen and tethered his horse. Father and son met mother and daughter, facing each other across the fence.

'I take it the admiral's visit isn't purely social,' said Helen, brushing some grass from her skirts.

'It is not.'

'What is it this time?'

'Not the usual affair. A delivery of sorts. A rather important document must be conveyed across the Atlantic.'

'The new world!' exclaimed Robert.

'When?' asked Helen, a look of resignation upon her face.

'I would have to leave tomorrow.'

Young Mary-Jane turned away, facing the field of flowers.

'There won't be any fighting then, Pa?' asked Robert.

'I shouldn't think so. Actually, we should be able to outrun any trouble. A frigate, stripped down and lightened for speed.'

'It will be months though,' said Helen.

Merriman nodded. He reached over the top of the fence and took her hands. 'I had hoped we would have a little longer but it is very urgent.'

'I suppose we should be glad that the court martial hasn't changed any minds in the Admiralty.'

The fact that his wife considered this made Merriman very happy. 'We should. There are other candidates but I'm led to believe it's mine if I want it.'

Helen squeezed his hands, then glanced at her children in turn. Still turned away, Mary-Jane's head was bowed. Robert seemed suddenly interested in his shoes.

'You're very quiet, young man,' said Helen.

'It's been nice having Pa with us.' Robert looked up at his parents. 'But he has to do his duty.'

'True,' said Helen.

Merriman climbed over the fence and walked around Mary-Jane so he could face her. He took out his handkerchief, knelt in front of his daughter and dried her tears.

'I am sorry, Mary-Jane. I did tell you this might happen.'

'I just thought we might have a few more days.'

'I know. I'll be back as soon as I can and in any case I'll write.'

Merriman straightened up. 'Once I've spoken to the admiral, I'll have Hopkins pack my gear and we can have a nice evening of singing and games. Now, let's ride back to the manor together.'

It was more than three hundred miles down to Plymouth, which Merriman managed in a creditable four days, thanks to more dry weather and a generous friend who supplied him with an excellent coach and two drivers.

Halting in Exeter, they took pity upon a harried engineer, whose own coach had thrown a wheel. This man was named George Matcham and he too was headed for Plymouth harbour. As the pair journeyed on together, Merriman was astonished to learn that Mr. Matcham was the brother-in-law of none other than the Admiral Lord Nelson, having married his sister Catherine in the year 1787. Merriman explained his own limited contact with the great man and they spent more than an hour lauding him, both barely able to believe that seven years had passed since his death at Trafalgar.

Merriman considered himself to be well-travelled fellow but Mr. Matcham has visited numerous exotic locales. Born in India, he had also visited Persia, Egypt, Greece, Turkey and Arabia, mainly in the employ of the East India Company. Hearing of these far-off places, Merriman thought of Helen and her late father, who had spent many years in the East.

They had been travelling together for almost two hours before getting around to the reasons why both were bound for Plymouth. Even in such esteemed company, Merriman had to be tight-lipped about the precise details of his mission, though he did admit that he would be crossing the Atlantic.

'And you, Mr. Matcham?' he asked as their carriage rolled on, the southern coast at last in view from Merriman's window.

'I will be discussing my plans for the breakwater to protect Plymouth Sound.'

'Ah, yes,' said Merriman. 'I have seen some of the works.'

'It is not my commission,' admitted Matcham. 'Lord St. Vincent has hired Mr. Rennie and Mr. Whidbey to lead the construction. They have asked to look at my original plans, which were drawn up some years ago. From our initial conversations, it appears they are to be even more ambitious than I. The breakwater is to run to more than seventeen hundred yards in length. They anticipate using more than three million tons of rock, would you believe?'

'Three million? By God, it hardly seems possible.'

'Talking of the possible, apparently some of the mining in nearby areas has unearthed novel types of fossil. In a recent letter, Mr. Whidbey explained that some scientists now theorise that these fossils are derived from a race of enormous reptiles that roamed the Earth before man.' Mr. Matcham chuckled and shook his head in disbelief. 'And this from scientific minds! Have you ever heard such bunkum?'

Chapter Seven

Crookhaven Bay and Brow Head

As anticipated by the barometer, the weather took a turn for the worse. By early afternoon, a strong wind was rising inexorably towards a gale. Even worse, it had shifted around to the south-west: right on the nose. With visibility worsening and sail reduced, HMS *Romulus* was just about able to make west-north-west. The lookouts were able to see only the merchantman, *Iona*.

Commander Shrigley could only hope that any signal from either HMS *Galway* or HMS *Zeus* would reach them at the rear of the convoy. Attending the quarterdeck with his boat-cloak about his shoulders, Shrigley wondered if he should have donned his oilskins. The first lieutenant was already in position, stationed behind the wheel alongside another of the midshipmen, Lange. Shrigley almost slipped as he joined them.

'They do roll, these brig-sloops, sir,' said Glanville.

'So I've noticed,' said Shrigley, who was missing the solidity and stability or the larger vessels he'd served on for so long. Looking forward, he was instantly concerned by what he saw.

'Why *Iona*'s a good half-mile away, Glanville.'

'Yes, sir. You want us nearer?'

'In these conditions, I do. Restore the flying jib and we'll see if that does the trick.'

'Aye, sir.' As the first lieutenant hurried forward to give the order, Lange came closer, narrowing his eyes against wind and rain. Though only eighteen, he was broad and rather fat, with a chubby face. The cutting summary of his abilities from Glanville and Ives was that he was capable but lazy.

'What do you think Captain Thorpe will do, sir?'

'Depending on the weather – which may be worse where he is – he could decide to reverse course. We are not all that far from Admiral Lord Keith's Western Squadron blockading Brest. Strength in numbers. He may also elect to turn north, head for Ireland with a more comfortable time of it, then back to the west or south-west as soon as conditions improve.'

Lange nodded as they watched the sailors attending to the flying jib under the supervision of Lieutenant Glanville.

'How did you find life aboard with Captain Stone?' asked Shrigley, who'd not had any time alone with the midshipman.

'The captain did love getting his whack, sir. They say he amassed over ten thousand pounds during his time at sea.'

'Exciting times, then?'

'Rather *too* exciting, sir,' said Lange, eyes widening. 'I've been on here barely two years. We've lost three lieutenants, two midshipmen, four petty officers. And the crew – I doubt half of them were aboard when I started. Last week, I dined with two schoolfriends in Chichester. They've hardly been in a scrape between them.'

'And the charges against Stone and the purser?'

Lange wiped water from his face and grimaced. 'With a man so obsessed with prize-money, it should not have been a surprise.'

'I was told that the evidence is irrefutable.'

'I too, sir. I suppose we didn't want to believe it.' Lange shook his head, several expressions passing over his face before he continued.

'The captain had a way of making everything sound like an…adventure. Even though he led us into danger at times, one…wanted to do well for him. It's hard to explain.'

The more he heard about Stone, the more Shrigley wished he had taken the place of someone far less interesting.

Lange grinned and shook his head at a memory. 'Do you know, sir, at the end of the court martial, as he was being led away – even though he knew what he faced – Captain Stone winked at us.'

The wind did not ease off and cold sheets of rain continued to scour the ship. Now all in their oilskins, Shrigley and his two lieutenants were on deck when news reached them from the lookout. All three watched with concern as one of the topmen carefully descended from the crosstrees. Once at the quarterdeck, he explained what he'd seen.

'Flag signals clear on the mainmast of *Iona*, captain. The fleet is ordered to turn to the north. *Iona*'s already bore away.'

For three hours they sailed towards Ireland, the speedy sloop flying along so well that they had to reduce sail once more. The wind dropped to twenty knots and the lookout soon reported that two merchantmen and HMS *Galway* were once again in view. Though none of the officers were sick, many men came up on deck to ease their nausea, with only limited success. Shrigley was grateful for the blasting wind and the salt in his nose.

Captain Thorpe later changed course to the north-west, having clearly decided to abandon the southerly route altogether. It was, Shrigley reflected, a very inefficient and slow beginning to the Atlantic crossing, but he could find no fault in Thorpe's decision-making.

Throughout the next day and night, the fleet continued north until the forward ships spied Cape Clear Island and the feared Fastnet Rock. By then the wind had backed to the south-east and so the convoy could lay a westerly course with ease. Shrigley went up the ratlines to the maintop himself and saw that, though all thirteen ships were in view, they had been somewhat scattered by the gale.

He had only been back in the great cabin for an hour when Lange came down to fetch him due to an alarming report. A minute later, a look through the spyglass given to him by Captain Merriman confirmed that, in escaping one danger, they had sailed straight into another.

Two masts bearing French tricolours had emerged from Crookhaven Bay, perhaps three miles north of their position.

'Must have been sheltering from the gale in there, sir,' said Lieutenant Ives, scowling as he scratched at a sideburn.

Shrigley nodded. 'No doubt lying in wait for well-laden ships heading for England but our charges will suit them well enough. Mr. Lange – ask the lookouts for the position of our frigates.'

'Aye, sir.'

Shrigley did not like the way that the heavy-set midshipman ambled around the deck.

'At pace, sir!'

Lange did his best to increase his speed.

'Shall we beat to quarters?' asked Lieutenant Ives.

'Let us first see where we stand.'

It was something else he had learned from Merriman. With the two French ships in sight, there was no doubt that *Romulus* would clear for action. And yet an immediate response to the danger invariably smacked of panic. Shrigley would pick his moment, if only to be seen to do so.

Five minutes later, he had a good idea of the situation as Lange reported back.

'Sir, *Galway* and *Zeus* are close together, two miles south-west of us.'

'They may have not seen the danger. Ives, find the gunner and have the six-pounders loaded. Lange, we shall need signal flags to alert them.'

'Aye, sir.'

Within two minutes, both six-pounders were ready. At a wave, Shrigley gave the order and the first shot went up, a puff of black smoke drifting from the forecastle. By the time he ordered the second shot, Lange had the flags up on the mainmast.

Lieutenant Cathcote of the marines appeared and listened carefully as Shrigley summarised their position. Cathcote summoned one of his corporals and passed on the order for his marines to prepare their muskets.

Within ten minutes, it was evident that the two frigates had turned and were heading straight towards *Romulus* and the French ships to the north. Glanville was now up on deck and had been monitoring them from the taffrail.

'Definitely two of them, sir. Fourth-raters, I should say.'

Shortly afterward, word came from the crosstrees of flag signals from HMS *Galway*. As Shrigley had expected, they were to close up with the convoy and screen the rear.

'Five hours of light,' said Shrigley. 'This could be interesting.'

'Looks like we might get that gunnery practice after all, sir.'

'It does at that. Lieutenant Cathcote, perhaps you'd have a word with your drummer. We shall clear for action.'

As there would be no immediate contact with the enemy, Shrigley felt it an appropriate time to show his face below deck. It was one thing to observe the crew in action during practice or firing drill, another when they knew an engagement was near.

Once at the bottom of the steps, he passed the marine drummer and was pleased to see Trelawney actually moving with a little haste as the partitions were removed. From here, he strode onto the gundeck and watched as the carronades were unchained and the men assembled into their crews. He could still not get used to the sight of the carronades, which were not even half the size of great guns. Though they carried a heavier ball and were more manoeuvrable, they lacked range and could be unreliable. He had met no officer or seaman who considered them superior to long guns, when all factors were taking into account.

It was by no means the swiftest clearing he had seen but neither was it the slowest.

Spying him, the gunner, a man named Newcastle, hurried over and the pair marched along the larboard side, doling out orders and guidance.

'Still a lot of roll out there, sir,' said Newcastle as they neared the bow. 'We shall have to be careful with our timing.'

'We shall,' said Shrigley, on the verge of lambasting two sailors wrestling with a hammock until they finally put it away.

Then he spotted something else he didn't like. 'There's nothing in that box.'

The empty container sat between two guns and both crews simultaneously claimed that it didn't belong to them.

'The less junk about, the less of it can splinter and stick you!'

Before Shrigley had finished, one of the young powder monkeys had grabbed the box and scurried away.

'That lad is showing some pride, at least,' remarked the captain.

He and the gunner encountered another misdeed as they hurried along the starboard side. The cook and his mate were hurriedly throwing various cuts of meat into two tubs.

'Apologies, sir,' said the cook. 'I was busy putting out the galley fire and forgot about all this.'

'You've a half-minute before I throw that over the side,' said Shrigley, though he had no intention of doing so: the meat looked very fresh.

Halfway back along the starboard side, he could see that the crews had prepared well enough.

'Now then, lads!' he shouted, loud enough so that all became quiet.

'French frigates sighted to the north. We're here to protect the merchantmen and that's what we'll do. I know we've only drilled a few times but you're experienced men and I know you'll do your best for me. The enemy might have size and guns on their side but we're fast and we're agile and there's not a ship afloat that doesn't fear a row of twenty-eight pounders.'

Struggling to finish his short speech, Shrigley recalled another line from Merriman, unable to recall who he'd stolen it from.

'When it's loud, when it's smoky, when it's bloody – stand by your gun, stand with your crew. Are you ready?'

The ensuing cheer was not the answer of a keen, loyal crew but it was loud enough for the new commander and he departed the gun deck feeling quite satisfied. He was glad to see they were ready but could not help hoping that *Zeus* and *Galway* would handle the interlopers.

On his way back to the hatch, Shrigley passed the tiny medical bay. A pale-looking Mr. Webster was unwrapping the tools of his trade.

'Captain, may I request a reminder for Mr. Peebles – that he is to report to me if the necessity becomes obvious.'

The crew of the brig-sloop was not large enough for a permanent surgeon's mate for Webster but an experienced idler, Peebles, had volunteered to assist if necessary. Shrigley was grateful for it; there were generally very few sailors who wished to descend into the bloody mess of a medical bay during battle.

'I will see to it that he is reminded, yes.'

Shrigley encountered Midshipman Haskell, who was holding the logbook.

'Made a note of the enemy?'

'Not yet, sir.'

'Do so. And the time that we cleared for action. You will remain with me on deck.'

'Yes, captain.'

Seeing Trelawney assisting the cook's mate with a cauldron of water, Shrigley ordered the servant to bring up his hat when he was free.

'A tot of something to steady the nerves, captain?' offered the Cornishman.

Shrigley ignored this idiotic comment. Up on deck, he was pleased to see that the nets were almost in place and the life-lines affixed. There was at least one advantage to captaining a smaller vessel: most tasks required less time and fewer crewmen.

'Er, sir.'

Lieutenant Glanville had just lowered his telescope and his face betrayed considerable concern.

'Two more. Frigates. Emerging from behind what I think is Brow Head, couple of miles west of Crookhaven.'

Shrigley took the telescope offered to him and trained it to the north. There could be no doubt about. Identical in appearance to the first pair, two more French warships were now coming out at them.

'Well,' said Shrigley. By now, *Zeus* and *Galway* were further north than *Romulus* and closing rapidly with the first pair. Whether this had been a joint action or not, it had worked out well for the French. His outmatched vessel was now the only thing between the raiders and the convoy.

Word had spread quickly and now every man aboard seemed to be gazing at the two clear tricolours to the north, including Lieutenant Ives.

'That bloody gale. We could have been sunning ourselves and well on our way to the Azores.'

Shrigley did not particularly approve of such unhelpful imaginings, which only served to distract. Just then, Trelawney appeared with his hat. Despite the stiff breeze, Shrigley pulled it on and checked his tunic buttons.

Mr. Diggs had been overseeing the preparations for battle and now returned from the mast, the wind tugging at his jacket and hair.

'Lookout reports that the convoy have put on sail and are reforming their line.'

Again, this was as expected and the sensible course of action.

'Thank you, Mr. Diggs. You have sufficient men on deck?'

'Yes, sir.'

With the fourteen guns all manned by a crew of four, that left around thirty sailors to handle the sails and other tasks. Lieutenant Cathcote's marines were currently down on the gundeck but could be spared if necessary.

The bosun looked to the east. 'At least they're not far away, captain. Might get back to help us out in a bit.'

'Let us hope so.'

With the weather gage, Shrigley turned directly towards the raiders, *Romulus* running hard before the wind as the close-hauled French beat towards them on a larboard tack. It was the first time he had seen the ship on a run and he was able to crowd on all plain sail. He ordered that the spanker be pulled slightly to starboard, allowing for the roll of ship in the swell, which was still from the south-west – a remnant of the storm.

The captain soon discovered that his new ship was unbalanced. With her backstays throbbing under thirty knots of wind, *Romulus* was digging in badly. The captain resolved to discuss the matter with the bosun after the engagement; they would need to shift ballast, guns, or both.

Lange came up with a report of a crushed foot from a moving gun: Mr. Webster's first casualty of the day. Knowing Glanville was popular with the men, Shrigley had already put him in charge of the guns and now sent him down early to ensure they would be ready. This was a devil of a sea to fight in but the same went for the French. Though they'd been unable to establish the exact class of the frigates, they were undoubtedly both thirty-two-gun vessels. Most of those guns would be twelve-pounders but they had far more of them.

'By God,' said Ives, slowly revealing himself to be the type unable to keep his fears to himself. 'Sixty-four guns between them.'

'Two big targets for us then,' countered Shrigley, pleased to see the eager grin from young Haskell. Despite his earlier misdemeanour, the midshipman had already showed some initiative; ordering a change to the life-lines, clearly unafraid of doling out orders to the sailors.

As the French vessels came near, Shrigley continued to consider his alternatives. The frigates were close together, no more than two hundred yards apart. They were bearing down on his starboard bow, and if they bore away at the last moment, *Romulus* would face a double broadside. She could return fire but had far fewer guns. In this sea, accurate gunnery would be difficult all round, but the damage might be severe. Even worse, if they passed him, he would be downwind and trailing the convoy.

He tried to shut out his surroundings and gazed out at the dark blue sea.

What do I do? What do I do?

Chapter Eight

Charmante and Gaillard

'We shall stay two points off their bows,' he announced to Ives and Haskell.

'Keep them hard on the wind you mean, sir?' answered Ives.

'Precisely?'

'Sir?' said Haskell with a frown.

Ives passed the order on to the helmsman, then took it upon himself to explain the tactic to the youngster:

'They can't turn too much to larboard or they'll luff up and slow – dead in the water. If they turn to starboard, we can match them and stay in the spot between their chasers and main battery. Should we ready *our* chasers, sir?'

'Yes.'

Mr. Newcastle was called up again and placed in charge of the six-pounders at the bow.

'How far, Mr. Haskell?' asked Shrigley as *Romulus* leaped on, her last recorded speed an impressive nine knots. This did, however, mean that the captain would have even less time to decide and act.

'A mile or so, sir?'

'A little more I should say,' replied Shrigley. 'Two points please, Mr. Diggs!'

Romulus was slowly turning to larboard as she matched the French ships, which also had the effect of filling the sails over the quarter as the run became a broad reach.

The bosun raised a hand in acknowledgement. He was standing with the helmsman and regularly ordering adjustments to lines and sails.

With Glanville now below, Ives had been tasked with monitoring the French. 'They have run out their guns, sir.'

A moment later, a cluster of dull reports suggested that the frigates had already opened fire. But there was no smoke. In fact, the noise had come from the east, where *Zeus* and *Galway* were close in with the French.

'Mr. Diggs, make ready to haul up the courses. And rig some running backstays on the starboard side.'

'Aye, sir.'

At his orders, dozens of sailors scurried across the deck while topmen worked frantically above.

'Will you go past them, sir?' asked Ives. 'Can we afford to give up the wind advantage?'

Shrigley had made his decision. *Romulus* was here to protect the convoy. And if she was closing with the French frigates, then she might as well make a fight of it, though the chances of victory seemed slim.

'We will go between them,' he announced. 'Turn across the bow of the first ship. They are both hard over: starboard gun ports will be closed lest they ship water. The risk of striking each other might also give them pause. Then we will quickly wear sail and run up their lee. That will push our starboard side up, helping us aim high – into the rigging.'

'Aim to strike the eastward vessel then,' said Ives.

'Precisely.'

'Shall I tell Glanville of your intent?' offered the second lieutenant.

'Please do.'

As Ives hurried towards the hatch, Shrigley looked back to the east. The four warring vessels were perhaps only two miles away, engaged in rapid turns, the sound of guns repeatedly reaching *Romulus,* despite the wind.

'We too shall begin.' Cupping his hands together, Shrigley hailed Mr. Newcastle. The gunner didn't hear but an idler near the mainmast did and got Newcastle's attention.

'Fire away!'

Ten seconds later, the two six-pounders released their shot in quick succession.

'Short, I think,' said Ives.

Shrigley wasn't sure how he could tell but hoped Mr. Newcastle at least had some idea.

He supposed it would all look rather ridiculous to the Frenchmen. This little terrier of a brig-sloop yapping at two bigger dogs and running straight for their throats.

'A hit!' yelled Haskell as a shout went up from the bow.

'At least we got the first one in,' remarked Ives.

Now came puffs of smoke from the enemy's bow-chasers. These whistled ahead of *Romulus* and did no damage. With the wind behind them, *Romulus* was running smoother than the French frigates, which were bouncing up and over the waves, making aiming much harder. Shrigley could see a good deal more of the them now: individual spars and sails, the vivid red and blue upon the fluttering tricolours.

'How far Mr. Haskell?'

'Eight hundred yards, sir.'

Shrigley approached Bosun Diggs and explained what he intended. When he saw the look upon the older man's face, he began to doubt himself. Was he simply trying to emulate Merriman with this bold, direct approach? Had he correctly thought it through? Did he have it all wrong?

Diggs, however, made no protest and soon had the sailors moving. The jib and staysail were now set out to starboard, as was the spanker. The main and foresails were braced around, allowing the sails to be set square by the wind.

Shrigley's doubts were not eased by the appearance of First Lieutenant Glanville on the deck.

'I'll keep this short, sir. *Between* them? Are you sure? Should we even be taking them on directly?'

'Taking them on?'

Glanville at least had the good grace to step away from the others and keep his voice down.

'Should we not retain the wind advantage, screen the convoy until help comes?'

'Help is not coming, Glanville. Our compatriots have already engaged the enemy.'

'They are in the same class as their foes. We are not.'

'We are all that stands between the French and the merchantmen.'

The French ship rounded up momentarily, bow-chasers exchanged fire. Shrigley had no idea if their shots struck home but there was a crash from the starboard side of the bow. He was not overly concerned: the small shot was most dangerous if it hit living targets.

Glanville replied: 'Is there not some wisdom in…picking our moment.'

'Or picking our *enemy*? Would you have us attack only weaker vessels? Only easy pickings? Easy prizes?'

A grim expression came over Glanville's face. 'I see you are set on your path, sir.'

'You see clearly, lieutenant. Ives explained what we are doing. You understand?'

'I do.'

'You will be able to see our target as well as I. Give the order when you see fit. I suggest you hurry.'

Mr. Diggs took it upon himself to have staysails set, then the forecourse and maincourse furled; these low sails were vulnerable to shot and fire. A few topmen remained aloft to assist those on deck.

They were now less than three hundred yards from the nearest frigate, in a position to turn and fire a broadside. But that would have been aimed at the bow, moving at speed, with little chance of landing many blows. As *Romulus* neared the first ship, it suddenly rounded up into the wind once more, bow chasers fired shot into the middle of the sloop. One cracked against the mainmast, causing the seamen to drop low, but was only a glancing blow. The Frenchmen seemed content to let *Romulus* come on, confident that they would fare better in an exchange of fire and would then have the weather.

At less than a hundred yards, Shrigley gave the order.

'To larboard!'

Assisted by Bosun Diggs, the helmsman threw the wheel over. *Romulus* veered to larboard, surging ahead as wind filled the staysails, they cut across the bow of the nearest frigate. Shrigley initially feared he had miscalculated and that a collision was inevitable. But, as *Romulus* crossed the enemy bow, there was nothing more damaging than the French bowsprit tearing a hole in the colours.

'Helm to starboard!'

Mr. Diggs and the helmsman furiously spun the wheel back to starboard. The spanker was hauled amidships and then freed off as the stern came through the wind, spilling air and losing power. The ship was further slowed by letting go the jib and staysail sheets. Due to the abrupt change of direction and speed, several sailors lost their grip and slid across the deck. The captain held tight to the taffrail as the larboard braces were freed and those to starboard were pulled. *Romulus* was now pressed over with the wind at her side.

Though unable to fire her great guns due to the angle of her deck, the French ship did have marines at the rails and in the rigging. Shrigley heard the order to fire in French and a musket ball thud into timber close by.

Glanville chose his moment well. *Romulus*'s seven starboard carronades all discharged within a second or two. With the starboard side up and the frigate still hard-pressed, the ships were soon past each other.

Shrigley saw little of his opponent until the sloop's bow went across the wind and she settled back down – hove-to.

Then came the blasts from the second French ship. But she was still hard over and, while *Romulus* had been close to her target, she was far. The cannonballs whistled away into the sky.

'Capital strikes!' yelled someone at the bow. Scrambling for'ard, Shrigley saw that Glanville's gunners had successfully targeted the French mizzen mast. Narrowest of the three masts, it then split with a satisfying crack, sending rigging and spars downward and dragging acres of sail with it.

'Huzzah!' came the cry from the few voices at the bow. Shrigley allowed himself not a moment of satisfaction.

The wrecked mast and rigging went over the stern, falling directly onto the rudder.

A grimacing Lieutenant Ives hopped to the rail and then fell. Looking down, Shrigley could see that something had gone through the white of his stockings just above his ankle.

'Haskell, what's the other one doing?' asked the captain as he went to assist Ives. The second lieutenant looked down, ashen-faced, as Shrigley checked the wound. A finger-sized shard of wood was sticking out of the skin.

'Stay there for now, Ives.' Shrigley stood up.

'She's turning to leeward, sir,' answered Haskell. 'Wearing sail.'

Shouts and cries went up from the closer French ship as she slowed. The fallen sails had covered the stern: they still did not know her name.

Diggs already had the sailors on the sheets, hauling the sails in, but for now *Romulus* was barely making way.

'She's helpless!' cried the helmsman.

He was quite right. They were ideally situated to rake their enemy's stern. Thankfully, there was soon enough in the topsails for the helmsmen to bring *Romulus* around a little and Glanville did not need encouragement to unleash the starboard battery once more.

By that point, the damaged French ship had travelled a quarter-mile but, with an easy target, most of the carronades struck home. A great chunk of wood was sent flying from the stern and two men fell into the morass of sails and rigging below.

'The second ship is around, sir,' announced Haskell. 'Reaching towards us.'

'Diggs, get us moving!' shouted Shrigley.

'Aye, captain, minute or two yet.'

Reaching the stern, Shrigley wasn't sure they had that long. In wearing sail, the French vessel had come around in a broad loop but the strong wind was propelling her along and she was no more than a half mile distant.

'The *Charmante*,' announced Haskell, now lowering his spyglass. 'Well done, sir. If it was just us and them, we might even take her.'

'Not today, I fancy.'

Pressing the attack against the *Charmante* would leave them completely exposed to the second ship. Having successfully damaged one and engaged them both – leaving the convoy clear – Shrigley adjudged that he needed boat speed and some space.

At last, the crew had the ship around and sails hauled in, *Romulus* began to move through the rolling waves once more: two knots, then four.

'West-south-west,' he ordered, hoping to at least stay between the frigate and the convoy. His course emulated the enemy ship, which was now directly behind them, slightly upwind, perhaps only four hundred yards away and closing fast. The bow chasers were already at it and a crash went up as a ball smashed through one of the great cabin's windows.

First Lieutenant Glanville came racing up through the hatch and to the quarterdeck. His right hand was slick with blood.

'Are you wounded?' asked Shrigley.

'Mr. Newcastle. We were so angled up that their sharpshooters had clear sight through the ports. A ball in the neck. He went quickly. Two others down.'

'Damn it.'

'You did well, Glanville,' said Ives, still slumped against the rail.

The first lieutenant was more interested in the pursuing frigate. 'He'll catch us before long.'

'Agreed,' said Shrigley.

'The carronades,' said Glanville. 'They're light enough that we can move some up here and to the stern. As least that way we can return fire.'

'You can do it without block and tackle?'

Glanville nodded. 'We did it before with Captain Stone.'

'Please do so. And have Lieutenant Cathcote come up. And Trelawney.'

'Aye, captain.'

Crouching over like everyone else to avoid the French sharpshooters, Shrigley approached Bosun Diggs, who spoke first:

'Sir, main topgallants' flapping. One of the balls must have done something to it. I'll get the topmen up there.'

'Do so. We'll need every bit of speed.'

'We're lucky the bottom's freshly coppered, sir. We got rid of the weed and barnacle too.'

Shrigley waited by the hatch for Lieutenant Cathcote to come up. He was only thirty-two but possessed a thick head of short grey hair that made him appear a decade older.

'We can spare your men from the guns for now. Please do all you can to assist Glanville in bringing up the carronades. Once that's done, have all of your marines come up with their muskets. I leave it to you to position yourselves and choose your shots but do whatever you can to put off our pursuers.'

Romulus was swift for a brig-sloop but the larger vessel could put up far more sail and the second frigate continued to gain. They saw gear going over the side and the water tanks being emptied. Shrigley might have done the same had he not been charged with crossing the Atlantic. Before long, the bow of the frigate was no more than two ship lengths from *Romulus*'s stern.

With some quickly strung lines and a lot of brute force, Glanville soon had the first of the carronades up through the hatch and mounted at the stern. The ammunition had come up first and the crew wasted no time in unleashing shot.

The French had also been busy moving their guns and they now had four at the bow, trained on *Romulus*. The exchange of fire was intermittent but they were concentrating on the rigging and had made the topmen's job very difficult. These brave fellows made the repair to the main royal barely a minute before another shot made a mess of the mizzen topgallant.

The great cabin had sustained more damage and the entire stern was now being peppered with shot. Shrigley had summoned Trelawney to help Ives below and he'd been instructed to keep all the crew out of the cabin.

After another great thud came a terrible exhalation of breath. Spinning around, the captain saw that one of Cathcote's sharpshooters had fallen from the rigging. The poor fellow had been shot in the chest and he was wheezing awfully, coughing blood up onto the deck. The French marines claimed another victim as a second man fell back from the stern, rolling in agony and gripping his shoulder.

Glanville came close to Shrigley. 'We have to do something, sir. I can prepare the larboard battery but we'll not fare well with a straight exchange of fire. We're too close to turn across his bow now.'

Shrigley watched as the injured, bleeding men were taken below. Mr. Newcastle was dead. Others would die. It was nothing unexpected. Nothing new.

Except they were members of *his* crew. *He* had made the decisions.

And, after that initial success, the pursuit seemed to have dulled his senses. A curious numbness had gripped him. He couldn't decide what do. As it happened, he was spared another decision.

'Movement at the ports!' shouted Lieutenant Cathcote, who was kneeling at the rail, his musket beside him on the deck.

'They can't bring them to bear yet,' said Glanville as both officers stood to watch the enemy.

'He's getting close,' replied Shrigley. 'A broadside now gives away his advantage. Why?'

'He may think he only needs one, sir. Sixteen guns.'

And then they all saw that the moment was now: the sailors moving, the sheets loosening, the bow turning away.

'Down!' shouted Glanville. 'Everyone down.'

Seconds later, the frigate unleashed the broadside and, at that range, Shrigley knew most of the shot would strike home. He was dropping low when something struck his left shoulder and head, throwing him to the deck. Ears ringing, head aching, he felt like lying there, eyes closed, hoping it would all go away.

Get up, man. Up!

Shrigley struggled to his knees and then his feet. In his nostrils, the familiar smell of shattered wood and dust. Despite his dazed state, he could see four clear holes in the rails. A third marine had been killed and two sailors were writhing around, blood leaking from their wounds. Hearing something above, he looked up and saw sails and lines and timbers hanging in the nets.

Suddenly Bosun Diggs was in front of him, gripping him by the shoulders.

'You all right, captain? You all right, sir?'

Shrigley managed to nod.

'A bit of block hit you, sir.' Diggs retrieved a handkerchief and put it against Shrigley's head. 'Hold this, sir. I suggest you go below for now.'

As Diggs moved on, Shrigley shakily crossed the quarterdeck, hand already wet with blood. Halfway there, he belatedly realised that he didn't know the state of the ship. He turned to see that the helmsman was at the wheel and that the sails were full, though a couple had been turned to rags.

Feeling a hand on his left arm, he allowed Haskell to help him to the stern. Glanville and Cathcote were already there, watching as the French ship veered away and let out her sails, now charging north-west with the wind at her stern.

'*Gaillard*,' said Haskell.

'Glad to see the back of her,' added Cathcote. 'Oh, you all right, sir?'

Shrigley nodded, still unable to form any thoughts or words. Black edged his eyes and he would have fallen if not for Haskell.

'Thank God for *Zeus*,' said Glanville.

Apparently aware of the fact that his captain was struggling, Haskell pointed out beyond the *Gaillard*.

'See her, sir?'

There, perhaps only a mile away, was the British frigate, sailing straight at their foe.

Chapter Nine

Committed To The Deep

The new captain fainted while he was being stitched up. Because Mr. Webster was occupied with no less than twelve wounded men, the task was carried out by Peebles in the great cabin. Sitting on a chair, surrounded by glass and debris, Shrigley was already woozy and had been given a great mug of strong rum to ease the pain. When he awoke, the surgeon's mate was still working on his head.

'Not sure how you managed that, sir,' said Peebles. 'Thought the pain would keep you awake.'

Gritting his teeth, Shrigley tried to think of anything other than the feeling of the needle sticking his skin.

'How much longer, Peebles? I must get back on deck.'

'It's not all that deep, captain, but it is long. Eight in already and the same again I would think. It's going to smart awhile.'

The captain reckoned that an understatement but he was more concerned about what was going on above. He guessed around half an hour had passed since *Gaillard*'s broadside. She and *Zeus* had clashed some distance away and – with blood pouring relentlessly from his head – he had instructed Glanville to take charge and pursue, with the intent of returning the favour. And yet *Romulus* had not used her guns again. Shrigley's ship and his crew had suffered considerable damage but they could not abandon those who had come to their aid.

Peebles puffed out a breath, then turned and washed his blood-soaked hands in a pail. Shrigley could feel that the needle was still in his scalp. He wanted to press the man but wasn't sure that he himself could have managed the task half as well.

Peebles returned to his work. After a time, the captain felt the ship slow and he heard a loud exchange of voices, though he could not make much out. This went on for some time, leaving him even more frustrated. He was about to summon one of the lieutenants when a harried-looking Mr. Lange appeared at the doorway.

'What's going on?' demanded Shrigley.

'Sir, Captain Halliwell just passed us. *Zeus* saw off the *Gaillard* with a couple of broadsides. The *Charmante* must have cleared the wreckage because she's headed east. We're too far for flags but Captain Halliwell assumes that *Galway* was badly damaged because she's fleeing to the coast. Might find better luck there, given her name.'

Shrigley grimaced, and not only because of the ongoing pain. The trio of escorts were barely in the Atlantic and had already lost one of their number.

'I assume Halliwell is pursuing the convoy?'

'He is, sir, and asks that we return to the rear at the earliest opportunity. Mr. Glanville is requesting permission to change course. Lookouts can still see two of our ships, close to the horizon.'

'Of course. And he is to put on all sail.'

'Sir, we are unable to raise the main topgallant and there is damage to the jib-boom but Mr. Diggs and Mr. Edmonds have a crew attending to both.'

'Very good. Dismissed.'

'Oh, and I found this, sir.' Midshipman Lange brought over Shrigley's hat and returned it to him.

'Thank you, Lange. Hurry now – pass on those orders!'

With his head stitched and bandaged, Shrigley left his hat in the cabin (not wishing to bloody it) and made his way up to the quarterdeck. He was not surprised to see the ship still covered by detritus. Even with all the gun crews on deck, there was a great deal to do: clearing and removing the nets, setting the sails and making the repairs. There was not a man to spare; Ives was helping with the nets and only Glanville stood behind the helm.

The sun was low now, the ship cloaked by murk, the blue sea turning black.

'Sir, are you feeling better?' asked Lieutenant Glanville.

Shrigley wasn't sure. On his way up the steps, he'd been struck by another dizzy spell and now held tight to the taffrail to steady himself. There had not yet been time for anyone to address the six cannonball holes in *Romulus*'s stern.

'Yes. Thank you. And for taking charge while I was below.'

'Not at all. There's the *Zeus*, sir.'

'Ah, yes.' Shrigley looked to the bow and saw that the frigate was only a few hundred yards ahead of them, the pale sails clear even in the gloom. The sight of *Zeus*'s ensign alerted him to the fact that theirs was missing.

'The colours?'

'Torn off, sir. We have a replacement. Damn that bloody quartet or skulkers. You'd think they'd be at Brest or elsewhere.'

'A crime of opportunity, perhaps,' said Shrigley. 'We fared well though. And thank God for Halliwell. His reputation is well deserved.'

'Look out below!'

A saw hit the deck just ahead of the wheel, causing the helmsman to swear at those working above.

'Sorry!' cried one of those stationed on the mast. This sailor was then subjected to a tirade of abuse from Mr. Edmonds, the carpenter.

His eyes now on a shredded section of the stern, Shrigley found himself transported back to the battle. 'Cathcote – was he shot?'

'No, sir, but several of the marines were. He's below with them now. Do you remember, sir, that Mr. Newcastle was slain?'

'I remember.' With that, Shrigley headed back toward the hatch.

The captain had not quite reached the medical bay when the scream went up. Shrigley had heard many such noises in his naval career but this one was so imbued with utter agony that it caused him to pause in the passageway. Lieutenant Cathcote lurched out of the medical bay, shaking his head and muttering oaths. He straightened and tried to regain his composure upon seeing his superior.

'Ah, captain. Sorry, I have never been able to endure the sight of the surgeon's work. Rather pathetic in a marine.'

'Hardly, sir. We are just fortunate that men such as Mr. Webster have the wherewithal to stand it.'

The noises did not cease. The two officers took several paces towards the stern.

'Are you all right, captain?' asked the grey-haired Cathcote, nodding up at the bandage around Shrigley's head. Putting his hand there, Shrigley was glad that the blood at least seemed to be drying.

'Fine. An amputation?'

'Dobson. Only nineteen. Left leg above the knee. The surgeon has already attended to another fellow in an awful state – not sure of his name. Mr. Webster said that everyone else can wait – which I suppose is good news of a sort.'

'He has Peebles back with him?'

'Aye, sir.'

'So other than Mr. Newcastle…'

'Fordham was killed also – the man who fell from the rigging. Two more marines wounded but they'll survive, I would think. Four sailors gone. I'm afraid I don't have the names. Another five or six wounded, none as bad as Dobson.'

'I see.'

'A brief affair, wasn't it?'

'But a costly one.'

'You should be proud, sir,' said Cathcote. 'The convoy proceeds unmolested. And it takes a bold fellow to throw a sloop at two frigates.'

'Ah, well…proud of the men certainly.'

Cathcote lowered his voice. 'I heard Glanville wasn't so keen.'

'It is always best to discuss decisions of such magnitude.'

Cathcote paused before nodding. 'Diplomatically done, captain.' The marine lowered his voice. 'Glanville, Ives, I wonder if they spent so much time under Captain Stone that they began to think like him. A voracious hunter of the prize, and I lost count of the times I heard him say, "orders be damned". Glad to be serving under you, sir.'

'Thank you, lieutenant.'

Returning once more to the deck, Shrigley found Glanville berating Mr. Diggs, who looked about ready to snap and return fire. Ives and Haskell were also present.

'What's going on?'

Glanville answered: 'Captain, we've already had tools raining from the rigging and now a man. If not for the nets still being up, we'd have another corpse on our hands.'

Shrigley saw that a man was being helped down from the nets at the bow. He could see little else, however, due to the much-reduced light.

'It's almost dark. Mr. Diggs, we have enough sail up to make what, five knots?'

'With this wind, certainly, sir. We don't have the main royal up yet.'

'That can wait until first light. The ship and the crew have been through more than enough today. We're quick enough to catch the backmarkers. Once the sails are set, keep only those you need on deck. Everyone else is to go below and get some food down. Mr. Haskell, I trust the logbook is up to date?'

'It is, sir,' answered the youngster.

'You will tell the cook to relight the galley fire and prepare a meal. See to it also that every man receives a double tot today.'

'Aye, captain.'

With that done, Shrigley turned to Glanville and Ives. 'Gentlemen, I shall take over for now. Please go below and check on the condition of the gundeck. Let us attain some sort of order before the dog watch is out.'

Shrigley remained on deck through the night. The salty Atlantic air seemed to keep his head clearer than the stuffy, sickly atmosphere below. He refused several offers to relieve him from Glanville and Ives, who seemed to have done a good job below.

As well as the human casualties, they had lost two guns. One had been struck by a French ball, the other had overheated on discharge. Fourteen main guns were now twelve. And having experienced battle against frigates while captaining a brig-sloop, Shrigley could only hope that the lengthy remainder of their journey would not include another engagement.

The night was at least a quiet one. The breeze had backed to a northerly and was steady at fifteen knots, putting *Romulus* on a solid reach. As had been decided before departure, the vessels of the convoy carried bow and stern lights. *Zeus* was visible throughout the hours of darkness and it was just after two o'clock when they sighted a second ship of the convoy. Relieved to be back in touch with them, Shrigley could not, however, resist regular glances over the stern, fearful that one or more of the French vessels was in pursuit.

At first light, the messmates of the six dead men brought up the bodies, wrapped in their hammocks; cannonballs at their feet and clothes put in with them to obscure their form, as dictated by tradition. They were placed at the rear of the quarterdeck.

Haskell and Lange came up soon after with the colours.

'Should we wait, captain?' asked Lange, warily eyeing the dead.

'Go ahead now,' said Shrigley.

Once the flag was flying, the midshipmen went below for breakfast. They offered to bring Shrigley something but he was not hungry. He did, however, ask them to tell Trelawney to bring him some coffee.

Before it arrived, John Webster came up. He had evidently cleaned his hands yet the stain of blood remained. His wispy red hair was blown about by the wind. He took himself to the starboard rail and planted his hands upon it, ingesting several long breaths.

'Morning, John. Did you manage any sleep at all?'

'None. Would you give me a moment, Alfred? I will brief you regarding the injured later.'

'Of course.'

Shrigley left him alone.

'Well done, Trelawney, it's almost as good as new.'

The dour servant nodded with the trace of a grateful smile. 'Took a while to get the blood out, sir.'

'Sorry about that.'

'Some old salts say it's good luck to have some of your claret in the ship's beams.'

'I've not heard that one before,' said Shrigley, placing his hat on the table as he slumped into his chair.

'Mr. Dyer will start on the windows this afternoon.'

'No hurry. I believe he's back at work on the rigging for the moment.'

Shrigley opened the desk's top drawer and retrieved a leather wallet containing the crew list.

'Some breakfast, sir?'

'Any eggs?'

'Not today, sir. One of the chickens was blown to bits and the other two are too scared to lay.'

'Can't say I blame them.'

'Bread's still just about palatable, captain. With some ham and cheese?'

'Very good.'

Trelawney withdrew. Shrigley detected a change in attitude from the man. Perhaps it was because he'd been injured. Perhaps it was because he'd led *Romulus* into their first engagement. Perhaps Trelawney was simply grateful for surviving the battle and feeling more generous towards his fellow man.

Shrigley went through the list, reading through the limited information on the gunner, the three sailors and the two marines. It had always been the habit of Captain Merriman to say a little more than was strictly required during a funeral ceremony. Shrigley always thought he had done it very well, judging the mood of officers and crew, leavening the sadness and sense of loss with a wise word or too. But he had been with this crew for only a few days, and he did not know the men well enough to speak with any warmth or certainty.

While he considered this, Trelawney returned with his breakfast and another cup of coffee. 'Funeral this morning, captain?'

'I should think so.'

Trelawney tarried a moment. ''Twas always the habit of Captain Stone to hold a funeral in the morning. Often early.'

Shrigley looked up from the list. 'What's your point?'

'The sharks, sir. It's well known. Bodies on board draw the sharks. Ill fortune too. Better to get them gone.'

Perhaps reading the expression on Shrigley's face, the servant continued: 'I'd expect the same, sir. Wouldn't take it personal if my time came.'

Wisely, Trelawney withdrew again swiftly. Shrigley looked down at the breakfast plate and pushed it away. He could not possibly count the number of dead compatriots he'd seen cast over the side. There was no other choice, he knew, but the thought of this fate had haunted him ever since the first time he'd seen it done.

He hoped and trusted that his soul would ascend to heaven. But he could hardly bear the thought of his body, wrapped up and rotting, drifting deep in the endless sea.

*

In order to have time for the funeral – short though it would be – *Romulus* put on more sail, including the newly-restored main topgallant. By ten o'clock she was less than a mile behind the convoy, with three other merchantmen (and *Zeus*) visible from the crosstrees. The captain waited until the last merchantman was only a quarter-mile ahead then ordered the sails furled.

This took longer than usual due to the damage but he was pleased to see the *Romulus* functioning normally. The speed at which sailors could restore a vessel's means of control and propulsion was a constant source of amazement to him. Then again, they all understood fully the fate of a warship unable to make way.

While men and officers gathered, Mr. Webster at last gave his report. Four of the injured were able to return to duty with limitations. Five others were expected to recover in due course. Three more – the marine Dobson included – had endured amputations and would need to be hospitalised upon landing. One, who had been struck by a ball that came through a gunport, had lost both legs below the knee. Mr. Webster remarked that he had never seen such haemorrhages and reckoned the man had lost three or four pints of blood. He believed his immaculately clean medical bay and instruments would guard against gangrene but he feared this fellow – an idler named Griggs – would be fortunate to survive.

Shrigley thanked Webster for all he had done and was glad to see the surgeon in better spirits. The Welshmen praised Peebles and two "loblolly boys" – sailors who had volunteered to assist when the medical crisis was at its worst. Shrigley made a note of their names and pledged to see them rewarded.

When the time came, Glanville offered to do the reading. He acted in a pious and humble manner but it did seem to Shrigley that he gained some satisfaction from being at the centre of things. The captain felt a tad guilty at this thought, especially when the lieutenant made some heartfelt comments about Mr. Newcastle, whose family he had met during their recent time ashore.

The service was interrupted by the arrival of a gull in the rigging. This was considered bad luck by all and the bird soon departed when Mr. Diggs cracked a pail against the mast.

Before the bodies were committed to the deep, Shrigley stepped forward.

'Thank you, Lieutenant Glanville, for those words. I am only sorry that I did not have longer to get to know the six fellows we have lost. They did their part and fought bravely in yesterday's engagement. So did you all, to a man.'

Chapter Ten

HMS Mercury

Merriman had only a day to familiarise himself with his new ship. She was at anchor in Plymouth harbour and he'd arrived late the previous night. A swift consultation with the first lieutenant established that they would leave before dawn to catch a favourable tide. The wind was weak and shifty. Over the years, Merriman had tried to train himself not to hope or pray for favourable conditions but it was difficult not to when the entire mission depended on haste.

Upon waking and dressing, he sat at the rear of the great cabin and watched with a wince as three members of *Mercury*'s crew departed. It had been close to midnight when he'd called in the sailing master and the bosun to inform them that their services would not be needed. Before taking a boat out to the *Mercury*, Merriman had been handed correspondence confirming that Tom Henderson, Bosun Brockle, and midshipmen Eades and Adkins would arrive before departure. With them was a fifth man: Peters, Merriman's long-serving attendant. Though reluctant to break up any crew, Merriman grinned at the thought of having his proven, loyal compatriots beside him.

One unforeseen result of the third dismissal – an attendant named Merrick – was that the captain was offered no breakfast. Calling in at the galley, he was told by the cook that he could have bacon and eggs whenever he needed it. Electing to get some essentials out of the way first, Merriman made for the gundeck. Though the ship felt warm on the sunny May morning, he collected his jacket and hat, thinking it important to make a good impression.

Though the ship was at anchor, it appeared that normal routine had been followed and the gundeck had been cleared of hammocks and gear. In fact, it appeared very clear indeed. Not only was the space empty of sailors, it contained only eight guns. A frigate of *Mercury*'s size would normally have been equipped with a minimum of thirty-two. His last ship, *Thunder*, had been a seventy-four.

'Eight?'

'Eight, sir, yes.'

Turning, he saw that it was his new first lieutenant, Ernest Hobbs. With first impressions in mind, Merriman admitted to himself that Hobbs did not present very well. Other than the fact that he was prone to an anxious expression, Hobbs was only a little younger than Merriman and had clearly never obtained a commission. Though many men never reached the rank of captain, this did not say a great deal for his ambition or skill.

'I thought there were to be sixteen.'

'I was told eight, sir. For the lightness and speed.'

'Well, yes, of course for the speed but...eight?'

'All the guns were taken off in the yard, sir, and this is what we got back.'

'Have you tested them?'

'No, sir. We have so little ammunition – I wanted to check with you before losing any.'

'I see. And where is everyone?'

'Deck, sir. Hauling up a new top for the foremast. For the bigger jobs, we need every hand. Orders direct from the Admiralty, sir – we followed it to the letter. Only ninety men aboard. Just about enough to handle the sails. For the speed, sir.'

'For the speed, yes,' said Merriman, rapidly losing patience. 'And on that subject, how are we faring? Not much point losing our guns and sailors if we neglect the fundamentals.'

'All the gear's new, sir, so she should fly along. She's been refitted after Ushant. This class was always quick and I've seen her do twelve knots fully laden when close-hauled.'

'Very good. And what exactly occurred at Ushant?'

As Hobbs spoke, the two officers marched along the deck, their footsteps echoing through the open space.

'We were on our way to escort merchantmen back from Portugal, sir, but we ran across a French eighty-gunner. *Formidable* and well-named she is too. We had a frigate and a couple of sloops with us but we couldn't make a dent in the thing. Only got clear by running in close to Ushant and following the coast where he wouldn't dare follow.'

'She was badly damaged?'

'Very badly, sir.' Hobbs aimed a thumb back over his shoulder. 'You can still see some of the fire damage back there. Couple of guns went up. We lost sixty-three men in one day.'

'By God. What a number.'

'Limped home, sir, and she was straight in the yard. Captain Gilfoyle was never the same. He was due to retire soon anyway so that was that. When she came out of the yard, we were recalled but most of the crew were long gone by then. They're mostly new too.'

'A disparate bunch then. And I have hardly made things better.'

'I'll admit something, sir. I wasn't disappointed to see Flint go.'

'The sailing master?'

'Fine man in his day but…' Hobbs mimed tipping a bottle.

'I see.'

'The bosun, James, had not been with us long.'

'Well, Mr. Hobbs, I can assure you that those joining us are men of the highest quality.'

'Very good, sir. This lot…well, a firm hand on the tiller and all that.'

Merriman thought this an odd thing to say.

Hobbs opened his mouth to continue but said nothing more as they turned and made their way back across the eerily quiet gundeck. The only noise came from above, the rhythmic cry of, "Heave!".

'Is there something you wish to add, Mr. Hobbs?'

The first lieutenant wrinkled his nose and scratched at his neck before replying. 'Well, sir, though many are new, we have a few dozen of the old crew. Nine are Irishmen. Hard workers to a man but there has been the odd…incident between them and the English sailors.'

'Nine, eh? That is quite a lot, especially with our reduced numbers. Pressed men?'

'A couple, sir. As I said, good workers and four of them topmen. None better, in my experience, but, well, if there's ever a reason to claim ill-treatment, they will do so.'

'It is not my first time encountering such a situation, Hobbs. Affairs between England and Ireland often cause ructions. Let us see how we fare.'

As they reached the rear of the gundeck, a young sailor entered, removing his hat at the sight of his captain.

'Boat at the nets, sir.'

Merriman felt sure that his old allies had arrived. 'Ah. Five of them is there?'

'No, sir, three. And only one joining us. Gentleman by the name of Brook.'

The captain admonished himself for thinking of his cohorts before his mission. He'd been told that Balthazar Brook was already in Plymouth and was glad that the Treasury agent – and his precious cargo – had arrived.

As Merriman and Hobbs made their way upward, the first lieutenant gave the captain more detail on his limited crew. The second lieutenant, a Dutchman named Van der Baan, was currently ashore, overseeing a final delivery of provisions. This task had fallen to him because they had no purser. *Mercury* also had no midshipmen (other than Eades and Atkins, assuming they arrived), no gunner, no armourer, no marines and no medical officer.

Though he'd known in advance of these deficiencies, Merriman shook his head as he climbed the steps towards the daylight. 'Do we have a physician of any kind? Even a surgeon's mate?'

'Not currently, sir.'

'Currently? Hobbs – we are departing before dawn!'

'Mr. Van der Baan was trying to round someone up, captain. I'm sure none of us wants to depart without a medical man.'

'On that we agree. And what of Van der Baan? He was with you in Captain Gilfoyle's time?'

'He was, sir. Very capable fellow. Speaks French and German as well as English and Dutch.'

'Always useful.'

They were met at the top of the steps by a man of around thirty years wearing anonymous dark clothing, his thick fringe of black hair almost covering his eyes. Over his shoulder was a large canvas bag of the type favoured by sailors.

'Captain Merriman?'

'Mr. Brook, I presume.'

As they shook hands, Merriman felt Brook's calculating eyes run over him and then Hobbs, who he introduced. Before Merriman could say anything more, Brook gestured to his left. Standing there were two men also wearing dark trousers and jackets, both with flintlock pistols hanging from their belts. On the deck between them was a small strongbox.

'We should get this below immediately. I'm sure you agree that the great cabin is the best location.'

Merriman couldn't really argue with that. There would be space for Brook and his precious cargo in the officers' cabin but that was a more exposed area and would invite unnecessary questions about the strongbox's contents. Even Hobbs had not been told of it: only that they were conveying an important passenger to Canada.

'Go ahead.'

Merriman stood aside and watched as Brook ordered his men down the steps, then followed close behind. The captain looked towards the foremast. A dozen sailors were on the mast itself, guiding the top section as two dozen more hauled it up. A portly fellow with a red neckerchief was directing operations.

'If we have no bosun, who is in charge?'

'Edmonds, sir,' replied Hobbs. 'Carpenter. Very experienced man. No one has been with *Mercury* longer.'

'Very good.'

Merriman looked out at the water, which was very calm. The other anchored ships and boats nearby were facing in various directions.

'We are in desperate need of a breeze.'

'May I ask our destination, captain? I was told only that we are to cross the Atlantic.'

'That we are,' said Merriman, seeing no need to disclose any more before they departed.

'We made our best guess with water and provisions: six weeks at sea seemed about right.'

'I concur. But I will be aiming for a considerably swifter passage than that.'

On his way down to his cabin, Merriman passed Brook's two assistants going the other way. They reminded him of some of the men employed by Sir Laurence over the years; one wouldn't take a second look at them in the street, but would also not wish to meet them on that street in the hours of darkness.

He found Brook standing over the strongbox, his bag on the floor beside it. The cabin contained no desk, no chair, no furniture of any kind.

'There is no marine detachment at all?'

Noting that Brook did not refer to him as captain, Merriman nonetheless replied cordially.

'None. We have only essential personnel aboard and, as you can see, all excess weight has been disposed of. I intend to spend the day ensuring that we retain any material essentials while removing anything we can afford to lose.'

'This room can be locked, I assume?'

'The door can. Many of the partitions have been taken off but I suppose we can keep these.' Merriman gestured to the movable walls that made up one end of the cabin.

'That will have to do. And are you happy for me to be accommodated here? It will make it a good deal easier for me to watch over the box.'

In normal circumstances, this would be out of the question; however, Merriman saw logic in Brook's request. 'Very well. I use the starboard side, generally. When my servant, Peters, arrives he can set up a bed for you to larboard.'

'Thank you. Now, what about the crew? Have you been through the books?'

'With what aim in mind?'

'I know there are dozens of sailors aboard but I must at least have a look: identify any possible criminal elements.'

Merriman thought it a bad moment to tell the Treasury man that he'd never been to sea on a ship that contained *no* criminal element.

'That will not be possible, Mr. Brook. The ship's books will provide only cursory information on each man.'

Brook scowled. 'This was all put together with such haste. I do wish the Treasury had been more precise with the Admiralty.'

'Do bear in mind that – once we depart – there is nowhere for any criminal to go. Any potential thief aboard also knows that theft from a captain's cabin would mean an appointment with the yardarm. And even in the unlikely event that they broke open your box, a treaty would hold little interest for them.'

'There are not only common criminals aboard His Majesty's vessels, captain. A French spy was discovered aboard a ship of the line only last week.'

'Mr. Brook, I appreciate that guarding the strongbox is your primary concern but please believe me when I tell you that we face far greater dangers; mainly in the form of the French navy and three thousand miles of a very, very dangerous ocean.'

Balthazar Brook rubbed his brow.

'The lockers at the rear there,' said Merriman, pointing to the area below the windows. 'We can have one of them padlocked.'

'Very good.'

'Now, to our precise destination. I was told that you would be given the location and that only we two are to know it.'

'The port of Halifax, Nova Scotia.'

Merriman was not surprised. 'That suits me well enough. Vice Admiral Sawyer is based there. He commands all the navy's forces from Halifax to Bermuda. He and his staff will know more than anyone about the movements of the American navy.'

'If war is declared, is there a danger of interception?'

'Certainly, though most of their vessels are based to the south.'

'The common consensus seems to be that their navy is quite weak.'

'Small, but I don't know about weak. And they have the luxury of not being involved in another, larger war. Let us hope that a conflict can be avoided.'

'Even if it is, my masters consider the alliance crucial.'

'Of course. I assume you are supposed to deliver it personally to this native leader?'

'It is my duty,' answered Brook, with a rather unnecessary air of drama.

'*Our* duty.'

Brook seemed to appreciate the sentiment.

'I am hungry,' announced Merriman. 'Would you like to join me for some bacon and eggs?'

'I would.'

'Very good. One more thing, Brook. I appreciate that you may be rather preoccupied at the moment but do remember to refer to me as "captain" or "sir"; and not only when we're in company. As of last evening, I am master of this vessel.'

Merriman soon concluded that the first lieutenant had done a fine job of limiting the ship's weight. Hobbs was unsure if more of the gravel used for ballast could be offloaded but – after a few calculations – the captain concluded that they could not risk it. Though the months of calmer weather were coming, the unforgiving Atlantic could still throw the heaviest of seas at them. The frigate was already under weight and he didn't want further instability. He was dismayed to find that *Mercury* was carrying less than three hundred cannonballs, plus some grapeshot and a commensurate amount of powder. The frigate would have to rely on its speed to get out of trouble.

Around one o'clock, the second lieutenant returned. Merriman was at the time running his eyes over the newly-complete foremast with the carpenter, Edmonds. Van der Baan was in a requisitioned boat laden with fresh provisions and would have been easily identified without his uniform. Tall and flaxen-haired like many Dutchmen of Merriman's acquaintance, he removed his hat as the boat passed the bow.

'Good morning, captain! Very pleased to meet you!'

Despite its heavy load, the boat rocked from side to side as the huge officer stood to greet Merriman.

'Good morning, Mister Van der Baan. Careful there, or you shall receive a dunking!'

The second lieutenant was accompanied by four sailors at the oars and another fellow sitting at the bow.

Concluding that Mr. Edmonds was indeed very capable and that the foremast was ready for full rig and sails, Merriman picked his way through the sailors preparing said rig until he reached the nets on the port side. Van der Baan climbed up, a great sack of grain on his shoulder, beaming at Merriman. He really was quite remarkably tall.

'Six feet, six inches, sir – before you ask.'

Merriman shook his hand. 'You must spend much of the day ducking.'

'I certainly prefer to be on deck. Captain Sir James, it is a privilege to be working with an officer of your standing.'

After the court martial, it was pleasant to hear such a comment.

'Thank you.'

Mr. Hobbs came up the steps and nodded to the Dutchman. They could hardly have been more different: the gregarious giant and the anxious, hunched figure. Merriman told himself to concentrate on a more important issue.

'Mr. Van der Baan, please tell me that one of those fellows has medical experience.'

'Indeed, sir.' The second lieutenant helped the man up the nets as other sailors crowded around to assist with the unloading. This fellow had his dunnage over his shoulder and removed his cap.

'Morning, captain. Morning, lieutenant.'

'Philip Askew,' announced Van der Baan. 'A very useful chap – originally an armourer's mate but he has also worked as a surgeon's mate.'

'Is that right?' said Merriman.

'Yes, sir. I was always below, in the same neck of the woods, and I developed an interest in it.'

'Some of the same skills, captain,' observed the second lieutenant. 'A steady hand and a knowledge of how things work.'

'I suppose so. Well, as you can see, Askew, we have only a small crew. You are very welcome.'

'If you'll excuse me, sir,' said Van der Baan. 'I shall oversee the provisions.'

'Of course.'

As the giant departed, First Lieutenant Hobbs licked his finger and held it in the air. 'It's getting up, captain. Ten knots at least. Northerly.'

Despite the reduced numbers aboard – or perhaps *because* of it – HMS *Mercury* continued to be a hive of activity throughout the day. Van der Baan busied himself with ensuring that the ship had sufficient provisions (but not *too* much). Merriman spent a few minutes with the new arrival, Askew, to assess his ability, and he concluded that the man was probably capable of patching holes but not a lot more. He found himself envious of Alfred Shrigley, who had the very intelligent and conscientious John Webster aboard his ship. He also spent a half-hour with First Lieutenant Hobbs, planning their route west, and how it might change according to the wind. When they had concluded, Van der Baan remarked in passing that the aged first lieutenant was the best naval navigator he had encountered.

Shortly afterwards, the two lieutenants came to the great cabin with another issue to consider. They had kept the ship's reserve anchor onboard, intending to ask the captain's opinion. After a good bit of debate between the three of them, Merriman decided to retain it. The second anchor weighed a ton and could be used as movable ballast. It was actually common to keep three, or even four aboard and he couldn't bear the thought of having no spare. His recent experience with *Thunder* only reinforced this view: without her anchors, the ship would have foundered on the African coast, long before facing the *Hercule*.

As the sun set, Merriman found himself growing uneasy. There was still no sign of his loyal crewmen. He supposed he would have to depart without them if they didn't appear but – comradeship aside – could he leave port without either sailing master or bosun?

He and Hobbs were working on a revised watch system when he heard another boat hailing the *Mercury*.

'That must be them, he said, pulling on his shoes and hurrying up on deck. Approaching the nets, he encountered Van der Baan talking to a man in a tiny rowing boat. The man was holding a lantern and appeared to be accompanied only by a woman, who looked up at the ship with wide, wary eyes.

'What's going on, Van der Baan?'

'It's a tad involved, sir. The woman there is the cousin of a Jack Lownes, carpenter's mate. He was killed during our encounter with the *Formidable*. He was well-known to Captain Gilfoyle on account of Lownes saving his life in a previous skirmish. His dying wish was that his son serve aboard *Mercury* like him. The captain did mention it to Hobbs and I but that was some months ago…'

'I see.' Merriman peered over the side. 'What's your name, miss?'

'Martha Lownes, sir.'

'And where is the boy?'

'Here, sir.' The boatman moved his lantern so that Merriman could see a rather pathetic sight: a shivering lad who looked no more than ten or twelve, clad in ragged clothes.

'How old are you, lad?'

The boy didn't answer.

'Ned don't speak much,' replied Martha, her Devon accent broad. 'He's been like this since he's been in the workhouse. They don't treat him right well at all.'

'And you can't care for him?'

'Got two of my own.'

The boatman muttered something, prompting Martha to speak again.

'Got two of my own, *captain*. Did try, sir, but I've many debts. That's why they put Ned in.'

'Well, lad?' demanded Van der Baan in his commanding tone. 'Can you speak at all? Not much use to us if you can't.'

Despite a clout around the head from his aunt, Ned Lownes said nothing.

'Captain, I'll happily throw down a couple of coins,' said Van der Baan.

Merriman reckoned he was getting sentimental in his old age. Before the children, he wouldn't have given a second thought to this matter, but Ned was not much younger than his Robert and he knew how awful the workhouse could be. At least this way, the debt to his father was paid and the boy had some possibility of advancement.

'No,' said Merriman. 'We should do right by the father and it's not as if he's going to add much weight.' He turned back to those floating below.

'We shall put him on the books as a Third Class Boy.'

'Much obliged, captain,' answered Martha. 'If he was with us, Jack would thank you too!'

The young boy was unable to climb the nets and so Van der Baan went down and climbed up one-handed, with Ned Lownes in the other. He was truly a pitiful specimen: barefoot and dirty, and apparently without any spare clothing or belongings at all.

'Tell cook to send up some hot water and have someone check the slops to see if there are any garments that might fit him. Well, young Ned, have you eaten today?'

The newest member of *Mercury*'s crew shook his head.

'Then you shall have some plum duff.'

Wishing to keep himself busy, Merriman worked with Hobbs on the new watch arrangements for a time before retiring. By that point, Balthazar Brook was already asleep in his bed on the larboard side of the cabin. Consulting his pocket-watch, Merriman saw that it was almost eleven o'clock. Given the tides, he knew he could wait until about seven in the morning, but no later. Climbing into bed in his nightshirt, he shook his head in disbelief. The thought of departing without his five compatriots was an awful one.

The captain was later awoken by the sound of footsteps echoing around the great cabin. Covering his face as light came near, he heard, 'shutter that lantern!'

These were the gruff tones of Peters, his servant of two decades, whose angular visage was soon illuminated by the dimmed light. Beside him were the keen faces of Eades and Adkins, the round features of Bosun Brockle and the lined profile of Tom Henderson.

'I do hope this isn't a dream,' said Merriman as he sat up.

'The journey was more like a nightmare, captain,' remarked Eades. 'Landslide blocked the coast road.'

With a grin, Merriman shook each hand offered to him.

'Gentlemen, it's a great relief to have you aboard HMS *Mercury*. Find somewhere to sleep and I shall make some introductions when we're underway. We depart at morning watch.'

Chapter Eleven

Danger Near and Far

While HMS *Romulus* had taken almost a week to leave the Irish coast behind, HMS *Mercury* completed the task in just three days. Mizen Head vanished into the gloom on the third evening and, from there, *Mercury* pushed on, the lightened ship faring well as the wind shifted all the way between a north-westerly and a southerly.

  Merriman was relieved and glad to see it but, with so little ballast and weight on the gun deck, the ship behaved quite differently: in a way none aboard had much experience with. She answered quicker to helm and sheet and sat high in the water. With the wind on those first three days not exceeding twenty knots, Merriman was concerned about how the ship would react to the heavy swells and blasting gales of the northern Atlantic. And yet, on the fourth evening, in a rougher sea, *Mercury* still seemed steady enough and he was informed by Lieutenant Hobbs that they'd achieved an average speed of nine knots, which he had seldom achieved on *Thunder*, a far larger vessel.

Everyone was kept busy. He tasked Hobbs and Van der Baan with introducing Bosun Brockle and Sailing Master Tom Henderson to ship and crew, which was also his way of ensuring the established officers befriended the newcomers. He also had a task for Eades and Adkins; asking them to keep an eye on the boy Ned Lownes. Knowing how such a vulnerable youngster might be taken advantage of – if thrown in immediately with the crew – he told the midshipmen to find a space for the lad in the officers' cabin. It was rare for them both to be there at the same time, so they told Ned he could use their bunks if they were absent. It seemed that matters of hygiene were a mystery to the boy so their first priority was to clean him up. Merriman heard from Eades that they almost lost Lownes overboard when he first used the roundhouse, which was designed for men. The pair confessed that they weren't sure what use to put him to (he was of course illiterate) but Merriman left that matter in their capable hands.

He had his own interloper to deal with in the form of Balthazar Brook. The Treasury man seemed embarrassed by the awful seasickness that struck him over the first few days and Merriman lost count of the times he apologised for the odour. The captain assured him that his sense of smell had been obliterated due to so many years at sea, which was half-true.

By the fifth day, however, Brook was able to move around. He ate something at last and was from then on often seen with his head buried in an instructional text. Merriman learned that, while he was fluent in French and German, his Portuguese was in great need of improvement. Merriman wondered if he expected to be sent on some intrigue in that embattled part of the world.

When he needed to speak to one of the officers within the cabin, Merriman asked Brook to leave, which the Treasury agent did only reluctantly. Even though the treaty was protected by two locks, he seemed concerned by the Irish contingent aboard and kept a loaded piece under his bed.

With his officers so busy, Merriman left their first dinner until the sixth evening. The midshipmen took charge on deck while the officers gathered in the great cabin with the captain and Brook. Peters was not impressed by the meagre provisioning but he and the cook formulated a decent turnip soup accompanied by some passable bread.

There was also a makeshift quality to their table, which was in fact a partition turned on its side and placed on gun mountings and kegs. Merriman found it strange to be in such a situation without Alfred Shrigley and he again thought of the man, as he invariably did when he gazed to the west.

Tom Henderson clearly felt somewhat sentimental too because he remarked on the absence of Lieutenant Jones and his violin. Hearing this, Van der Baan pointed to the large bottle he had brought with him. 'No musical instrument I'm afraid, but that is best Dutch gin.'

'A very large bottle that,' said Henderson. 'I'm surprised it was allowed on our lightweight vessel.'

'If we were being that particular, Tom,' said Merriman, 'we would have to offload Mr. Van der Baan himself.'

The Dutchman took this in good heart and Mr. Hobbs made his own contribution: 'Having seen Van der Baan in the middle of a brawl outside a Plymouth hostelry, I can assure you that he is worth at least two men when it comes to fisticuffs.'

Finishing his soup, Merriman asked Van der Baan to explain how he came to be serving aboard a British ship of war.

'By all means,' said the Dutchman, planting his great arms on the table. 'With apologies to Mr. Hobbs – who has heard the tale on more than one occasion. I was sixteen, serving on a merchantman returning from Java when the French invaded. Like many, I returned to my homeland to fight but, as you know, we did not last long.

'I have a mother and a sister to support and so I returned to the high seas, sending back what I could, when I could. Then came the Walcheren campaign, what is it…three years ago now. I was approached by a British fellow' – at this, Van der Baan pointed across the table at Brook – 'I suppose he might have been a Treasury man like you, sir. In any case, they were looking for Dutch speakers to act as liaisons between the Earl of Chatham's forces and nationalists like myself.

'Along with some others, I was tasked with accompanying the first landings on South Beveland island. As is often the case onboard ship, our chief enemy was disease. Beveland and Walcheren are swampy places, not good for health, and our soldiers suffered. We all know how it is once these afflictions take hold. The French forces were weak to begin with but eventually reinforced under Marshal Bernadotte. The city of Flushing was to be the limit of our advance and the whole venture foundered from there.'

'I recall it well,' said Merriman with a shake of his head. 'Something of an embarrassment for Lord Castlereagh.'

'Indeed. And what I saw convinced me that the lot of the soldier is even worse than the least fortunate sailor. However, I also saw the determination of the British to see Napoleon defeated. And, though that campaign was a failure, I realised that only the British have the means to defeat him. At sea. With the greatest naval force in the world. Upon my return to England, I volunteered my services.'

'And now you find yourself sailing *away* from Europe,' said Brook.

'True. I am subject to the demands of His Majesty's Navy and that does not concern me at all. For one day I will return to my homeland and – unlike most Dutchmen – will be able to say I fought the forces of Bonaparte until the inevitable day of his defeat.'

'Let us all drink to that,' said Merriman, raising his glass.

*

With *Mercury* romping along at ten knots, Merriman felt able to stay in bed longer than usual, feeling himself possessed by a familiar weariness. Experience told him that the cause was more than drink: it was the frenetic, draining period of a ship's departure followed by the inevitable problems that arose once at sea. Considering *Mercury*'s new configuration, these had not been too numerous, and most had now been amended by the established crew plus Henderson and Brockle. It was after such trials, Merriman felt, that one's mind and body began to relax; and then the true deficiencies of vigour and vim revealed themselves.

'Are you ill, sir?' asked Peters, entering the great cabin after a knock.

'No. Just weary. I'll take another hour.'

'Very well, captain.'

In the event, he couldn't find sleep again and knew it was useless to try when the bell rang for the morning watch, even though the tiny crew made less noise than most. Noting that Mr. Brook was absent and wearing only his nightshirt, Merriman roused himself and slumped onto the back bench beside an open window. A swift inhalation of the briny air did him some good and he gratefully took the cup of coffee swiftly delivered by Peters.

'Sorry about the quality, sir – looks like an uneven roast to me.'

'No matter.'

As Peters turned away, Merriman realised how little he'd said to his long-serving attendant since they'd been reunited. Not for the first time, he had taken him for granted.

'Peters, take a seat a moment.'

Spinning around, the servant frowned. 'Sir?'

'Come and sit.'

His expression turning to befuddlement, Peters sat several feet away, hands clasped awkwardly in his lap.

'Well...I should have taken the time to thank you for standing by me. We have, after all, been through quite a lot together.'

'We have, sir. To be honest, my wife was telling me to seek another post.'

'Is that right?'

'On account of how – with respect, captain – you always seem to get mixed up in the most dangerous assignments. Bloody battles, perilous voyages, nasty intrigues, that sort of thing. "That Captain Merriman – he's damn near killed you a dozen times". That's what the old girl said.'

'I see.'

'She wanted me to take a post at some local manor.'

'Ah. You live in Sussex, correct?'

'That's it, sir. Shoreham. But I said to her, "better the devil you know." Captain Merriman might find his way into trouble but he always finds his way out.'

Merriman just nodded. He was starting to wish he hadn't started this conversation but at least Peters had something pleasant to say.

'But the main thing is the prize money,' added the servant. 'Even the share of a lowly attendant goes quite a way. And there are no prizes to be found in the counties, are there, sir?'

'Indeed not, Peters.'

Merriman sipped his coffee. The servant was quite right about the uneven roast; some cups tasted merely mediocre, while others were really quite unpleasant.

'Will that be all, sir?'

'Yes. Thank you.'

The French ships were sighted just before midday. At the time, Merriman was with Lieutenant Hobbs, who was preparing to take his noon readings with the sextant and discussing their location. It was already evident to Merriman that Van der Baan was right about the quiet officer. Like many, Merriman had only grasped the intricacies of navigation (the mathematical element in particular) through guidance and constant repetition. Hobbs obviously possessed an innate understanding of the discipline and he handled the sextant more like a clockmaker than an officer of the navy.

As the ship was settled on an efficient reach, Merriman decided to take a rare trip up to the crosstrees. Upon hearing of this, Balthazar Brook asked if he could accompany him. Wondering if the Treasury man wished to bolster his reputation after his bout of seasickness, Merriman nonetheless acceded. Leaving his jacket and hat with Midshipman Eades, he rubbed some sand onto his hands for grip and set off up the mainmast.

He wasn't sure when he'd last climbed a mast but soon reckoned it was longer than he might have imagined. Stopping after about thirty feet, he looked down to see Brook close behind him. The deck already appeared alarmingly small below but he cleared his throat and pressed on, soon passing a pair of topmen lounging on yards, as relaxed as dogs lying in the sun.

'Morning, men,' said Merriman, trying to sound enthusiastic.

'Morning, captain,' said one of them, his Irish accent clear. 'Almost halfway.'

Forcing a grin, Merriman continued on, his hands and knees now starting to ache. The breeze seemed to grow as they climbed higher but he stuck to his task until the eager face of Adkins appeared above.

'Well done, sir. Would you like a hand?'

'No thank you, Adkins.' Merriman climbed around the overhang of the crosstree spars, up onto his knees. He nodded to Adkins but said nothing while he tried to regain his breath. Annoyingly, Brook, sprang instantly to his feet and gazed out at the sea.

'By God, what a view.'

Anxious not to lose yet more ground to the youngsters, Merriman hauled himself up.

'Glass, sir?'

'Yes, thank you, Adkins.' Merriman put the telescope to his eye but found that he was still rather dizzy. Steadying himself on the mast, he took a few breaths before looking to the south once again.

'Distance, Adkins?'

'Five miles,' said Brook, though he hadn't been asked.

'Twelve miles, captain,' said Adkins.

'Around that, I agree,' said Merriman.

'Really?' questioned Brook.

'It takes many years at sea to become accurate regarding distance,' said Merriman. 'Even close in. Two vessels. Same size, Adkins?'

'I think so, sir. Frigates perhaps.'

'Could well be.' Though he could see no more than dabs of dark hull and smudges of white sail, Merriman felt sure that Adkins was right.

'How on Earth can you tell that at this range?' asked Brook.

'We could both be wrong,' replied the captain, 'but one acquires an instinct for these things. Something we do not realise the eye has taken in perhaps.'

'More likely to be French than ours I suppose, captain?'

'In this area, I should say so, Adkins, yes.'

Merriman returned the glass to the midshipman, then perused the scene below, glad to see that all seemed as he would like it. He then turned his attention to the upper rigging and saw that all was well there too.

'The topmen appear to be as proficient as Lieutenant Hobbs suggested.'

'Mostly Irishmen,' said Adkins neutrally.

Brook was far from neutral in the way that he shook his head and glanced downward at the sailors stationed on the mainmast below them.

'How does one become a Treasury agent, Mr. Brook?' asked Adkins.

Merriman got the impression that Brook would have ignored the youth in other circumstances.

'One must be selected,' he replied gruffly, flicking his dark fringe away from his eyes. 'One must come to the attention of those in authority as a capable individual.'

'I think I'll stick to the navy,' said Adkins, still gazing southward towards the two ships. 'I like my enemies where I can see them.'

Merriman found his downward trip even less to his liking and reminded himself that there was probably a good reason why captains didn't often climb masts. Still, he received some admiring glances and compliments on his return to the deck. Meeting briefly with Brockle and Henderson, he was pleased to hear they shared his view that there was little wrong with the performance of *Mercury*'s crew. Merriman was immensely relieved by this, because each man would be needed when conditions inevitably worsened and the lightly-manned ship required more work. Indeed, he thought it inevitable that all but himself might have to put their hand to a rope at some point.

His satisfied mood was broken in late afternoon.

Lieutenant Van der Baan dragged one man up on deck and was soon followed by Brockle and Henderson, who were dragging another. Both of the apprehended sailors were injured, the first bleeding from his nose and mouth, the second holding a damaged jaw.

'What's going on here?' demanded the captain.

'We heard a racket and found these two brawling, sir,' said Van der Baan. 'Others seemed keen to join in so we nipped it in the bud.'

'Well done. And what is at issue?'

'A familiar tale, I'm afraid,' said Van der Baan. 'Melrose here is a Scotsman but friendly with our Irish contingent.'

Merriman knew that religion was likely the reason for that alliance.

'Apparently, a comment was made about them by Spears here.'

Melrose was a brawny fellow with a thick, brown beard. Merriman first turned to him.

'What have you to say for yourself?'

'I'll admit I struck first, captain, but only under provocation. Spears here was muttering about *kerns*.'

Merriman knew the term: an archaic word for a foot soldier who hailed from Scotland and Ireland, it had become a pejorative over time.

'Spears?'

'Aye, sir. I said it. But I have my reasons.'

He was one of those unfortunate fellows whose hair was thinning outward from the top of his head, creating an unusually wide parting.

'I have no time for guessing games, Spears. Why?'

'Heard them talking when we passed Ireland, captain. They said they wished a gale would blow us onto the shore so that they had a chance of going home. And we've heard plenty worse than that over the years. I tell you, captain, their first loyalty is not to the ship, nor to the crown. We'd be better off without them.'

Van der Baan exchanged an exasperated shake of the head with Hobbs.

'I assume this isn't the first time such a matter has arisen?'

'Far from it, captain,' said Hobbs. 'Nor is it only these two that have been involved. Unfortunately, with our reduced numbers, it's not possible to keep them apart.'

Merriman noted Balthazar Brook lurking just below the hatch. He knew this long-running issue couldn't be solved immediately but he needed to make a swift judgement on these two. As the sailors were of equal rank, he saw no need to resort to flogging.

'Melrose, you have used violence against a compatriot, yet at least you admitted it. Spears, you used a term that you must have known would provoke your crewmates.'

Spears seemed to think about speaking up but caught himself in time. Merriman was concerned about what he'd heard regarding the Irishmen but, until he saw evidence to the contrary, he could hardly question long-serving crewmen.

'Melrose, you shall be tied to the shrouds from now until sunset tomorrow and you will go without sustenance. Spears, you shall join him from sunset today, which is not far away. Lieutenant Van der Baan, please see to it.'

'Aye, sir.'

Merriman detected a certain disapproval in the Dutchman's manner. Hobbs was harder to read. Merriman didn't care if they thought the punishment insufficient. This crew were new to him and he wanted to leave himself room for manoeuvre. The trouble with swift, hard justice was that it often left the dispenser with nowhere to go.

As the offenders were led away, he saw that more of the sailors had gathered at the hatch with Brook. They were soon dispersed by a thunderous volley from the bosun, while Brook came up and withdrew to the quarterdeck.

'Tomorrow is Sunday, isn't it,' said Merriman when later approached by Adkins.

'It is.'

'Good. I think the crew would benefit from a sermon of a very specific nature. What news of those ships to the south?'

'Turned away, sir,' said Adkins with a grin. 'And I do believe I glimpsed a tricolour. I expect they realised they'd never catch us.'

*

The captain planned his sermon for the afternoon but was forced to bring it forward. He was woken to the news that another brawl had broken out between the Irish and English contingents. Apparently, an Irish carpenter's mate had been tipped out of his hammock. Due to the darkness, no one could identify the offender but it had led to more accusation, insult-flinging and unrest.

Merriman was on his way to the gun deck when the passageway ahead of him was blocked by the hulking form of Lieutenant Van der Baan. The normally composed officer was clearly embarrassed by the ructions afflicting the crew.

'Sincere apologies captain. It is under control now.'

'Not your fault, Van der Baan. Any offenders identified?'

'It is difficult, what with the dark and the…lack of clarity.'

'I'm sure.'

Van der Baan looked back over his shoulder and snapped at a sailor to make himself scarce. He lowered his voice.

'If I may, sir, I do wonder if a sanction of a rather harsher nature could be employed. That is how Captain Gilfoyle dealt with these divisions and it was generally effective.'

Even in the shadowy passageway, the Dutchman could see enough of his superior's expression to know he had erred. Merriman gave him time to change course.

'Sir, I…I again find myself apologising. On this occasion for my own conduct. These decisions are yours alone.'

Merriman chose not to answer this and move on to the more important issue. 'Mr. Henderson tells me that we should wear sail soon. That we will do once I've addressed the men. You and Mr. Hobbs have ten minutes to assemble them.'

Overnight, *Mercury* had sailed through a great patch of weed that clung to the bow. Watching as two sailors hurriedly removed it, Merriman waited for his officers to organise the men into neat lines as instructed. For religious services, it was common for benches to be used but there were of course none aboard the speedy ship, nor did the captain consider this a religious occasion. He stood alone by the mainmast, his hat firmly pressed onto his head, hands clasped behind him. He had purposefully chosen not to address, or even look at, the two men tied loosely to the shrouds on opposite sides of the ship. They too would hear him.

'Ready, captain,' said Hobbs.

Merriman turned and walked back to address the men.

He glanced speculatively at Tom Henderson, and received a nod to assure him that all was well with the ship. Even Balthazar Brook was present, leaning against the larboard rail, as ever surveying affairs with those dark eyes below that dark fringe.

Merriman found it hard to believe that the few dozen arrayed before him constituted the entire crew. Still, his approach would not change. As a young officer, he had seen some captains pick one face to address or stare into the middle distance while they spoke. He preferred to get close and move his eyes slowly from one man to another, sailors and officers alike. Some within each class seemed to find it unsettling but it was yet another way Merriman had found to impose himself and his rule. He supposed he had learned a few things in his many years as a master.

'The prime occupation of this mission is speed. The movement of this vessel from one side of the Atlantic to the other. That can only be achieved by an efficient crew and, as ours is a small one, a *united* crew.'

He paused, and heard only the sound of sheets under strain and water frothing from the bow.

'Must we all be friends aboard ship? No. Must we like and admire every last one of our compatriots? No. Must we all be in agreement about matters political or religious or even nautical? No. Must we follow the same god, the same faith? No. But we *must* work together, and in a peaceful and effective fashion.'

Merriman paused again, locked eyes with a few more of his crew. 'In the last day or so, there have been some incidents of unruliness and disobedience. The results of that are clear to see behind me. I of course also reserve the right to invoke the Articles of War and remind you of article twenty-two, which states that " if any officer, mariner, soldier or other person in the fleet, shall presume to quarrel with any of his superior officers, or shall disobey any lawful command of any of his superior officers; every such person being convicted of any such offence, by the sentence of a court martial, shall suffer death, or such other punishment."

Merriman let that sink in and then continued. 'Those "other punishments" are ordered entirely at my discretion. And let's not forget article twenty-three, which iterates the same consequences for "any person who shall quarrel or fight with any other person in the fleet, or use reproachful or provoking speeches or gestures, tending to make any quarrel or disturbance."

Merriman paced slowly back and forth as he spoke.

'But I want you to know something else. I have acquired many a prize in my career, and it may be that we soon find ourselves at war and in fertile hunting grounds. The American navy is generally considered to be no match for us and opportunities may well arise.'

Merriman had heard this said repeatedly and, while he was reserving his own judgement, the sentiment suited his current purposes. He saw that a few expressions had changed.

'The name of any offender mentioned to me in the coming days and weeks will be remembered. Perhaps he will be spoken to and punished openly, perhaps not. The first he will know of the *true* cost of his actions is when the time comes for this crew to receive its two-eighths of any prize. For some, their pockets will be heavy with coins. Others may be lighter. Or empty.'

Now he had the active attention of every man before him.

'Think on that.'

At a nod from Merriman, Hobbs dismissed the crew. The captain turned away and strolled towards the bow.

Chapter Twelve

The Invisible Enemy

HMS Romulus had been at sea for eleven days and four had passed since the battle with the French ships. Almost all the damage had been repaired by the carpenters and there had also been time to make the ship better balanced, which had involved a day and a half of experimentation with ballast, sails and rig. The injured men were all on the mend too, with the exception of poor Griggs who – as Mr. Webster had feared – had been unable to recover from his terrible wounds.

All in all, they had lost men, material and time and gained nothing save the safety of their charges. This was clearly an unwelcome situation for officers and men well used to taking prizes and Captain Shrigley was told of numerous complaints. He cared not. Nor did he care what those officers and men were used to or what they expected. His first command was a ship of His Majesty's Navy and she would conduct herself accordingly.

'By God,' said First Lieutenant Glanville. 'That accursed crew are making a right bawbels of this. Excuse my language, captain.'

Glanville was referring not to the crew of *Romulus* but that of the *Diane*, a merchant ship that had dropped gradually to the rear of the convoy. The wind had shifted during the afternoon and, while *Romulus* had executed a tack in a respectable six minutes, *Diane* had now exceeded ten. Half a mile behind her, the two officers on the quarterdeck watched sails and sheets continuing to flutter and flap.

'She's over-laden,' added Glanville. 'It's clear as day.'

He had been complaining for several hours, suggesting that, as Captain Halliwell and the *Zeus* (and indeed the rest of the fleet) were so far ahead, that they should take charge and do something about the *Diane*. It didn't seem to occur to the first lieutenant that his captain was considering the same issues without articulating them.

'A mule and no mistake,' added Glanville.

Shrigley decided on a clear announcement, if only to shut the man up.

'If we've lost sight of *Iona* by morning, we shall take action.'

'Leave her behind?' suggested Glanville eagerly.

'Or she can dump some cargo. Perhaps they will rediscover their earlier form – she started the voyage well enough.'

'Can there be anything worse than convoy duty?'

'I think we both know the answer to that.'

Alfred Shrigley did not often dream while aboard ship, which he ascribed to exhaustion and a preoccupied mind. When he did dream, what he saw and felt was seldom good. This dream was the exception and might have been a recollection, so real and reassuring did it seem.

He stood in a doorway, doing nothing more than looking on as his precious wife nursed his precious son in the familiar surroundings of their parlour. Late evening perhaps. A low fire was glowing and Parsnip, the family cat, sat on a chair nearby.

The captain was snatched from this reverie by the servant Trelawney, who told him there was a message of distress from the *Diane*. Well used to such unwelcome transitions, Shrigley had cleared his mind of dreams and memories by the time he joined Ives at the bow.

'A mile or so, sir. We've put more sail on – we'll be with her before long.'

Shrigley pulled on his cloak. It was very cold on deck, with a chill wind and a clear sky above.

Glanville appeared and was soon complaining once more.

'Lieutenant, it is the middle of the night and there is no need for all three of us to be on deck. I might well need you to take charge in the morning. Please return to the officers' quarters.'

Glanville bristled at this. 'Sir, perhaps I should wait until we know the nature of the *Diane*'s predicament?'

'I'm sure we can handle it. If you please.'

It did not take long for *Romulus* to reach the stricken vessel. Though the sea was not a large one, *Diane* was wallowing in the broad ocean waves. She had only a little sail up to steady her and appeared even lower in the water than usual.

With Mr. Diggs stationed at the mainmast to relay instructions to the helm, Shrigley had his brig-sloop come alongside before reducing sail. Accompanied by Ives, he spoke to a man who announced himself as Tobias Hamm, *Diane*'s second in command.

'Captain Wynn is down in the after-hold. We knew we'd sprung a leak but hadn't been able to find it. Right under a load of ballast. We think we struck a whale or some other obstacle the night before last. Ballast pressing down has probably made it worse.'

'Can the captain come up?'

'Not at the moment, sir. It's looking bad down there and the carpenter's out of commission: spiked himself through the hand two days out of Plymouth. A dozen hands down too – ill.'

'How high is the water?'

'Eight feet at the well.'

'The size of the hole?'

'Around three feet.'

'Stand by.'

Shrigley turned to Ives, who had a suggestion:

'Send Mr. Dyer and his crew across, sir?'

'Possibly.' Shrigley shouted across the water again. 'Mr. Hamm, what ails your men?'

'Surgeon says an ague of some kind. A few have recovered already so we hope the others will too.'

Shrigley addressed Ives once more. 'Will you take the work party across? Rouse Mr. Dyer, both his mates, and ask him to nominate half a dozen other skilled men. In my experience, the tradesmen on vessels such as this aren't a patch on ours. In any case, he should be able to tell us the state of affairs.'

'Aye, sir.'

A quarter-hour later, Ives and four sailors rowed across with the carpenter and his eight subordinates. In the swell, moving between the two ships, this was a task best accomplished with care rather than haste. Mr. Ives acquitted himself well.

Waiting at the bow with the bosun, Shrigley later saw his second lieutenant in the glow of a lantern held by Mr. Hamm.

'Sir, Dyer describes it as serious but not fatal. He believes there is a good chance that they might have the repair in place by dawn. He has asked me to fetch some materials. This ship is not equipped as it should be.'

Mr. Hamm bowed his head at this in a gesture of what appeared to be shame.

'Very well. Please do so.'

As Ives withdrew, Shrigley heard a sigh from Mr. Diggs.

'We will fall even further behind, sir.'

'That can't be helped. We are obliged to assist.'

Having sent Glanville below, Shrigley elected to remain on deck. In addition to the *Diane*'s woes, he was wary of the ships' proximity. Not long after the arrival of the morning watch at four o'clock, the swell became higher and, an hour or so later, the wind shifted around to the south and grew to twenty knots. Shrigley had *Romulus* dropped back a hundred yards and was relieved to have the capable Diggs on duty; the bosun oversaw the modifications necessary to hold the ship in place amidst a changeable sea.

It had already been a long night and the hours of darkness dragged on, the rain intensifying. Shrigley went below only once, to exchange his drenched cloak for his oilskins. His discomfort was amplified by his stitched-up head which ached doubly when cold. Trelawney had just boiled a kettle and the captain returned to the deck with a mug of steaming tea.

With the merchantman and the warship pinned below dark cloud, dawn brought little relief other than the appearance of Lieutenant Ives upon *Diane*'s quarterdeck. He was accompanied by Captain Wynn, a white-haired man who announced that the repairs were largely complete. His sincere thanks at least made Shrigley feel that the effort had been worthwhile.

By the time Glanville came on deck and took charge, Ives and his work party were back aboard *Romulus*. The second lieutenant assured Shrigley that *Diane* would be ready to get underway again within the hour. The captain sent he, Mr. Dyer and the others below to warm up and ordered a double ration of rum for them all. Shrigley remained on deck long enough to see both ships lower wet sails that were soon filled by the southerly and allowed them to set a north-westerly course. Ideally, he would have stayed longer but his head was by now troubling him so badly that his vision was blurring and his thoughts seemed muddled.

Once in the great cabin, the ache seemed to lessen a bit. Changing out of his wet clothes, he refused an offer of food from Trelawney and collapsed into his bunk, immediately falling into a deep, restful sleep.

It took the two ships three full days to catch the convoy. Having lambasted the *Diane* and its complement for many days, even Lieutenant Glanville had to credit Captain Wynn and his crew for their recovery and resilience. Many aboard *Romulus* seemed convinced that they would never regain contact with their compatriots until they struck land.

When the line of ships was sighted, a cry of 'huzzah' went up. The convoy was far to the south, but a change of course and a concerted effort from both crews saw them within signalling range by nightfall. Later that night came a message passed back along the line from HMS *Zeus* and Captain Halliwell.

'Welcome back *Romulus* and *Diane*.'

Captain Shrigley was very grateful for the message and relieved to be back with the fleet but by then he was already aware of another problem; a problem of a type that alarmed him more than any other.

Two of the men who'd gone aboard *Diane* were ill: both very fatigued and suffering a high fever. But what concerned Mr. Webster was the subsequent vomiting and overall body aches, which could indicate a more serious ailment. The physician had already expressed his dismay that the men were allowed aboard a vessel with so many ill. Shrigley had countered that the alternative – leaving *Diane* to fend for herself – was simply impossible. Even so, the thought that he had allowed a serious disease aboard was a terrible one. He knew, as every captain knew, that the Royal Navy lost scores of men to disease for every one killed in combat.

On a sunny morning with favourable wind, he received the surgeon's latest report. John Webster entered the great cabin with a handkerchief around his neck, which he often employed to cover his mouth and nose.

'Captain, I regret to inform you that I have discovered red spots in the mouth and throat of Knapp. They are yet to appear upon Smith.'

Shrigley knew enough to realise what that might mean.

'Smallpox.'

'There may be other explanations but, given their other symptoms, I feel that is most likely.'

'By God. And we're hundreds of miles from land. You were right about *Diane*. I should have consulted you.'

'Not necessarily,' countered Webster. 'It is believed that the disease manifests itself between seven and seventeen days. That means that either man may have acquired it before we set sail.'

'Tell me what we must do.'

'I have already established a quarantined area beside the medical bay. I am using my store room. It is not very comfortable for the poor souls but I must keep the bay clear.'

'Of course. What of Flood?'

The sailmaker's mate was still recovering from two nasty wounds and had shown remarkable endurance.

'He is with his messmates. It was evident from their visits that they care for their friend and he's well past the worst. I would, however, appreciate your support in ensuring that they don't let him have any grog. They seem to think it's a laughing matter, including Flood himself.'

'Of course.'

'I have already examined Knapp and Smith's messmates as well as their close colleagues but we must continue to do so. I cannot believe that these will be the last of our patients.'

'It can kill, yes?'

'Typically, one in three of those affected. And the pain it causes can be unbearable. After the red spots come sores and then scabs that can cover almost the entire body. If patients survive, it is believed that they cease to be infectious only when the last of those scabs have disappeared. This matter will concern us for the remainder of our voyage, captain.'

Shrigley let out a long sigh. 'Understood. Have you told them?'

'Not yet. I will do so now.'

'Doctor, you must not expose yourself any more than is necessary. Is there any more you can do for them?'

'Very little other than endeavouring to ease their suffering. They will require plenty of fluid and whatever food they can manage.'

'In that case, I suggest you leave their care to your assistants.'

Shrigley knew that he had been fortunate in avoiding serious outbreaks of disease during his naval career. The thought of managing one without the expertise of John Webster was truly terrifying.

The surgeon produced a list of names from his pocket and handed it over. Though ashamed, Shrigley worried that even the paper might convey the disease and he was grateful that the great cabin was spacious and airy.

'The messmates and colleagues. My suggestion is that – for the next few days – they are stationed at the bow, not too close to each other. They should not be permitted below decks at all. My assistants and I can then monitor them.'

'That is rather…unpractical but I shall see to it.'

'I would suggest isolating them in the boat but that might merely ensure that one case becomes ten.'

'Of course. Fortunately, the wind has been steady for some time. We can keep work at the bow to a minimum.'

'Will you notify the officers?'

'I will notify them and then the entire crew.'

'We must also inform the *Diane*,' added Webster. 'It is of course possible that *our* men transmitted the disease to *theirs*.'

The only pleasant aspect of the next few days was the weather. The convoy having dropped further south, the prevailing winds were now becoming more southerly, ranging between fifteen knots and twenty-five, the weather gods smiled upon the convoy, allowing even the troubled *Diane* to average six knots, which meant over a hundred and forty miles covered per day.

This good fortune was barely discussed by either officers or men aboard *Romulus*. On the day following the confinement of Knapp and Smith, two others manifested the red spots on their mouths – this being discovered when they checked each other. Dr. Webster had encouraged the whole crew to monitor themselves and their cohorts for symptoms. On the following day, Mr. Lange, the midshipman; and a thirteen-year-old powder monkey became the next crewmen to face isolation.

There was no longer sufficient room for the six and so Shrigley had the bosun's storeroom cleared. This involved a good deal of work but it was of sufficient size and, being up near the bow, well out of the way. Eight hammocks were placed there along with two casks of water, a box full of raisins and another of tack. The patients entered the shadowy room and were joined the following day by two more men.

'An awful scene,' said Mr. Webster, when he reported back to Shrigley and the lieutenants, who had gathered in the great cabin. 'Knapp appears to be close to death. If he survives, he will owe a great debt to Smith, who is trying to get him to drink, despite his own discomfort.'

Ives shook his head. 'It's true that Smith is now covered by the pustules too?'

'He is. But Knapp is suffering greatly. Often crying out. And now the others must watch, knowing what awaits them. And then there's the boy.'

'Why he only joined us in Plymouth,' said Ives. 'What a fate.'

'Some of them should survive,' said Dr. Webster.

'By God, will they want to go on?' asked Glanville, who was leaning against the larboard wall, arms crossed. 'We have all seen the scars that survivors bear.'

'Better that then death,' said Ives.

'I'm not so sure.'

Webster shot a rare glance of anger at Glanville. 'You invoke the name of God often, Mr. Glanville, yet I've seldom heard a less Christian attitude. You would have suggested to the Lord Jesus that he turn his back on the lepers, I suppose?'

Glanville at least made no reply, for which Shrigley was grateful. The well-bred officer could be very tactless at times, and it was quite evident that the whole episode had taken a great toll on the physician.

Lieutenant Ives spoke up: 'If I haven't already said so, my thanks, Mr. Webster. I hate to think how this affliction might have run amok had you not seen the signs at so early a stage.'

'A drink perhaps, John,' suggested Shrigley, who was in dire need of one himself.

'No, thank you. I shall retire to my quarters, rest awhile.'

'Very wise.'

'Ives? Glanville?' said Shrigley, already on his way to a bottle of port he had taken out the previous evening. As both answered in the affirmative, Shrigley called out to Trelawney, asking him to bring some hot food at the earliest opportunity.

The three of them sat around the desk at the cabin's centre, soon all drinking in silence. It had become the habit of all aboard to maintain distance where possible, though this was virtually impossible for those who dwelt on the gundeck. Shrigley felt almost ashamed at the space he had to himself.

'So much for the old captain's good luck charm,' said Shrigley. 'What was that fellow's name?'

'Greaves,' answered Ives. 'We did do well in the battle though, sir.'

'I should not have spoken like that to the doctor,' admitted Glanville as – with Shrigley's permission – he refilled their glasses. 'Why those learned fellows should be paid whatever they require.'

'If they are at Webster's standard,' agreed Ives. 'Though I'm sure we've all met many who are not.'

'Damned insidious these afflictions,' said Glanville, loosening his collar. 'Any cough or rash draws suspicion and fear. One can feel it among the men.'

'If the number rises no further, I shall consider us fortunate,' said Shrigley. 'On my last voyage, I passed the West African coast. There are fevers there that have decimated entire crews.'

Ives slugged down some more port. Like many Shrigley had met, the generally quiet fellow quickly became voluble after a bit of drink.

'It was a great satisfaction to me – being at sea aboard *Romulus* again. And I'm sure it was a great satisfaction to us all that we saw off that French attack.'

He aimed his glass towards Shrigley then, which the new captain did appreciate.

'But now,' continued Ives, 'I can hardly wait until I set foot on land and am no longer trapped aboard ship with a lethal disease.'

Chapter Thirteen

Weather Luck

'A blessed passage so far, and no mistake.'

This was the conclusion of Mr. Van der Baan, offered to Merriman as he and his officers drank coffee. The midshipmen were present too, though Eades and Adkins preferred tea. They had all been drawn on deck by a sighting of flying fish and had remained there, enjoying yet another sunny day. Better still was the wind, steady at eighteen knots and blasting them along from the north-east.

Mr. Hobbs continued to reveal yet more navigational prowess. As well as naval texts, he consulted the tables of the Hudson Bay Company and also employed a technique using "lunar distance", a method Merriman had heard of but didn't entirely grasp. Hobbs had also kept a very close eye on their distance made good. After just ten days at sea, they had covered in excess of fourteen hundred miles, which meant a remarkable average speed of six knots. First sight of land would be Newfoundland, and that was around seven hundred miles more. Their destination, Halifax, was another five hundred miles beyond that. All was going well – even the taciturn Balthazar Brook seemed satisfied – but Merriman was always reluctant to tempt fate.

'I'm certainly pleased with our progress to date,' he remarked. 'But that is all. In my experience, when at sea, it is seldom wise to expect anything other than the unexpected. Remember the whale we sighted while hunting the *Hercule*, Adkins?'

'I do, captain,' said the midshipman.

'You thought the slap of its tail was the boom of a gun,' said Eades.

Van der Baan laughed at this.

'Also true,' admitted Adkins.

Bosun Brockle was ahead of them, inspecting the deck, which had been scoured with the holystones that morning. The wily Brockle had kept the men very busy and – to the captain's knowledge – there'd been no further incidents between the English and Irish rivals. Merriman supposed that his words regarding prize-money might also have had some effect. Tom Henderson, meanwhile, was not content to sit on his laurels. Though HMS *Mercury* continued to fly along, he had suggested several adjustments to ballast and the sails that had demonstrably improved performance. The four familiar faces were hugely reassuring to Merriman, and he was glad to see them getting on with the frigate's old hands.

Mr. Hobbs strolled towards the bow, causing Adkins and Eades to approach Merriman. Eades was the elder at eighteen (Adkins was sixteen) but both appeared preoccupied.

'What is it, you two?' asked Merriman.

'Sir, it's Mr. Hobbs,' replied Adkins. 'We…well, we've tried keeping up with his teachings but I'm not sure…'

'It's not going in, sir,' said Adkins, tapping his head. 'More often than not, we don't follow what he explains and then he's on to the next thing.'

Merriman had not specifically asked Hobbs to instruct the young pair. It was the responsibility of all officers to assist the midshipmen with their training, though some took this duty more seriously than others.

'It is often the way with very capable men that they don't appreciate the limitations of others. Find a way to tell Mr. Hobbs that you are struggling. And count yourselves lucky that you have an opportunity to learn from a man of such skill. Especially you, Eades, didn't you tell me that you aim to take the lieutenant's exam upon our return?'

'Perhaps that was the rum talking, sir,' offered Van der Baan.

'Not at all!' exclaimed Eades. 'Thank you for the advice. captain. We will of course endeavour to be diplomatic.'

'Another necessity in an officer,' said Merriman.

Then came a pause in the conversation. The officers watched as four topmen climbed the ratlines of the mainmast to attend to the main topgallant.

Eades had a question: 'Captain, do you think we might have passed Commander Shrigley and the *Romulus*?'

'It's possible, I suppose.'

'At Plymouth, they said the convoy contained several ships slow even by the standards of merchantmen. While we have been speeding along.'

Merriman finished his coffee, idly perusing the black sludge at the bottom of his cup.

'This is my first voyage without him, sir,' said Eades. 'I remember him in my prayers.'

'As do I,' said Merriman. 'Now then, you two, what of the assignment I gave you in the form of young Ned Lownes? I've not seen hide or hair of him.'

'Well, he's a lot cleaner now, sir,' said Adkins. 'And the smell in our cabin is not half so bad. We found him two sets of clothes that just about fit. For the first three days, he hardly said a word. But Eades read him some of the Tales of the Arabian Nights. Ned pretended not to be listening but we could tell he was because the following night he asked to hear another.'

Merriman couldn't help grinning at this. Some of the midshipmen he'd encountered had been from wealthy backgrounds and concerned solely with their own advancement. He had given Eades and Adkins this task because both young men were considerate and kind.

'From there, we asked about the workhouse,' continued Adkins. 'It turned out he worked regularly in the kitchens there. Cook gave him some peeling to do and, apparently, he's very handy at chopping and dicing. He did eight hours straight yesterday, sir. Not afraid of hard work.'

'Then he should make a fine sailor.'

'We tried to explain that he's actually earning his own money, sir,' added Eades. 'But we're not sure he grasped the idea.'

'I'm sure he understands it,' said Merriman. 'He might just not be able to believe it.'

On the twelfth and thirteenth day of the journey, sails were sighted to the south. They were too far to discern any flags but the common consensus was that the distant vessels were not ships of war. Both were spotted from the crosstrees by Lieutenant Hobbs and then Midshipman Eades. They confided in Merriman first, wary of alerting the crew to potential prizes that they were passing by. The captain told them that he cared not. The *Mercury* was no privateer and, if he ever elected to try and take a vessel, naval or not, it would be at a time and location of his choosing.

Aware that they could run into hostiles at any point – but unable to slow the frigate for a proper gun drill – he nevertheless put his skeleton crew through their paces. Unsurprisingly, given the mercenary nature of their previous master, the sailors proved themselves efficient and hardworking, despite the reduced numbers of guns and men to operate them. He could not measure accuracy but was very pleased by the rate of fire.

On the fourteenth day, his inspection of the main hold was interrupted by an anxious-looking Lieutenant Hobbs.

'What is it?' asked the captain, surrounded by boxes and kegs, despite the *Mercury*'s light load.

'Mr. Brook, sir. Has a sailor by the ear. Claims he's seen him twice lingering outside the great cabin.'

Not only did the Treasury agent have the sailor by the ear, he also had a dagger in his hand. The pair were in the passageway outside the cabin and were accompanied by Van der Baan, who let Merriman past. The captain recognised the sailor from the firing drills of the previous day: an Irish idler of about thirty years named O'Shaughnessy.

'The *second* time, captain,' declared Brook, his angular face tight with anger. 'I've observed this man loitering hereabouts. Crafty of him – allowing time to pass before trying to get a look at the strongbox.'

'Mr. Brook, please let go of the man's ear. He is not going anywhere.'

'He might have a weapon on him.'

'Lieutenant Van der Baan can establish that.'

Brook let go, causing O'Shaughnessy to grimace and whisper something in what sounded like Gaelic.

'Watch your mouth, you swine,' uttered the Treasury man.

The sailor raised his arms and allowed Van der Baan to search him.

'What have you to say for yourself?' demanded Merriman. 'I cannot think of any good reason for you to be in this area.'

The captain reflected that this wouldn't have been a problem in normal circumstances: it was usual practice for a marine to be stationed outside a great cabin.

'I...I wasn't trying to get inside, captain, I swear it,' said O'Shaughnessy. 'And I didn't even know Mr. Brook was in there.'

'Clearly not,' retorted the agent, 'or you wouldn't have been sneaking around.'

'So, what *were* you doing?' said Merriman.

O'Shaughnessy rubbed his brow and squeezed his eyes closed.

'I...I was hiding, sir.'

'From who?'

'From the bosun, sir?'

'Brockle? Why?'

'I've not done my turn cleaning the roundhouse, sir.'

'Well, it's hardly a duty anyone enjoys...'

'It's nothing to do with the filth, captain.'

'What is it then?'

O'Shaughnessy looked along the passageway, where several were now looking on.

Merriman wanted a swift conclusion to this odd incident. 'Mr. Van der Baan, get rid of them.'

A single bellow from the giant was enough to clear the passageway.

As Merriman had experienced on his last voyage and many other before it, a ship was a complicated place. While a captain was generally concerned about sailing the vessel and any obstacle in his path, he presided over a large community of men, all with their own concerns, foibles, aims and anxieties.

'I'm running out of patience, man.'

'Yes, captain,' said the Irishman, straightening up. 'It's the water. The water below. I'm all right inside the rail but when I'm looking down into it…last time, I felt faint. I thought I might fall.'

'Is this to do with Newhaven?' asked Van der Baan.

'What happened there?' replied Merriman.

'Newhaven was a sailor,' explained the Dutchman. 'He fell from the bowsprit during our last voyage with Captain Stone. We went back for him, put out the boats. He must have injured himself when he fell because there was blood in the water. His body popped up and we thought he was alive but it was the sharks…fighting over him.'

'I see,' said Merriman.

'You knew him didn't you, O'Shaughnessy?'

'I did, lieutenant. But I don't know if it's that. I have these dreams, captain. These terrible dreams.'

Balthazar Brook, who had remained close to the sailor, now stepped back, towards the great cabin.

'Let's get you some air,' said Van der Baan. 'Perhaps a shot of rum.'

Merriman nodded his approval. 'I'll have a word with Brockle. We'll find another duty for you.'

As the pair departed – O'Shaughnessy with head bowed – Brook finally put away his knife.

'I would have thought a Treasury agent would rely more on evidence than supposition.'

'I could not have known he is infirm, captain.'

'He is not infirm. Life aboard ship does strange things to us sometimes. Some are overcome by their fears. Some vomit for days on end. We all have our crosses to bear.'

Seventeen days after her departure from Plymouth, the *Mercury* endured the most singular event of the trip. Merriman and his officers were fixated on the imminent sighting of Newfoundland but before that they faced something very different.

The wind dropped to ten knots then backed and veered violently for an hour as rain began to fall. The sky grew gloomy around them, particularly a patch to the north. That patch resembled a great circular cloud of pale grey that rapidly became dark. The rain seemed heavier beneath this spot and the area was soon more clearly defined by what appeared to be wind whirling in a circular motion.

'Waterspout,' said Tom Henderson confidently. The sailing master stood beside Merriman and the two lieutenants on the quarterdeck. All were clad in their boat-cloaks.

'I've never seen one,' said the captain.

'I've only seen one other,' replied Henderson. 'Bermuda. Missed us but hit a sloop. Knocked her mizzen down.'

Their attempts to sail *Mercury* clear of the waterspout proved ineffectual. Blanketed by rain, the wind shifted with such regularity that the sails could hardly be set. All those on deck watched as what had been an indistinct mass narrowed to a swirling tower that was now moving ominously towards them.

As the waterspout got closer, the sails, yards and lines were blasted by the wind. As the lines whipped back and forth, all those on deck put up their arms to protect their faces from the stinging spray. The tower became almost white and seemed to be sucking the sea upward into a watery web.

Merriman was on the verge of ordering men into the boat to pull them clear when the waterspout shifted again, clearing the starboard quarter by mere yards.

'Our good fortune continues,' said Lieutenant Hobbs as the waterspout wheeled away to the east before dissipating as rapidly as it had formed.

Within an hour, the rain had ceased and *Mercury* was able to continue westward in a moderate south-easterly. Two hours before dusk, Midshipman Adkins ventured up to the crosstrees and reported news that brought a beaming smile to the usually reserved Lieutenant Hobbs. Newfoundland was dead ahead.

Chapter Fourteen

North American Station

The southern tip of Cape Race was a rocky promontory. Further inland, the cape was covered by lush grass and Merriman found the whole scene rather reminiscent of the Cornish coast. This somehow seemed both a reassurance and a disappointment.

'Gilbert claimed this land for the crown,' said Lieutenant Hobbs, who was with him when they passed the cape in clear weather.

'Gilbert, sir?' enquired Adkins, who was once again undergoing navigational tuition.

'Sir Humphrey Gilbert,' answered Merriman. '1585 was it, Hobbs?'

'1583, I believe, captain.'

'As I recall, he fought off some fishing fleet, landed and claimed it for England. One of the man's few successes. Known mainly for nautical failures earlier in his career. Sailed back to England on a ship that went down with all hands. Silly name.'

'*Squirrel*, sir,' said Hobbs.

'That's it.'

'He would have known Sir Walter Raleigh, I suppose?' said Adkins.

'I believe they sailed together,' said Merriman.

'I wonder what Raleigh would have made of all that's happened in the colonies,' said Hobbs.

Merriman nodded vaguely, now desperate to reach Halifax and continue on to conclude their mission.

Hobbs turned to Adkins. 'Do you know how the colony of Virginia acquired its name?'

Adkins shook his head.

'Named by Raleigh for his queen. The *Virgin* Queen Elizabeth.'

That night, Merriman feared that their much-discussed weather luck had deserted them. It was now early summer and the winds seemed to become weaker and less reliable. But, with dawn near, and Cape Race still visible from the crosstrees, a light northerly strengthened to fifteen knots. *Mercury* was just able to lay a direct course for Halifax, and she bounded on over the next two days, Mr. Hobbs soon able to navigate with more accuracy using an almanac describing the Nova Scotian coast.

Twenty-three days after her departure, the frigate entered Halifax harbour, all aboard aware that they had missed the best recorded crossing by only two days. Immensely proud of his makeshift crew, Merriman encouraged them all on deck as they approached their destination. Also mentioned in the almanac were the fortifications built six decades earlier. One of them, Fort George, was shaped like a star and clearly visible from the sea. *Mercury* passed the low lying McNab's Island, upon which was a round Martello tower of the type constructed all across the British Isles in recent years. Soon the frigate was approaching the harbour, which was located on the west side of a promontory.

Mercury's larger sails were furled as a boat came out to the new arrival. Not for the first time, Merriman felt a warm pride at the sight of the red ensign. It never ceased to amaze him how far the bold men of his country had spread; men like Gilbert and Raleigh. Ironically, the assistant harbour master in the boat turned out to have a French accent but he gave them instructions on where to anchor and *Mercury* was soon dropping her cables not far from a great ship of the line named *Africa*, and the smaller Frigate *Shannon*. Along with Bermuda, Halifax was the other key base of the Royal Navy's Atlantic fleet and there were two other frigates anchored close by.

All around him he saw smiles and even Balthazar Brook's expression seemed hopeful when he appeared on deck. Despite a bracing breeze, the June sunshine was warm, and the densely-packed buildings that lined the harbour looked most inviting. Many of the unoccupied crew remained at the bow to survey the town.

'Don't like the look of that,' remarked Tom Henderson.

'Really?' said Van der Baan. 'Small perhaps, but it looks a fine enough place.'

'I think he means the men,' said Bosun Brockle.

'I agree,' said Merriman. 'Until I know the situation, I cannot be sure there will be a chance for them to go ashore. Brockle, if you would oblige.'

'Fear not, captain. I can always find work for idle hands.'

'Very good.'

Merriman was pleased with his officers and crew but felt he simply had to reward Lieutenant Hobbs for his navigation and Tom Henderson for his outstanding handling of a new, unusual ship. He also felt it wise to keep the imposing Van der Baan onboard. The Dutchman took the decision in good heart and was soon helping Brockle to keep the men and petty officers occupied.

Peters had already laid out Merriman's spare jacket and he'd done a fine job with the metal and braid. The captain's shoes were also well polished and – once back on deck – he was pleased to see both Hobbs and Henderson well turned out. Knowing this would not be the final destination for his cargo, Balthazar Brook elected to remain in the great cabin, though he requested that the captain pass on all relevant intelligence immediately upon his return.

Conveyed ashore by the harbour master's boat, Merriman received an early taste of intense questioning that would soon become a barrage. The assistant harbour master asked him firstly about their crossing and was astounded by the twenty-three- day voyage, initially expressing disbelief. From there, his questions moved on to Anglo-American relations and Merriman professed that he had no new information to offer.

Once on the quay, Merriman and his two officers were immediately surrounded by a selection of locals, sailors and naval officers. Again, they faced a barrage of questions until rescued by a portly commander who bellowed at the interrogators to "cease their noise!" and then conducted the under-fire trio to the harbour master's office. Here, a small crowd gathered outside, while the commander had a clerk bring them some brandy.

'My apologies,' said the helpful fellow, who had identified himself as Commander Brunswick, a staff officer of Vice-Admiral Sawyer. 'I hurried down as soon as I heard of your approach. I shall be most surprised if the admiral doesn't want to see you immediately.'

'Have you heard anything here?' asked Merriman.

'The American Congress has voted for war,' answered Brunswick, his expression grave. 'But the Senate must also agree and apparently that vote may well be closer. No new arrivals from the mainland in three days, however, so we know nothing beyond that. We are rather stuck out on a limb here in Halifax.'

The commander jutted his chin towards the office window. 'There is a good deal of anxiety from the locals and interest from our fellow Navy men. Even if war is declared, we might not receive specific orders for eight weeks or more. I've not never heard of a ship cross with the speed that you did, captain, and I would not expect it to happen again. Now then, our vehicle is ready so we shall go and see Vice-Admiral Sawyer.'

The trio and their new acquaintance hopped into the carriage in a courtyard at the rear of the office. From there, they were conveyed along only three streets. Unsurprised by the odd feelings in his stomach and legs, Merriman now also found himself gripped by a sense of displacement. He could not avoid the feeling that his return to England would be much more protracted and difficult than his arrival in these far-off lands.

Admiralty House was also busy. A selection of officers had gathered outside and, having saluted Merriman, they looked on as the arrivals were led inside. Tom Henderson had time only for a brief exchange with a lieutenant he had served with over a decade earlier.

Commander Brunswick introduced Merriman to the admiral's personal clerk, who explained that Sawyer was in a meeting but would join them shortly. The trio were taken through to a well-appointed reception room, where they were provided with coffee and a plate of little cakes.

'Gentlemen, when I am called in, I'd be much obliged if you would introduce yourself to the locals. Tom, that old compatriot of yours might be a useful source for us. We're here only briefly. Let's learn as much as we can, particularly about the American Navy.'

'Intelligence-gathering,' said Hobbs, an excited look upon his face. 'Mr. Brook will be impressed.'

'I'm not sure anything impresses Mr. Brook much,' said Merriman.

'Other than Mr. Brook,' came the withering aside from Tom Henderson.

Perhaps a minute later, Merriman was summoned to Admiral Sawyer's office. Already present there was a fellow captain.

'Captain Merriman!' exclaimed Sawyer. 'You and your ship possess the speed of Hermes if this morning's intelligence is to be believed.'

'Very pleased to meet you, sir,' said Merriman, shaking his superior's hand.

Sawyer seemed quite young considering his rank – younger than Merriman, certainly – his most notable features his pronounced chin and thick, dark eyebrows. He gestured to the captain.

'And may I introduce Captain Sir Philip Broke, master of HMS *Shannon*.'

Broke looked to be in his late thirties; a fellow with a genial face and a head of wavy brown hair.

'Honoured, sir,' said Broke. 'I have heard of your exploits in many a club.'

'A mark of my age perhaps,' said Merriman.

'Merely your repute,' countered Broke. 'I'm afraid I must leave you. The admiral has just delivered my orders and I'd like to have the *Shannon* away swiftly.'

Sawyer gestured to Broke. 'Between you and I, Merriman, the finest captain under my command. If it comes to blows, the Yankees won't know what's hit them.'

'Glad to hear it, admiral. Best of luck, Captain Broke.'

'Best to you, Captain Merriman. I hope our paths cross again soon and we can exchange a tale or two.'

As Broke departed, Admiral Sawyer invited Merriman to take the seat his fellow captain had just vacated. As he sat down, Merriman noticed something about a large portrait mounted behind Sawyer.

The admiral smiled. 'No doubt you've seen the resemblance. My father. He too occupied this post.'

'Ah. I see.'

'He was active in both the Seven Years War' and the War of Independence. I only hope I can serve with such distinction.'

Merriman wasn't sure what to say to that.

'Well,' continued Sawyer. 'Twenty-three days. Remarkable. I received no despatch ahead of your arrival, captain, so please tell me of your orders.'

'Admiral, back aboard the *Mercury* is a strongbox under the protection of a Treasury agent named Balthazar Brook. In it is a treaty signed by both His Majesty the King and the native leader named Tecumseh, who I believe represents a great confederation of tribes in Upper Canada. The treaty promises mutual support in the event of a war with America.'

Frowning, Admiral Sawyer leaned back into his chair. 'I did not expect that. What I do know is that, without native assistance, we have little chance of holding back the Americans. I assume then, that you will be sailing onward?'

'I will, sir. At dawn. But I depend on you for my next destination. I was given my orders by Vice Admiral Pertwee and there was no accurate information in England about Tecumseh's current location.'

'I see. Well, I cannot claim to know much about that myself, but we have some very well-informed fellows here so let's see what we can find out for you.'

Merriman then endured a rather frustrating two hours spent in the admiral's office. Even though Sawyer went back and forth and kept him informed, Merriman rather wished he'd taken charge himself. Unused to such passivity, he was on the verge of announcing his departure when Sawyer returned for the last time.

'Well, Merriman, we've done what we can. My clerks have spoken to Indian agents, fishermen, trappers, all sorts. There is no accurate intelligence on the location of this man Tecumseh. However, two sources agreed that there was recently talk of him meeting Governor-General Prevost, who is based in Quebec. We cannot know if that is accurate, if the meeting has occurred or will occur. I'm afraid that is best we can do.'

'Understood. Thank you, sir.'

'Please.' Admiral Sawyer led Merriman over to a large nautical map on the wall. 'As you'll know, Quebec can be reached via the St. Lawrence but that is a journey of some eight hundred nautical miles and not an easy one. We've had reports of French ships in the Gulf of St. Lawrence as recently as April. Additionally, the river itself can throw up obstacles, especially without local knowledge. Here is what I propose.'

Admiral Sawyer pointed to Halifax, on the eastern side of Nova Scotia, and ran a finger downward and around the island's southern end. 'This route takes you into the Bay of Fundy and I suggest you dock at Saint John. You are likely to obtain much more accurate and timely intelligence there and your Treasury friend might secure the services of an Indian agent or a native guide. There are army units there too who may be able to assist.'

Merriman examined the map. 'A hundred and forty miles or so.'

'A little less,' said Sawyer, returning to his desk and taking up a pen. 'With that speedy ship of yours, you should do it in a day or two. But do be careful in the Bay. Some of the strongest tides in the world. One of my clerks will provide you with a navigational guide. There are also the Americans to consider, of course. The border is not far from Saint John.'

Merriman thought the admiral's suggestion entirely sensible. They had been so fortunate with the crossing. The thought of trying for the St. Lawrence, with many more days at sea in unknown waters was not appealing.

Sawyer scribbled a few lines, signed his note, and handed it to Merriman, who held it carefully in order to let the ink dry.

'Governor Smith is an old friend. He will assist in any way he can.'

'Much appreciated, admiral.'

Sawyer offered his hand. 'I hope your agent finds his man. By the way, I have a second mission for you. It seems war is coming, and a frigate captained by a veteran would be a great boon to the Atlantic Fleet. If some more guns and crew can be arranged for you, will the *Mercury* join us?'

'I was given no further orders beyond my mission of delivery, Admiral Sawyer. If that is your wish, please consider myself and my ship to be at your disposal.'

Chapter Fifteen

The Dead and the Dying

It was as grim a sight as Alfred Shrigley had beheld on a ship.

He stood alongside eighty officers and crew, packed onto the bow of the *Romulus* as the smallpox patients disposed of the first fatality. Only Mr. Diggs, the helmsman, and a couple of trusted others remained stationed at the sheets, in case of emergency.

Under the supervision of Dr. Webster, every area other than the bosun's storeroom below deck had been cleared and every hatch opened to aid ventilation. Smith, who had cared so well for Knapp, was now too ill himself to assist. It was therefore left to the three most recent additions to the quarantine area to take Knapp's body up on deck and then to the larboard nets.

John Webster moved forward and said a few words, as agreed with Shrigley beforehand. The trio, two of whom were not moving well at all, then disposed of the dead man. *Romulus* was clipping along at five knots and Shrigley winced as the body hit the water with a crash. Most of the sailors looked for the weighted hammock, which swiftly slipped beneath the waves.

The captain noted several men shake their heads, and another curse under his breath.

'I hear so much as another whisper, there'll be hell to pay!' hissed Lieutenant Glanville. 'This is how it has to be done.'

Shrigley wished the man would keep his outbursts to himself. This was one occasion where there was more to be lost than gained by sanctioning the men for minor indiscretions. It did not surprise Shrigley that the dead man's friends and many others did not approve of this treatment.

The infected sailors walked back to the hatch. All had covered their heads with hoods and their mouths with handkerchiefs. Talbot, the armourer's mate, was only seventeen. Though he walked well enough, the visible sections of his face were now covered with pustules.

'Strength, lad!' cried Mr. Appleton, the armourer. 'You're in our prayers. All of you.'

This gave rise to a number of similar calls from other men. Glanville was clearly considering a response when Shrigley caught his eye and indicated with a subtle shake of his head that the lieutenant should say nothing.

Once the trio had disappeared below deck, Dr. Webster followed them downward, then returned to signal that they were back in the quarantined area. At his suggestion, the crewmen were to remain on deck for another half hour before going below.

As Mr. Diggs began dispersing the men, clearly aiming to keep as many occupied as he could, a grey-haired sailor approached Shrigley. Removing his hat, he bowed his head.

'Permission to speak, captain?'

'Move along, Rowley,' said Lieutenant Glanville, a hand on the sailor's shoulder.

'It's all right, Glanville,' said the captain. 'What do you wish to say, Rowley?'

'Sir, the lads asked me to speak on their behalf. About the men in quarantine. Sir, it just don't seem right. Leaving them to die in there like that.'

'It's a difficult situation for all concerned, Rowley. We must defer to Dr. Webster in these matters. All that he – that *we* – are doing is designed to prevent the spread of infection.'

'Sir, can it really be that the affliction is spread through the air? If so, why don't we all have it?'

'I don't know, Rowley. But then, I am not an expert physician and neither are you. If you're a godly man, then I suggest you pray for the poor fellows like Mr. Appleton. I certainly am.'

Old Rowley said nothing, but he bowed his head once more before replacing his hat and withdrawing.

That night, Shrigley did more than pray. The sight of the three patients had made him even more determined to do anything he could to ease their suffering. John Webster had been making regular visits to offer advice from the other side of the storeroom door and, that night, Shrigley joined him. He did not look forward to the prospect but he felt it was something that Captain Merriman would have done; and something he should.

He met Webster outside the medical bay and found the surgeon holding two bottles of rum.

'They keep asking for more. The truth is that too much will weaken them, though it will ease the pain a little. Perhaps you could bring the lantern, captain?'

'Of course.'

Shrigley followed Webster forward, passing through the cramped confines of the gundeck. First watch was underway and so those not on duty were either sleeping or gathered in small groups. Many gave a greeting to the physician and the captain and – as ever – Shrigley found the world of the crew a strange place. No matter how many times he passed through their quarters, he could never quite grasp what it was like to live and eat and sleep as the Jack Tars did.

The bosun's storeroom was situated on the lowest deck, close to the bow. Mr. Webster had asked for Cathcote to place a permanent guard there and they found a Corporal Raskin on duty. Just as the marine moved aside to let them through, an awful cry went up from inside the storeroom. His young face caught in the lantern's glow, Raskin's anguished expression was clear.

'Thinking I might find something to block my ears, sir. Gets wearing, it does.'

'I've no doubt,' said Webster.

'You're relieved for the next half-hour,' said Shrigley.

'Sir.'

Before announcing their presence, Webster spoke quietly. 'I shall pass the rum through and then check on them as usual. What are you going to say?'

Shrigley found himself somewhat caught out. 'I'm not sure. I suppose I'd just like to…show some camaraderie; show that they're not alone.'

Webster nodded, then knocked on the door.

'It's Dr. Webster. I'm opening up.' He took the key from his pocket and did so. Shrigley, who was holding the lantern to help him, saw that there were two more lanterns alight inside the store. Most of the men were lying on their beds and they did not move as Webster carefully placed the bottles on the floor.

'Is that the captain there?' asked a deep voice.

'It is,' said Shrigley.

'Good of you to come down, sir,' said another voice.

'The least I can do.'

Having deposited the rum, Webster withdrew.

'Now then, that is to last you all for the next day. Howard, you will ensure it is shared fairly and for those in need?'

'I will, sir,' croaked Howard. With the death of Knapp, the quarter gunner was the senior sailor amongst the ailing men. Shrigley was glad that there was a respected leader among them. He found it oddly moving that, even in their desperate state, the sailors honoured such things.

'How are you today, Howard?' asked Webster.

'More of 'em, Mr. Webster. More of 'em in my throat. Bowels ain't good either.'

'Have you eaten anything?'

'Can't hold anything down.'

Mr. Webster spoke to four more men, including Talbot and the even younger Isaac Hamble, who was just thirteen. The remaining men, Midshipman Lange included, were not capable of speech but Howard was able to report on their condition. Webster listened carefully and gave specific advice. Once that was done, he turned to Shrigley. But before the captain could say anything, Hamble spoke up.

'Captain Shrigley, sir, can I ask about my wages?'

'Your wages, Hamble?'

'If I'm taken, sir. Will my money go to my mother?'

'Well…we can certainly make arrangements, yes.'

'Remember what I've told you,' said Webster. 'All of you. More folk survive this condition than do not.'

'But what life do they have?' asked Talbot, easily identifiable by his broad Dorset accent. 'Looking like…as I do now.'

Shrigley remembered what Glanville had said, about their lives not being worth living. He thought also of Jesus and the leper.

He and Webster heard weeping and whispering.

'Trust in the Lord,' said Howard after a time. 'That's all we can do.'

'And what did he do for Knapp?' cried Talbot. 'Poor Smith won't even last the night!'

'Shut up!' shouted someone else. 'Shut your mouth.'

Shrigley was trying desperately to find some words. He knew that Captain Merriman would have said the right thing. Suddenly, they came to him.

When he spoke, his voice faltered but he pressed on: 'Men, we all here are sailors and every sailor knows that many things are outside our control. This is another. You at least have Dr. Webster here and all the rest of us aboard praying for you. Think of this as another battle. In a battle, we stay together. We just try to survive.'

Some of the men thanked him, which somehow made Shrigley feel even more hopeless.

'A tot or two might help you sleep,' said Webster. 'I'll come again in the morning.'

As they withdrew along the passageway, Shrigley felt obliged to apologise for the inadequacy of his words.

'Not at all,' said Webster. 'This…powerlessness is a familiar feeling for physicians. One we must become used to.'

Midshipman Lange was the next to succumb to the disease and then, a few hours later, Talbot. Just as he had carried a dead man up to the deck, his turn came, and again the crew gathered at the bow while their bodies were committed to the deep.

Shrigley had been unable to face another visit to the storeroom but Webster told him that, despite the recent losses, Howard and the others were holding up well. The single ray of hope came from the fact that no other cases had been identified and Mr. Webster was beginning to sound confident that the outbreak had been isolated. If that was the case, Shrigley knew that the physician would have once again acquitted himself well. It was by no means unheard of for entire ships to be infected and lose half or more of the crew to disease.

Only an hour or so after Talbot's funeral, message flags were sighted on the mast of the *Iona*, the ship in front of *Romulus*. The message was from Captain Halliwell and summoned the brig-sloop to the front of the column. So began a day of slow progress as *Romulus* passed six of the merchantmen before receiving new orders passed back just as *HMS Zeus* was finally spotted around five miles ahead.

VESSELS UNKNOWN TO SOUTH. SCREEN COLUMN TWO MILES SOUTH OF BENGAL.

Bengal was the seventh ship they passed and Shrigley stopped to converse with the second officer. He learned that a trio of ships had been sighted the previous afternoon and seen sailing north towards the column before they were lost to the darkness.

As the ships parted, Shrigley looked to the south and saw nothing more than an empty horizon. There were no reports of any sightings from the crosstrees.

'Rather odd,' said Lieutenant Glanville.

'There's a haze,' said Lieutenant Ives. 'It's possible that *Zeus* can see them but we can't.'

'A message to the *Zeus*, sir?' suggested Glanville. 'For clarification?'

'That will be slow,' said Shrigley. 'We have our orders. South it is.'

This meant a series of tacks and an onerous period of work for the entire crew. Shrigley did not mind that. The arrival of the disease had cast a pall of gloom across the entire ship and he was satisfied to keep the men hard at it.

Once two miles to the south, *Romulus* turned to the west and fulfilled her shielding role for the remainder of the day. That day was a warm one, for the previous week seemed to have heralded the arrival of summer. Keen to stay on deck, Shrigley was tempted to remove his jacket as Glanville had but he wished to keep up appearances, even though his shirt clung to him and his brow was clammy with sweat.

The first lieutenant remained another irritant. Glanville seemed convinced that the message was now out of date and that *Romulus* would be better off returning to her previous position and protecting the rear of the column from the ships that were clearly now elsewhere. However, with a reduction in wind throughout the day, the haze became more of a fog and soon only *Bengal* was visible. Shrigley drew comfort from the knowledge that the mysterious ships would be equally disadvantaged.

An hour before dusk, a possible clue as to their identity was revealed. One of the topmen spotted something floating in the water nearby and, as *Romulus* was making only three knots, Shrigley again kept the men busy by launching the boat. It would have been an ideal opportunity for gunnery practice but he did not wish to alarm the *Bengal* or other allies that might hear the gunfire.

The object turned out to be a large barrel. It was too heavy for the boat-crew to manually lift out of the water but they were able to read some faint writing.

'Well?' asked Shrigley as the crew returned to the *Romulus*.

'French, sir.'

'You're sure?'

'Armanac, sir. Saint-Sever. Weed on it. Been in the water a time.'

'Maybe we should rig a crane and pull it out?' said Ives with a grin.

'Tempting,' said Shrigley.

It was to be their only discovery of the day and, as night fell, the *Romulus* continued west, still guarding the southern flank of the slow-moving convoy.

Not long after midnight, the captain sat at the rear of the cabin, gazing at the desk. It was not in fact the desk he was gazing at, precisely, but a bottle of brandy, one side gleaming under lamp-light. The sight of the armanac had somehow prompted him to open a bottle earlier brought to the cabin by one of the officers – he couldn't remember which. Shrigley had downed several glasses in quick succession. Vision blurring, head lolling, he now dropped the glass to the floor.

Miraculously, it did not break, but the noise of it caused Trelawney to knock on the door.

'All well, captain?'

'All well.'

He heard the servant retreat. Now struck by guilt, Shrigley replaced glass and bottle in the cabinet. While drinking, he had sat beside an open window, enjoying the cool night air, feeling comfortable for the first time since the morning.

Men were dead and dying and here was he, seeking refuge in the bottle.

Shrigley had never done it before; never succumbed to the temptation.

'Fool. Bloody fool.'

He knocked a fist against his forehead, shamed at the thought of what Captain Merriman would have said. He almost dozed off before standing and shakily making his way to bed.

Shrigley awoke to a bad headache and good news. The mist had cleared and a message had been passed on via the *Bengal* from HMS *Zeus*. *Romulus* was to return to the rear of the column. Better still, land had been sighted.

Chapter Sixteen

Arrival at Saint John

For a time, it seemed that the *Mercury*'s outrageous weather-luck would continue. A steady easterly propelled them south-west until they rounded the southern end of Nova Scotia. The frigate then had to tack its way into the notorious Bay of Fundy, a process made rather easier by an immensely strong tide that pushed them towards Saint John for six hours. During this time, Lieutenant Hobbs used landmarks in the navigational text provided by Admiral Sawyer's staff to count off mile after mile.

While he was preoccupied with the guide and what could be seen from the crosstrees, Merriman, Van der Baan, and many others kept their attention on the western shore. For the majority aboard, this was their first sight of American territory. Officers and crew knew of the Congress's decision for war and that hostilities could break out at any time. Large vessels were only seen venturing out once the tide had turned, using the immense force of the current to coast southwards. During the slack period, *Mercury* had made some progress, but once water began to flow back out of the bay, she became embroiled in a battle she could not win.

With her sails hauled in and her nose pointed north, the speedy frigate was pressed back at what Hobbs calculated to be at least four knots over the ground. The navigational guide suggested trying to use the eastern side of the bay, where the currents were weaker. Given the wind direction – and the fact that their destination was on the western side – Merriman elected that they would stay there.

He remained on deck as *Mercury* battled the tide through the hours of dark. He was less concerned about enemy vessels at night and desperate to give his ship the best chance of regaining her position once the tide turned again. Hobbs did a splendid job of monitoring the nearby coastline using only the light of a half-moon. Henderson matched him, guiding the frigate through a series of tacks as she fought wind and tide. The usually reserved Hobbs gave a whoop of excitement when Tom Henderson alerted him to a change in the wind direction. Still blowing at around twenty knots, the wind had shifted to a southerly, meaning they could just about lay a direct course for Saint John.

The return of the flood coincided roughly with the arrival of the morning watch and the fresh men soon had the frigate going well. Though the commensurate loss of tidal strength by the coast cost them some speed, the remarkable flow nonetheless swept them towards their destination.

Merriman didn't need Hobbs or Henderson to tell him it would be a close-run thing. After a couple of hours of sleep, he returned to the quarterdeck at dawn, finding the pair apparently joined at the hip. If they weren't examining the sails and rig and ordering some refinement, they were checking the coast with a spyglass, running out the log or consulting the navigational guide.

At Merriman's order, Adkins fetched them each a cup of coffee and the pair continued their crucial work. With slack water upon them, *Mercury* eventually found herself in the lee of Cape Spencer and out of the strongest currents at last. Henderson and Hobbs announced that they would reach their destination safely, which caused a great cheer from those on deck.

Approaching Saint John, which seemed a busy place with a well-developed harbour containing many ships, *Mercury* joined the dozen or so other vessels at anchor just outside the port. Again, they found themselves the object of attention and were soon being addressed by a merchant officer in a tender returning to his ship.

'I am somewhat relieved!' he cried in an odd-sounding accent. 'We thought you might be an advance force of Yankees until we saw your colours.'

'We are very close to the border, are we not?' answered Van der Baan in his booming tone.

'Quite close, yes, so we at least get news from the south quickly. I must tell you that the latest news is not good. The Senate approved the vote by nineteen to thirteen. It's war.'

Balthazar Brook was like a man possessed. His single bag already packed, he asked that the boat be launched immediately and that Van der Baan and Merriman personally accompany him to shore. Merriman of course agreed but found himself annoyed once again by the demanding agent. Brook didn't seem to care that only an extreme element of good fortune and the excellent performance of the crew had allowed him to reach his destination in such good time.

Radiating impatience, Brook stood by the great cabin door, strongbox at his feet, as Merriman put on a fresh jacket and took his hat from Peters. Brook had recruited the midshipmen to carry the strongbox and, as they made their way along the passageway, Lieutenant Hobbs came down from the hatch, stumbling on the penultimate step and narrowly avoiding the midshipmen and their precious load.

'Careful there,' snapped Brook, at which point Merriman finally lost his temper with the man. As Adkins and Eades carried the box upward, Merriman gripped Brook by the arm, causing a flash of anger from those dark eyes.

'Captain?'

'I suggest another selection of words for Lieutenant Hobbs, Mr. Brook. If not for the outstanding effort of he and Mr. Henderson, we might not have reached Saint John at all. He has not slept for a whole day and night.'

Brook took a breath. 'You are right, captain, of course. Thank you, Mr. Hobbs. And to you and all your officers and men, Captain Merriman.'

Merriman nodded and remained below for a moment while Brook hurried after the strongbox.

'I would normally encourage you straight to your bunk, Hobbs, but I've another task for you.'

Despite his red-rimmed eyes and pale visage, the lieutenant straightened. 'Of course, sir.'

'If the men aren't assured of time ashore, we might have a mutiny on our hands. Spread the word that they'll all get a turn before the day is out. If I'm not back by midday, send half of them ashore. You know the form – good mix of officers and men, standing orders and all that.'

'Aye, sir.'

Brook and Van der Baan were both conspicuously armed with pistols and it was just as well. Upon reaching the quay at the southern end of Saint John's harbour, the five climbed up the steps and beheld a scene of some confusion. The harbour was exceptionally busy with sailors, local folk and a good number of uniformed men. Brook took the lead and immediately intercepted a corporal of infantry, requesting directions to the nearest army post.

The corporal was not from Saint John himself but did disclose that he was part of the 104th Regiment of Foot, which was now being deployed across the Canadian province of New Brunswick. His knowledge of the town was limited because he and his men were from another part of the state, though he did know that the highest-ranking soldier in the town was a Scottish major named Campbell. He was not, however, sure where he could be found.

'Ridiculous,' said Balthazar Brook as the corporal and his platoon departed, their orders to secure an American privateer whose skipper had been accused of spying.

'Are you from that new ship?' The lady's voice held an accent that seemed to Merriman both English and American. The speaker was dressed in a fine green gown and a broad-brimmed hat. With her were a female servant and a young boy.

Balthazar Brook ignored her, instead glancing around for another source of information.

'We are, madam,' said Merriman. 'I wonder if you could direct us to someone in authority? The local governor, perhaps, or an infantry officer.'

'Governor Smith is sadly at death's door,' said the lady. 'Though I can probably locate Major Campbell if you wish.'

Brook was now considerably more interested in this conversation.

'My name is Anne Humbert,' said the lady. 'My husband is Stephen Humbert, a member of the Common Council. We also have interests in shipping and provisioning. Our music shop is just over there. Perhaps you would like to come and have some tea while I have Matthew fetch his father?'

'Most kind, Mrs. Humbert,' said Merriman, before introducing himself and the others. 'Thank you.'

'Humbert – sounds French,' grumbled Brook as Van der Baan and the midshipmen followed their new friend.

'Do not look a gift horse in the mouth, Brook,' replied Merriman. 'A well-connected woman can be as useful as a well-connected man. And, unlike some, they possess excellent manners.'

Sitting close to a piano and surrounded by at least two dozen stringed instruments, the captain, the lieutenant, the midshipmen and the agent drank tea. Mrs. Humbert had tasked her servant with preparing the refreshments while her son was despatched homeward. Her husband was apparently so busy with the business of the town's council and state legislature that he'd acquired a nasty headache. He had ignored his wife's imprecations to get some fresh air and Anne Humbert admitted that calling him down to the harbour was not an entirely altruistic gesture.

'This delivery of yours, Mr. Brook,' she said, cradling a cup and saucer in her lap only feet from the strongbox. 'Should I assume it is monetary?'

'I'd rather not go into the details,' said Brook.

'How long has the governor been ill?' asked Van der Baan.

'It was a riding accident,' answered Mrs. Humbert, shaking her head. 'Some stray dog startled his mount. Tuesday last.'

From beyond the shop door came a string of oaths as some ruffian fought his way through the crowd.

Mrs. Humbert tutted. 'Dear oh dear. Now is not the time for panic. Cool heads are required at times like this.'

'Mrs. Humbert, what's all this about Kentuckians?'

This came from Adkins, a reference to a shouted discussion they had heard outside.

'You know nothing of them, young man?'

'I know Kentucky is a state but that's all.'

'Militiaman,' said Mrs. Humbert. 'Known to be as vicious as any native and, likewise, not averse to scalping their enemies. The Indians call them "big knives".'

Adkins looked as if he wished he hadn't asked.

Coming from their refined host in their genteel surroundings, the statement somehow seemed even more shocking.

'Terror is a powerful weapon here,' added Mrs. Humbert. 'It has always been so.'

'Did you say you were born in America?' asked Brook.

'We both were. We moved here after the war. Couldn't be part of that rebellious rabble to the south. You'll find many like us here and across the rest of Canada.'

Stephen Humbert entered the music shop, along with his son. A well-dressed man of around Merriman's age, he was tall and rather portly. He removed his black hat and politely greeted the guests.

'My son tells me that you are in need of assistance.'

'We are, sir,' said Balthazar Brook as he stood. 'Can you convey me to Major Campbell? I am in need of intelligence and a guide.'

'Intelligence regarding what?'

'The location of a tribal leader by the name of Tecumseh. We were told that he is due to meet with Governor-General Prevost in Quebec.'

'Ah. So that's what Hokolesqua is doing here.'

'Hoko-who?' asked Brook, drawing smiles from Anne Humbert and her son.

'Hokolesqua. He's been here for the last week or so; asking everyone about new ships and reports from elsewhere along the coast. I imagine Tecumseh sent him to ensure the treaty reaches him.'

Brook was looking rather hopeful but the last sentence seemed to alarm him.

'Come now, Mr. Brook,' said Humbert. 'A crucial object sent from London via a Treasury agent and meant for Tecumseh. I have solved far more thorny puzzles than that one in my time.'

Anne Humbert spoke up again. 'One wouldn't imagine that my Stephen started his working life as a humble baker, would one?'

'Can you introduce me to this Hokolesqua?' asked Brook.

'Oh, certainly,' said Humbert. 'I believe he's residing at the Villiers Guest House.'

'He is an associate of Tecumseh?' asked Brook.

'Closer than that. His cousin.'

'I thought he'd have feathers in his hair.'
'Or a bone through his nose.'
'Or at least an axe on his belt.'

Merriman almost chuckled at the comments of the two midshipmen. The party had been conducted around half a mile to the guest house, which was a middling place that seemed an oasis of calm amidst the general uproar. Now, standing with Stephen Humbert, the navy men looked on as Brook and Hokolesqua conversed on the other side of the inn's courtyard.

The Shawnee tribesman was in fact quite distinctive, wearing moccasins, trousers and a tunic that all seemed to be made of the same pale brown hide. His long black hair hung over his shoulders and he nodded occasionally while he listened to Balthazar Brook. At their initial meeting, Merriman had heard enough to establish that Hokolesqua spoke good English and was quite relieved at the arrival of the precious document. He had insisted on seeing the paper itself and Merriman and the others had peered down curiously as Brook removed the wooden case in which the treaty was mounted. Merriman had seen the signature of the king several times over the years and noted that it seemed to have changed somewhat.

Balthazar Brook and Hokolesqua walked back across the courtyard. It seemed to Merriman that the tribesman was very used to curious eyes upon him and that – though no more than twenty-five – he was a composed and capable character.

'We have made an agreement,' declared Brook. 'Hokolesqua was told by his cousin that he will be in Quebec for the entirety of the month of June. It is a journey of around four hundred miles but, on horseback, we might manage it in eight or nine days.'

'That is *most* optimistic,' said Stephen Humbert. 'These fellows fly along but you are not a Shawnee, Mr. Brook.'

'I can ride well enough,' replied the Treasury man.

'You mean to go alone?' asked Van der Baan. 'Just the two of you? No military escort?'

'If we had time, perhaps,' said Hokolesqua. 'But infantry will slow us down and draw attention.' The tribesman spoke in a low, even tone. 'I will give Mr. Brook some of my clothes. His hair is almost as black as mine.'

'You could give him one of your weapons!' declared Adkins. 'Do you have an axe?'

'Several,' said Hokolesqua.

At a tut from Eades, the younger midshipman clammed up.

'Mr. Humbert, your thoughts?'

Noting an expression of annoyance from Brook, Merriman turned and waited for his answer.

'For all we know, American troops may be coming our way.'

'All the more reason for haste,' countered Brook.

Humbert addressed his next question to Hokolesqua. 'Do you plan to cut across Maine? That will take several days off your trip.'

'Possibly.'

Humbert turned towards Merriman. 'Captain, I have travelled all across our province and beyond but I cannot claim to know the lands as well as this fellow. As riders and readers of terrain, the Shawnee have no equal. Nor can I argue against the fact that a larger unit might draw unwelcome attention. But it is a long way, and the declaration of war throws everything into flux.'

'I did not travel here in the expectation of avoiding risk,' said Brook. 'Gentlemen, I would like to begin my preparations so that we can depart in daylight.'

While Brook shook hands with Van der Baan and the midshipmen, Merriman joined Humbert in wishing Hokolesqua well.

'My cousin told me to deliver this to him at any cost,' said the Shawnee tribesman. 'Rest assured I will do so.'

Merriman then shook hands with Brook. 'Please be careful. I hope to God you will soon be in Quebec and with Governor-General Prevost.'

With that, the captain and his officers walked back through the busy streets of Saint John. As he was rowed out to *Mercury*, Merriman experienced mixed feelings. On the one hand, he was greatly relieved to have done his part in taking the treaty this far. On the other, he was very concerned about the task facing the two men he had just left. He imagined Vice Admiral Pertwee and all the others luminaries waiting back in London for news that the crucial document had been delivered; that their alliance had been secured.

Once back aboard *Mercury*, he called all the officers and petty officers into the great cabin.

'Now, as promised, we must give the men some time ashore. But I want them in groups of no more than ten, each with one of you in attendance. They can drink of course but I want no reports of rough stuff. These people are under threat of invasion. The last thing they need is some troublesome Tars in their midst. Now what's the time?'

'Just gone eleven, sir,' said Adkins.

'All right. Take half the men and give them until four. The other half can go after dinner until dusk. Off you go. Not you, Eades.'

The midshipman looked rather concerned that he had been singled out so Merriman smiled.

'Nothing to worry about. I'm correct in thinking that you're not too keen on the drink?'

'No, sir. I try to keep up with the others and I just make myself ill.'

'Very sensible,' said the captain as the last of the others filed out. 'I've an important task for you. Admiral Sawyer asked if we would assist his ships and something tells me they will be seeing action imminently. If we join them, I have no wish to do so on an undermanned and under-armed vessel. I would like to make some enquiries regarding both personnel and long guns. I myself will do so tomorrow but perhaps you can make a start?'

Eades seemed enthused by his assignment. 'Of course, captain. I can begin with the ships we passed in the harbour. There was a sloop and a brig.'

'Very good.'

'I shall report to you immediately upon my return, sir.'

'One more thing, send Ned Lownes along, would you?'

Once the midshipman had shut the great cabin door behind him, Merriman summoned his attendant.

'Peters, talk to cook and ensure that we've some decent fresh food for an officers' dinner tomorrow.'

'Aye, captain. Some wine and rum too, I would think.'

'Quite so.'

As Peters left, he held the door open and pointed down at a small figure. Merriman walked over.

'Thank you, Peters. Ah, here's young Ned. How are you?'

'Well, sir,' said Ned, tapping a knuckle against his forehead.

'Very good. I've a job for you. I am extremely tired and I am going to sleep. You will guard my door. If anyone comes along, tell them I am not to be disturbed.'

Chapter Seventeen

A New Mission

The next two days unfolded largely to the captain's satisfaction. Only one of the *Mercury*'s crew disgraced himself during his run ashore. The miscreant had to be extracted by the lieutenants from Saint John's prison, having manhandled several barmaids. Merriman considered flogging him but, upon seeing the black eye that Van der Baan had administered, he instead – as promised – informed the sailor that he could expect no prize-money.

Eades had done his best in terms of securing sailors but, unsurprisingly, there were only slim pickings to be had. However, with Adkins' assistance, he put the word about and a dozen men offered their services. Assessed by Bosun Brockle, eight were identified as sufficiently useful and entered onto *Mercury*'s books. Stephen Humbert continued to be of assistance and one of his colleagues on the common council advised Merriman to impress men if necessary. This fellow seemed convinced that the maritime theatre would be crucial to the outcome of the war.

The captain and his lieutenants calculated that they could effectively manage six more guns. The problem was finding those guns. Saint John had a naval workshop but any piece in working order had already been seized by local warships. However, on the third day in port, a solution presented itself in the form of a fellow captain.

His name was Caleb Perry, master of the frigate HMS *London*, and he visited the *Mercury* barely an hour after his own ship arrived. He was very young for a captain and came bounding aboard alone. Short but powerfully built, he removed his hat to reveal a head of curly hair identical in colour to Van der Baan's. His otherwise handsome face had been disfigured by an ugly pit of a scar on his right cheek. The injury had evidently not affected the man's confidence.

'Captain Sir James Merriman, pleased to make your acquaintance.'

'Likewise, Captain Perry. I've just been inspecting your ship through my glass. She looks very smart indeed.'

'Barely a year old, fresh from Chatham. Admiral Sawyer asked for four frigates but he got only us. We bagged a French merchantman three months back but that's it. Keen for action – myself and the men. Will you join us, captain?'

'Join you where exactly?'

'We passed the *Shannon* just beyond the bay. She's aiming to sit off New York and watch for Yankees. Captain Broke asked me to muster whoever I could to patrol the bay. Could be a fertile hunting ground for us – those tides have caught out many a ship.'

'Mine included.'

'There will be strength in numbers, Captain Merriman. My *London*, of course. The *Crocodile* too.'

'I'm tempted to say she's a mere sloop but she of course has more guns than I do.'

'How many do you need?'

'Six is all we can handle with the present complement.'

'Your total then would be?'

'Just fourteen.'

'Oh no. That simply won't do. You must have eighteen, at least. If I can find you the guns and the men, will you accompany me out into the bay for the hunt?'

'Captain, if you can manage that, I should feel duty-bound to follow you just about anywhere.'

The energetic Caleb Perry was true to his word. Later that afternoon, Merriman looked on as the sloop *Alexander* drew alongside. He was astonished that the captain would willingly give up all ten of his twelve-pounders but they were soon being loaded using a crane assembled under the supervision of Bosun Brockle. Also coming aboard were a pair of bronze bow-chasers donated by *London*.

'The skipper's not even aboard,' said Van der Baan as he and Merriman looked on from the quarterdeck. 'Perry said he's an odd fellow, lost his nerve. He was supposed to sail *Alexander* around to Quebec months ago. If Sawyer knew, I daresay he'd replace the milksop immediately.'

'In that case, the guns are better employed with us,' said Merriman, 'small though they are.'

It wasn't just the guns coming aboard. Perry had also persuaded the unseen captain to temporarily part with his gunner and a dozen more men. The gunner, who was named Milton, introduced himself and was soon swinging across on a spare halyard, followed by the sailors. All seemed very keen to contribute, no doubt eager for an opportunity at a prize, which was far more likely to be attained by *Mercury* than *Alexander*.

'An early start tomorrow then, sir?' said Van der Baan.

'Yes, indeed. Perry wants to catch the outgoing tide which means everyone up at morning watch.'

From the south came the sound of long guns. *London* and *Crocodile* were conducting firing exercises off Cape Spencer. Merriman found himself envious. Due to their lack of practice and makeshift crew, he felt very much underprepared. And yet he also felt confident in his men, and *very* confident in his officers. They had enjoyed a fine dinner on the second night in Saint John. An evening of amity and good cheer. Not bad, he thought, for a group thrown together around a month earlier. Now would come a different test.

The fleet of three departed on time, hauled out by the ebbing tide once more. Captain Moresby of the *Crocodile* had been in Canada for some years and used a neat trick to help the trio avoid losing progress fighting the flood. For five hours, the ships anchored in Long Island Bay, an anchorage on the eastern side of a large island named Grand Manan, which was situated on the western side of the Bay of Fundy.

With the captain resting and under the command of Lieutenant Van der Baan, *Mercury* then followed *Crocodile* and *London* southward until they were beyond the worst of the tides and able to monitor the fifty-mile gap from west of Grand Manan to the coast of Nova Scotia.

The following day, Merriman put the gun crews through their paces. The new twelve-pounders were mixed in with the eighteen-pounders and Mr. Milton and the other men from the *Alexandria* did quite well. The rate of fire was as good as could be expected and there were thankfully no accidents. One of the new guns required a minor repair to the firing mechanism but Milton soon solved that.

On the third morning, Merriman awoke to the smell of frying bacon, which put a smile on his face and caused him to reflect on the many benefits of landfall. In Saint John, the cook had been able to obtain fresh meat, fruit, vegetables and water. There were also two pigs and a dozen chickens aboard. Peters had promised him a pork joint for roasting that he was also looking forward to.

As he dressed, the captain's thoughts turned to Alfred Shrigley. No one they had spoken to in Saint John had any news about the convoy. Even given the differences in speed, Merriman was concerned at the lack of information. He wondered if fate might bring him together with his compatriot and friend during this patrol.

'Mornin' sir,' said Peters, after knocking and entering. 'I've got your coffee, and there's some bacon on the go.'

'My nose has already told me that, Peters. Anything else?'

'Freshly baked bread, and some cheese, sir. I'll get a plate ready for you.'

Though hungry, Merriman had slept later than usual and was keen to show his face and see that all was well.

'Belay that for now. I'll have my coffee and take in the deck. Have the food ready in say, a quarter-hour.'

On the quarterdeck, he found Hobbs leaning up against the starboard rail.

'All well?' asked Merriman.

'Good morning, captain. Yes indeed. A quiet morning under easy sail. Wind's been steady from west-south-west. Morning mist has burned off.'

Merriman didn't have his hat on, so he shaded his eyes with hand and looked out at the sea. There was only a slight chop and he reckoned he was lucky to find himself in this hazardous region during summer rather than winter.

'Odd to be out here again so soon, isn't it, captain?' said Bosun Brockle, who was standing by the helm.

'It is, Brockle. I've always found that, in the service, it's best not to look too far ahead – because you never know where you're going to be.'

The three vessels were well spread and patrolling from north-west to south-east, between Grand Manan and Brier Island, which was just off Nova Scotia. By using this method, they would hope to intercept vessels entering the bay and would pass each other regularly for communication.

Hobbs spoke up again. 'I also took the liberty of adjusting the chronometer, sir, based on the lunar distances. I calculated that it was nearly five minutes fast. I can show you my workings if you like?'

'Thank you, Hobbs, but not now. I have some letters and reports to attend to.'

This was only half-true but Merriman did not wish to get bogged down in obscure statistics and calculations this early in the day.

'Coming up on three miles from Brier Island, sir,' asked Hobbs. 'Shall we turn at one mile again?'

'At your discretion. Thank you.'

Merriman was soon back down below. As he was still without a desk, he sat on the bench by the window, his shoulders warmed by the sun. He had located a pen and some paper and was currently formulating the first lines of a letter to Helen while setting about a second rasher of bacon.

'Crispy as you like it, sir,' said Peters, who was sitting on a stool on the far side of the cabin, making a repair to one of the captain's stockings.

Merriman then heard fast-moving steps outside his door and the inevitable knock.

'Come in,' he said, trying to hide his displeasure at being disturbed.

Adkins quickly dragged off his hat and hurried across the near-empty cabin.

'Mr. Hobbs' compliments, sir, but the lookout reports ships sighted and gun smoke. He thinks they're at one another.'

Peters shook his head and tutted.

Merriman sighed and put down the plate. 'Very well, Adkins. Compliments to Mr. Hobbs and I shall be there presently.'

With his shoes back on, Merriman met Peters at the door, still munching his second rasher of bacon. The servant put on his jacket and handed him his hat.

'Never bloody ends, does it, sir?'

Moments later, Merriman was back on deck, glad to be properly attired if action was imminent. He was aware that Mercury had made her turn and headed back to the north-west while he was penning his lines to Helen.

Hobbs had been joined by Van der Baan and Tom Henderson.

'What do we have, Mr. Hobbs?'

'A topman spotted some sails off to larboard, sir. About four points off the bow. Hull down, so a good distance off, but he thinks he saw some bright flashes on the sails and possibly smoke. He can't be sure, though, not without a glass.'

Merriman saw that young Eades was already climbing aloft with a brass telescope under his arm.

'Don't fancy it today, sir?' asked Henderson with a grin.

'I think once a year suits me well enough, Tom. Feel free to take my place.'

'Young man's game, sir.'

'Now you tell me.'

Wishing he'd had time to finish his bacon, Merriman saw that Eades had become a proficient climber. The midshipman used the lubber's hole on the way up but – having surveyed the situation through his glass – was brave enough to shim down the main-topmast back stay, landing smartly on deck before hurrying to the stern to make his report.

'Three ships, sir, heading into the bay from the south-west. Looks like two smaller ships being attacked by a third-rater. Too far to see colours, sir.'

'Given our location and the declaration of war, our intervention may well be required, wouldn't you agree, gentlemen?'

'A third-rater, sir?' said Hobbs. 'If she's fully armed, it would be helpful to have *London* with us.'

'It would. Let's hope Captain Perry also has some keen-eyed fellows aboard. Tom, can we lay a course of interception?'

Henderson glanced up at the clouds, then the sails, then the wake left by *Mercury*. 'Not quite, sir. We can make two points closer to the wind but that tide running out of the bay will set us off by a few miles. Coming off the wind puts *Mercury* on her best point of sail. Faster, balanced and we won't be fighting to keep her straight. About two hours to reach them. Should bring us up on their quarter too – keep the weather and the tide to our advantage.'

One of the many things Merriman admired about Tom Henderson was that – like any good student – he showed his workings. Better still, his conclusions were invariably sound.

Merriman nodded his approval. 'Well then, let's be about it. Mr. Hobbs, lay that course. Master Henderson, please plot that out and Mr. Mr. Eades can practice to work it up. Mr. Adkins, please rouse the other officers and ask the cook to feed the men. We will clear for action at the third turn of the hourglass. If needed, I will be in the great cabin, finishing my breakfast.'

Merriman completed not only a review of the ship's recent accounts but three pages of a letter to Helen. Writing of their speedy crossing and general good fortune to date made him wary of the impending encounter. What he heard once back in the breeze and sunlight confirmed that this would be an engagement fraught with danger.

Mr. Van der Baan had the deck and gave his report. 'Afternoon captain. We have one American frigate chasing two British merchant ships. The American vessel is clearly undeterred by our presence and is keeping up steady fire with her chasers.'

'Positioned well for the engagement, lieutenant?'

'We'll be off the American's starboard quarter in about fifteen minutes, sir. With Mr. Hobbs' calculations and Mr. Henderson's sea-knowledge, we're right we they said we would be.'

'We are quite blessed with that pair,' agreed Merriman. 'We may be under-manned but I'm very pleased with those we have.'

'As we're still short, perhaps we can impress a few Yankees, sir.'

'Well, as they're already upset about that issue, we might as well keep at it!'

Captain and second lieutenant exchanged a grin but Van der Baan's expression darkened when he looked northwards once more.

'One of these big fellows we were told about, sir. Frigate only in name really.'

'Well, the Royal Navy is a match for any vessel.'

'Of course, captain.'

Despite his bold talk, as Merriman gazed at their opponent, his mind turned to what had been discussed at the officers' dinner. Henderson and Hobbs had passed on what they had learned while he'd been with Admiral Sawyer in Halifax and much of the discussion revolved around these new vessels. The American frigates were very long, deep-keeled, narrow at the beam, with a tall rig, and unusually well-armed. They were the creation of an American naval architect named Humphreys, who'd aimed to create a ship powerful enough to take on any British vessel but quick enough to outrun a ship of the line.

'The USS *President*,' said Eades, reporting back from the bow.

'Well, well,' said Merriman. 'She of the *Little Belt* affair last year.'

This infamous incident was still the subject of controversy. HMS *Little Belt* was a Royal Navy frigate that had been fired upon by *President* near Cape Hatteras. Both sides claimed that the other had initiated the action but *Little Belt* came off far worse, losing eleven men and sustaining considerable damage.

The USS *President* was fifty feet longer than *Mercury*, but only a couple of feet wider. If fully armed and manned, she possessed more than twice the guns and twice the crew. Tugging on his ear, looking around at officers and crew, Merriman could see that they shared his anxieties about taking on a far superior vessel. He also reminded himself that he was not facing the French this time. Despite so many years of war, they were still known for their poor training and lax discipline. Generally, the Americans were considered to be more capable.

'As Captain Perry was generous enough to furnish us with some bow-chasers, we may as well try them out. All hands to action!'

'Aye, captain.'

Mercury still didn't have a drummer but Van der Baan passed on the orders and the crew went swiftly to their business. Mr. Milton came up to assist with the bow-chasers, the crews went to their guns, and the officers joined Merriman on the quarterdeck.

Removing his hat momentarily to mop his brow, Henderson grimaced. 'We are losing the wind, sir. The water and the clouds tell me we've only a few minutes left. Don't much like the thought of being becalmed with these tides.'

'And our quarry?' Merriman now saw that the *President*'s masts indeed looked very high. Just like *Mercury*, the pale paint of the gun ports formed a stripe between solid black above and below.

'Them too, sir,' answered Henderson. 'Courses are already shivering. Men going aloft.'

'Stopped firing as well, haven't they?' said Merriman.

'Last volley two minutes ago,' confirmed Hobbs.

Merriman saw that the merchant ships were perhaps a mile clear of the *President*. Raising his telescope, he saw objects being thrown over the side, others floating in their wake. Sailors were tightening sheets and clewlines to flatten the sails. Others were wetting the sails with buckets of water and firing it upward with a hand-cranked pump.

'One cannot say that our compatriots aren't trying everything to get away.'

Now he could hear the lines and sails of his own vessel as they sagged and dropped. He swung the telescope back to the *President*, which had virtually stopped in the water. The rolling swell caused huge swathes of canvas to bang and slap against *Mercury*'s masts. As Brockle sent his sailors upward, the Americans scaled their own masts to furl away and prevent wear and damage.

Merriman continued to move his telescope until it was trained on another man looking back at him, sunlight sparkling on his glass. Instinctively, the captain raised his hat in salute and received the same gesture in return. Merriman had done this many times before but such a cordial exchange always struck him as ironic.

For some reason, his thoughts turned to home and his son Robert, who wanted so much to go to sea. It seemed to him at that moment a terrible notion to allow his own flesh and blood to participate in the insanity of war.

'Beggin' your pardon, sir, and ress-pects from Mr. Eades.'

Merriman turned to see the diminutive figure of Ned Lownes looking up at him, squinting in the sunshine.

'Er…yes?'

'The gun crew is ready and askin' if they can have per…permission to fire?'

'*Captain*,' corrected Van der Baan, causing Lownes' narrow eyes to widen with fear.

'Captain,' stammered the youngster. With the officers staring at him, he now began to tremble and seemed on the verge of crying.

'You can tell the gun crew to go ahead,' said Merriman.

Lownes responded with a half-bow, half-curtsey that had the officers struggling to contain their laughter.

'Better go and tell Mr. Eades,' suggested Lieutenant Hobbs, who had maintained his composure.

Ned trotted away.

Merriman glanced speculatively at Van der Baan. 'I wonder if Eades and Adkins might have got rather carried away with finding a role for the lad.'

'I'll have a word with them, sir.'

'If you would.'

From the bow came the sound of hammering and Merriman saw that Mr. Milton was knocking some metallic imperfection off one of the cannonballs for the two bow-chasers. There had been ambitious talk from some quarters about adapting the ship to place heavier guns here, offering an unusual advantage, but Merriman thought the nine-pounders would do the job well enough. Recalling a similar situation twenty years earlier in the Irish Sea, he didn't wish to place the scantlings under excessive strain.

A minute later, both belched fire, and smoke momentarily hung in the air ahead of the ship before being swept away. Merriman didn't see the balls land himself but word came back that they'd dropped short.

Snatching up his telescope, he trained his lens on the big frigate, then turned it towards the nearby island of Grand Manan. He did so three times in the next minute to make sure he was right, then addressed the sailing master.

'Tom, it appears we have a new problem.'

Chapter Eighteen

Time and Tide

'Yes, captain,' replied Henderson. 'Flood's got us. Scanty wind, currents, shoals and banks in this area.' His lined face broke into a grim smile. 'At least there's no fog.'

'A challenge and no mistake. Still, nothing on the Menai Strait, eh?'

'You've sailed through it, captain?' asked Van der Baan.

'Aye. Tom and I both have. And more than once.'

Adkins spoke up proudly: 'Lord Nelson trained his crews there. He said that if they could handle the Strait, they could sail anywhere in the world!'

'Quite so,' said Van der Baan.

Tom Henderson rubbed his chin for a while, then spoke. 'I'll take bearings off Grand Manan and White Head Island. We'll pass south of there. Shoals. But we have those notes from Captain Perry on the currents and I can work out where we'll be at each turn of the hourglass.'

'Then we are already working to find an advantage. Please get to it, Tom. Mr. Hobbs, please assist where necessary. Mr. Van der Baan, please accompany me to the bow. I wish to see what we can do with these new popguns.'

Merriman and Hobbs were there to see the next volley from the bow-chasers. Those aboard the *President*, drifting on the flood like the *Mercury* around eight hundred yards away, seemed unconcerned by the volleys. The giant frigate was currently stern on to the British ship, main guns useless, and showing no signs of mounting any guns to return fire.

No doubt many eyes were still on the merchantmen, or perhaps the Americans were also concerned by the effects of the tide.

It was possible, Merriman supposed, that the merchant ships might have originated from Shrigley's convoy. He planned to ask any friendly vessel they encountered about HMS *Romulus*.

Even after Mr. Milton had overseen the elevation of the barrels and an extra allocation of powder, the balls from the nine-pounders continued to drop short or fall wide. There was hardly a breath of wind now and it was an eerie scene, the two warships unable to touch each other and both in the grip of the elements. As the minutes passed, Merriman could feel the fear and uneasiness amongst the crew, most of whom had nothing to do.

True to his word, Henderson quickly worked out their current position, placing *Mercury* within a very small triangle upon the chart, four miles south of a location called Gannet Rock. Fifteen minutes later, a second set of sightings confirmed their speed and direction; they were already being pushed northeast at over two knots. With this information, he and Hobbs were able to plot where they would be every half hour until the top of the tide nearly five hours later.

Merriman joined the pair below an awning swiftly raised by Brockle and some hands to shield them from the sun and aid their efforts.

'Here, sir,' said Henderson. 'We will pass over Proprietor Shoal. It will be tight – just a few feet of clearance under the keel.'

Merriman straightened up and looked over the bow at the stern of *President*.

'I do not wish to simply drift and wait. Let's see what we can do with the sweeps.' He then grimaced, recalling how much had been removed due to weight. 'Do we have any?'

'Only four, sir,' said Van der Baan.

'It will have to do.'

Two long oars were put out from the middle of the ship on both sides, manned initially by topmen who had nothing else to do. The first few strokes had little effect but soon the frigate was moving, a faint wake visible at the stern. Slowly, inch by inch, minute by minute, the *Mercury* began to move closer to the *President*.

'We're getting there,' said Merriman. 'Mr. Van der Baan, please pass on the word to Milton and monitor. Chase guns to be fired at every five minutes. That will save shot and powder and keep them cool.'

Wind remained elusive. All within clear view of each other, the two warships and the two trade ships were pushed further north-east, Grand Manan to the north, the broad bay stretching away to the east. Even if *London* and *Crocodile* had been within sight, they'd have been unable to do much with so little wind.

After an hour, the sixteen oarsmen were changed. Merriman was very glad to see the English and Irish contingent still getting along.

And after two hours, their great effort was at last rewarded. One of the nine-pound balls cracked into the stern of the American ship, eliciting a mighty 'Huzzah!' from officers and crew.

The next volley sent splinters flying from the mizzen boom.

Any sense of jubilation left Merriman when Adkins announced that the lookout had spied a boat on the larboard side of *President*. Somehow, they had launched it and kept it hidden without their enemy noticing.

'They're turning,' said Hobbs.

'They let us get close,' breathed Merriman, knowing he had made a mistake. 'Damn it.'

He watched in horror as the little boat rounded the bow of the *President*. There were only six oarsmen (and a man at the tiller) but their effort was sufficient. As the line pulled tight, the ship's bow began to turn.

'Gun ports open,' said Hobbs. He cupped his hands around his mouth but Bosun Brockle beat him to it.

'All hands take cover!'

Yet the onslaught didn't come. Still being dragged into the bay at four knots by the tide, the crewmen in the American boat were having trouble as whirling currents tugged at their oars. The same issue afflicted those at the *Mercury*'s sweeps.

'The shoal,' said Hobbs. 'We reckoned on another five minutes or so but I think we're over it *now*!'

Like him, Henderson was crouching low but he stood to gaze at Grand Manan. 'Could be.'

Merriman locked eyes with the sailing master and Henderson knew instantly what to say. 'Ranges from two fathoms to ten, sir.'

Merriman nodded. There was no time to waste. 'Eades, get up to Van der Baan. Tell him to forget the guns. We will unlash the bower anchor and make ready to let go.'

The two vessels continued north-eastwards, one trying to present the side of their ship, the other trying to do the opposite. Merriman called down various commands to the oarsmen, endeavouring to escape the inevitable broadside. If anything, the *President* was closer now – no more than two hundred yards. Even worse, the individual gunners had enjoyed plenty of time to mark their target.

Lieutenant Van der Baan called all spare men to the cable locker on the orlop deck. Here, the cable was run back to the mainmast and wrapped around it three times in order to mitigate the huge forces the line would be subjected to.

'I've a feeling we'll get it on the next swing,' said Henderson, hand gripping the rail, eyes fixed on the *President*.

Merriman had just passed Brockle and the helmsman when the guns flashed.

Before he knew it, he was on the deck, the sound of crashing impacts and splintering wood all around. Someone landed beside him and then *something* landed on them both. Legs and back pinned, Merriman could not get up. All he could do was look towards the bow and see the devastation wrought by several hundred pounds of shot.

A spar and a swathe of canvas landed beside the mast, knocking more men over. One poor soul was staggering around, blood pouring from a stomach wound, mouth frozen open in agony.

'The anchor,' said a voice that Merriman did not instantly recognise. Only when he tried to speak did he realised that the weight on top of him was crushing his chest.

'Yes. The anchor. Now!'

No one heard him but – thankfully – the order was given.

'Anchor away!'

'Away, aye!'

Despite the noise, Merriman heard the impacts of axes releasing the lashings and then the throbbing against the timbers beneath him as the anchor fell into the water and dragged its cable with it. He just hoped that no part of that equipment had been damaged.

He was just able to turn his head to the right and he saw that it was Lieutenant Hobbs lying next to him. Hobbs had a nasty gash in the side of his neck that was leaking blood at an alarming rate. His eyes were closed.

'Hobbs! Hobbs, can you hear me!'

Merriman knew the second volley would be coming. All around him were the horribly familiar chorus of shouts and groans and screams. At least twenty guns had opened up from short range. By the sounds of it, the masts were intact but the Americans might easily finish them off. Tides or no tides, they could return later and complete the job. Merriman fought off the terrible thought of losing another ship.

Hearing a grunt of effort, he felt the weight lift off him. Turning, he saw Van der Baan with a great piece of wood in his hands. Puffing hard, the Dutchman managed to turn and drop the heavy chunk of timber.

'Captain?'

'I'm all right. See to Hobbs.'

Merriman was struggling for breath. He was greatly relieved to see an apparently unhurt Tom Henderson getting to his feet only yards away.

'Tom, where's the *President*?'

A sudden lurch of the ship caused the sailing master to stumble. The anchor cable groaned. Two other men nearby fell to the deck atop a pile of canvas. Others slid past. A yard came flying downward but was thankfully caught by the nets, narrowly missing Henderson and the helmsman, who staggered back to the wheel.

'Tom?'

Henderson stood up, one hand on the yard that had almost taken his head off.

'*President*'s spinning, sir. Must be the shoal. Tide's hauling her away. Can't bring her guns to bear. I think our anchor's dug in. Let me…yes…anchor's holding for now, captain.'

Thank God for the shoal and the anchor.

Merriman turned on to his side, realised his breathing was a little easier now.

Thank God.

*

The captain had not heard the name Philip Askew since the former surgeon's mate had come aboard in Plymouth. Now the lives of three men were in the hands of a man with no formal training whatsoever. One of those men was Lieutenant Hobbs, whose blood still stained the deck where Merriman had lain trapped beside him. Hobbs and two others were now down below in the medical bay.

Five others had perished and their bodies remained on deck, covered by spare canvas. Merriman was only yards from them and he could not forget the sight of poor O'Shaughnessy, the topman falsely accused by Brook. The heavy shot from the *President* had gone straight through the sailor's chest. Merriman told himself that it would at least have been quick.

There were a number of other injuries, including to Mr. Milton and to Midshipman Adkins, who had a metal bolt lodged in his thigh. Bosun Brockle was certain that he had broken his arm but was still doling out orders, gingerly holding the arm as he moved around.

As for the captain, he suspected he had broken a rib or two but the only visible damage was some bruising.

He stood now, leaning against the larboard rail, where he had stationed himself to keep an eye on the *President*, which was now at least a mile away. It seemed the American captain realised he was back in deep water and that trying to set his anchor would be futile.

'I know, captain. I know.'

This from Van der Baan, who – along with two dozen sailors – was desperately trying to clear wreckage that had fallen from the mizzen mast.

'We must get under way,' added the Dutchman.

'We have a little time now,' said Merriman, wincing every time he spoke. 'I must thank you for lifting that timber off myself and Hobbs. Astonishing you did it alone.'

'Once we're under way, I shall check on Ernest. Askew will help him. I'm sure of it.'

Merriman was far from sure that Hobbs would survive but said nothing. It had already become evident to him that – despite their innumerable differences – the two lieutenants had a very strong friendship.

'Ah, the man of the hour,' said Merriman when young Eades came back from the bow. 'I hear it was you that ordered the anchor be dropped.'

'Seemed the right thing to do, sir.' Eades now pointed at the colours, which were fluttering. 'Bit of breeze if I'm not mistaken.'

As he spoke, Tom Henderson came up from below, still pulling on a new shirt in place of another blood-stained garment. He had taken charge of moving and covering the dead.

'You're not mistaken,' he said, eyes scanning the sky then the sea. Six, maybe even eight knots and building. A south-westerly and that will do us well enough. Captain, I suggest we get up what we can, then lift our anchor.'

'Agreed, Tom. There's a bit more flood to come and it'll push us towards the *President*. And she still has three good masts.'

Despite the ongoing pain from his ribs, Merriman took personal charge, insisting that Brockle go below and leave him to organise the sailors. Two topmen were injured but the remainder were swiftly up the ratlines, loosing gaskets and making ready to drop the sails. With jibs backing, the head of the ship tried to fall away from the wind.

Eades had kept an eye on *President* and noted that she was now heading south-east to clear the shoals, sails full once more. Merriman was prepared to sacrifice the anchor in order to get away promptly. He had to keep his wounded vessel out of the *President*'s reach until nightfall, which gave him around four hours.

Two sailors stood ready at the bow with heavy knives, ready to cut through the cable.

'You are sure, captain?' said Henderson, coming forward with a chart grasped in one hand. 'We will have no spare.'

'What do you think, Tom?'

He glanced momentarily to the north. 'I agree, sir. We have no time.'

At a nod from the captain, the sailors set about their work, chopping through the heavy fibres of the thick cable.

'Topsails and topgallants will be ready as soon as we're off the wind,' said Merriman to Henderson. 'But he'll have two or three knots on us.'

'We can lay south-south-east, sir. Hope to find *London* or *Crocodile*.'

In two minutes, the cable was severed - the final strands parting with a bang - and *Mercury* was away. Within another five, every sail upon the foremast and mainmast had been unfurled. As for the mizzen, frantic repairs were underway.

Merriman was on his way back to the quarterdeck when Brockle came up through the hatch, his arm now bound by a sling. He didn't wish to ask about the sick bay but the bosun told him anyway.

'Another's passed away, sir. Askew seems to have stopped the bleeding with Mr. Hobbs but he can't get all the wood out.'

'Is he conscious?'

'He is. Asked for strong drink and Askew has allowed it. Adkins is bearing his wound well.'

Merriman looked to his left, at the high, rocky coast of Grand Manan Island. He did not much like the thought of seeking refuge close to those rocks in the darkness but it might be a risk they'd have to take. Watching as Tom Henderson studied his chart, he then saw Peters, Ned Lownes and a couple of others come up to start scrubbing the blood out of the deck.

Merriman did not regret attacking the *President*. He had followed direct orders and they had at least deterred the attack on the merchantmen. But his ship but suffered considerable human and material cost while inflicting virtually no damage on their enemy. It had not been a successful day.

And yet, two hours later, *Mercury*'s prospects began to improve. With both warships now in the grip of the ebb, *President* was gaining enough to have Merriman consider moving the chase guns to the stern. Just as he discussed this with Henderson, one of the topmen spotted sails to the south. Rather shamefully, the officers and crew had been too preoccupied to notice a vessel no more than three miles from their position. Eades soon established that it was the *Crocodile*, running in on a direct course for the American frigate.

Twenty minutes later came another sighting that brought even more cheer to the men of the *Mercury*: HMS *London*. This caused Merriman to hurry forward and join Eades at the bow.

'And another ship to the north-west, sir,' said the midshipman. 'Not much sail up.'

'One of our friends from earlier? No, they'll be well into the bay by now.'

Merriman hurried back to the quarterdeck. 'Tom, I'd like to have a word with Captain Perry.'

'Sir.' Henderson was instantly back at his chart and soon had a new course for the helmsman.

Merriman thanked Peters for leading the cleaning efforts as the attendant led his little crew below, the deck now largely clean of blood.

In no time at all, *Mercury* had shifted course again, in order to pass close to *London*. As the two naval vessels neared each other, Brockle ordered that the sails be loosened and *London* did the same.

'We mustn't get too close,' said Merriman. 'Not that with that bloody current.'

Evidently untarnished by battle, the fully-crewed *London* looked in fine fettle. At a distance of around a hundred feet, Merriman bellowed to Captain Perry, who was also at the rail.

'Good afternoon, Captain Perry!'

'You seem to have led the Yankees straight to us, Captain Merriman!' answered the energetic Perry. 'Might I suggest a bargain?'

'Please do.'

'That ship to the north is American. Fully laden and rolling like a barrel. Dreadful seamanship. Greedy captain. Take her in and we share the prize?'

'Happily. And the frigate?'

'*Crocodile* has the weather and you have no mizzen. Leave him to us – I'm inclined to catch him in a pincer. What do you know of him?'

'*The President*. We had a narrow escape.'

Perry then said something that no one aboard *Mercury* heard but the captain gave a cheery wave then returned to his watching officers and trained his telescope on the American warship.

Merriman turned to find that Van der Baan had returned to the quarterdeck.

'You heard that?'

'I did, sir. Perhaps we should be grateful. Without the mizzen, we'll likely do more harm than good.'

'Agreed thought it still doesn't seem quite right. How's Hobbs?'

'Passed out again. An awful wound. He lost a lot of blood before Askew stitched him up and it's still leaking. He needs a proper surgeon.'

'Then we must make all haste. The wind's still light – we can start repairs while underway. Brockle, keep at it with the mizzen.'

'Aye, captain.'

'I shall go and see Hobbs and the others. Let us repay our allies by at least seizing this merchantman. Assuming we can catch them, that is.'

Chapter Nineteen

The Prize

That question remained unresolved until dusk. In a scene reminiscent of the initial clash with *President*, *Mercury* employed her bow-chasers, with no less than twelve cannonballs falling short until one finally cracked into the stern.

The merchantman was not large – no more than seventy feet – but she had a full complement of sail and crew. She was named *Blessings of the Bay* and her captain obstinately refused to give in until Merriman had the gun ports opened and prepared a broadside. He felt an immense sense of relief when he saw the Stars and Stripes lowered. Ordered to drop her courses, *Blessings of the Bay* was soon falling back towards *Mercury*.

During this lengthy pursuit, Midshipman Eades had followed the engagement to the south. After an exchange with first *London* and then *Crocodile*, *President* had turned westward and they had lost sight of all three ships south of Grand Manan.

With an already minimal crew denuded by injuries and sailors still working on the mizzen mast, Merriman had Van der Baan chose his prize-crew carefully. The imposing Dutchman was the obvious choice to lead it but he had only a dozen men (and almost every musket).

With the ships drifting along together, the second lieutenant took the boat across, three sailors aiming the remaining muskets at the Americans until the prize crew was safely aboard. Merriman could see the hateful expressions of the Yankees and was not surprised when one launched a tirade of insults at Van der Baan. Though the ship's master bawled at the sailor, the Dutchman took charge, reversing his musket and jabbing the miscreant in the head. This seemed to be sufficient to calm the rest and he was soon seen shaking hands with the captain. Shortly afterward the boat was sent back.

Soon, the sails of both vessels were full again as they ran north, pushed along once more by the flood. As night fell, Merriman left Henderson in charge, asking him to keep *Mercury* close to their prize. Lights were placed at the bow and stern of both vessels. No others could be seen.

Once below, Merriman's first stop was the medical bay. He first encountered Adkins, who was helping Mr. Milton put on a new shirt. The young midshipman had a bloody bandage around his thigh and was dripping with sweat. Though the darkness had brought a chill on deck, below the June heat seemed to remain, along with the usual noxious odours. It was a mark of how preoccupied Philip Askew was that he did not look up at Merriman's arrival. Askew was stitching up a wound on the shoulder of a sailor who was biting down on his scarf to avoid crying out.

'How are we faring, gentlemen?

'Not too bad, sir,' said Milton, who had been struck with splinters on the front of both legs. He was wearing only his underwear, his skin from the knees downward covered with trails of dried blood.

'Got most of them out?'

'The big ones, sir, yes. Mr. Adkins here has been a great help.'

'A fine young officer,' said Merriman, placing a hand on the young man's shoulder. 'And you, Clarence?'

'Well, I'll be hopping for a while, sir. Mr. Askew got the bolt out but there's quite a hole there. I will have to careful to keep it dry and clean.'

'Quite so. I believe we will have you both to Saint John in daylight tomorrow.'

'And we have a prize, sir?' said Milton.

Merriman was not surprised that the man who'd volunteered for this hazardous patrolling mission was keen to know more.

'Half of one, at least. We don't know what she's carrying but looks well-laden. You two hungry? Thirsty?'

'Both, sir,' said Adkins. 'We've not had a thing.'

'What 's that bloody cook playing at? I'll give him a kick up the backside.'

Merriman then moved on to Askew and his patient. The amateur physician couldn't have been more than thirty but appeared to have visibly aged since the captain had last seen him.

'A fine effort, Askew. My thanks.'

'Too much guesswork, I'm afraid captain, and my texts don't cover half of it.'

'The men are grateful, I'm sure.'

'I am, captain,' said the sailor with the shoulder wound, his eyes glazed. ''Specially for the rum.'

'Always helps,' said Merriman.

The two beds in the bay were occupied by an unconscious man with bandages around his entire middle. Beside him was Ernest Hobbs, lying completely still, propped up on several pillows. His neck was also bandaged but the cotton was soaked through. Hobbs was an awful colour; almost pale green, his pupils dark and small.

'Do you have some fresh bandages, Askew?'

'I know they're sodden, captain. He's next on my list. Mr. Hobbs can't speak. I couldn't get it all out.'

Merriman knelt by the bed, embarrassed at the grimace caused by his aching ribs.

'Ernest, I can see you're in great pain. We're heading straight for Saint John on the flood. Even when the tide turns, we have a south-westerly to help us. We'll be there quickly, I promise. Remember Mr. Humbert? I'm sure he'll know an excellent surgeon.'

The first lieutenant could do no more than nod, his teeth scraping as he fought the pain.

Merriman gripped Hobbs' arm. 'Just hold on. I'll be along to see you again soon.'

Cloaked by darkness and now fighting the Bay of Fundy's ebb-tide, the warship and the merchantman reached northward. Merriman did not unleash a full broadside on the cook because the man had been earlier preoccupied in his second role as member of a gun-crew. The captain did, however, ensure that every man received some hot food and a double allocation of rum. He was pleased to see that, despite their losses, morale was fair, due doubtless to their recent good fortune.

Leaving Henderson in charge on deck, Merriman summoned Eades to his cabin to assist with a reorganisation of the watches. The loss of the dead and injured combined with the prize-crew meant quite a bit of work but the list was soon complete, ready for implementation the following day. Merriman got a few hours' sleep before replacing Henderson with the morning watch at four o'clock.

Mercury now had all available sail up in order to reach Saint John as quickly as possible. Philip Askew was gravely concerned about Ernest Hobbs and two other men needed urgent treatment. Bosun Brockle stated that he could have the mizzen repairs completed by midday but, even without them, the frigate was soon overtaking the *Blessings of the Bay*. The captain made Lieutenant Van der Baan aware of his intentions and was in turn reassured that there had been no further incidents aboard the seized ship.

At dawn, Merriman was assured to see no trace of enemy vessels and he toured the deck, imploring the men to do their best for Mr. Hobbs. This indeed spurred them on for, in his way, the quiet officer was as popular as the avuncular Van der Baan.

Brockle was true to his word and, with all but her mizzen royal and mizzen topgallant flying, *Mercury* made the most of the flood. With no other vessels visible, she sped towards Saint John at ten knots over the ground, Henderson again proving his inestimable worth even without the assistance of Lieutenant Hobbs. Merriman fulfilled his promise of calling in on the ailing officer and was dismayed to find him unconscious, with Askew agonising over whether to operate on his throat again. Merriman dared not offer any advice but, when told that they would reach Saint John just after dusk, Askew elected to leave the officer be.

In the event, with lights at stern and bow, *Mercury* returned to Saint John at eight in the evening. Met by the harbour-master's boat, Merriman explained the loss of the anchor and was told there were no more places in the harbour for such a large ship. When pressed, the local man said that the last place had been taken by a newly-arrived frigate: HMS *Romulus*.

'Shrigley!' exclaimed Eades, who was with Merriman and Henderson at the taffrail.

Merriman was also excited to hear this news but there was a more pressing concern. 'He has a physician named Webster with him?'

'He does. Mr. Webster came ashore today to organise the care of the infected men.'

'Infected with what?'

'Smallpox. The *Romulus*'s boat took them to Partridge Island this afternoon where they're to be quarantined.'

'And he's on *Romulus* now?'

'I should think so, captain. I gather they've had a rough time of it.'

'Is Shrigley well?' asked young Eades.

'The captain? Yes, I met him today. The surgeon had the ill fellows isolated and stopped the spread.'

'I have an urgent request,' said Merriman. 'The weather is fair so we can tie up at your careening wharf for now. I would ask you to proceed directly to the *Romulus* and inform Dr. Webster that Captain Merriman requests his urgent assistance aboard this vessel. Perhaps you would convey him back here?'

The harbour-master's boat was manned by four sturdy oarsmen and Merriman had previously seen it speeding around the harbour. It was without doubt the swiftest method of getting the physician to Mr. Hobbs.

One of the oarsmen was currently holding a lantern that illuminated the harbour-master's frown. 'I will direct you and pass on the message but that is all. I do have other business, captain.'

Both hands on the rail, Merriman fixed his gaze on the man in the bobbing boat below.

'Sir, one of my lieutenants is near death. I must tell you that if you refuse my request, you will make an enemy of me.'

Merriman did not much like throwing his weight around but – as he'd observed over the years – there were few men prepared to refuse a captain of the Royal Navy.

'Very well, captain. He shall be with you presently.'

Less than an hour later, with *Mercury* tied with long springs to the wharf, the harbour-master's boat reappeared. Bosun Brockle, Midshipman Eades and Master Henderson all joined the captain at the nets to greet their former compatriot. Dr. John Webster came up first, followed by another familiar face.

'I do hope you don't mind, captain,' said Alfred Shrigley, as he stepped onto the deck. 'I thought I might come along and bid you all good evening.'

Merriman had rarely felt such emotion at the sight of someone outside his immediate family. He darted forward, shook Shrigley's hand and squeezed his shoulder. 'And I'm bloody well glad you did, captain.'

The pair stood there for a moment, regarding each other, and Merriman found he didn't know what more to say. As Henderson and the others crowded around, he moved on to John Webster and shook his hand also. Two sailors from the *Romulus* had come up behind him, each holding one side of the physician's medical chest.

'John, I'm very relieved to see you. My first lieutenant, Mr. Hobbs, is in great need of your skills.'

'So I hear, captain. Please show me the way.'

Merriman turned to the others. 'Tom, please take Alfred down to the great cabin and I'll join you there.'

If the captain was relieved to have John Webster aboard, Philip Askew must have experienced the same feeling tenfold. He greeted the surgeon with great enthusiasm and took him straight to Ernest Hobbs, who had already been laid out flat on a table, with four lanterns placed on the ceiling. Merriman felt close to vomiting when Askew removed the bandage to reveal the gory, swollen wound on the left side of Hobb's neck.

'Two or three large splinters,' explained Askew as Webster peered closely at the wound. 'I took out some but I dare not go any deeper for fear of damaging his throat.'

'I *must* operate,' said Webster. 'The wound is leaking with every breath. I doubt there's any way to avoid the trachea but we must take out whatever we can or he won't last much longer.' The surgeon moved swiftly to his already open chest and selected a probe and a scoop. We have plenty of light, at least. Mr. Askew, will you assist?'

'Gladly, doctor.'

With that, Merriman withdrew. On his way to the great cabin, he passed three crewmen who asked how Hobbs was faring. While he told them that Mr. Webster was operating, he listened to other discussions going on: all related to *Blessings of the Bay* and when their prize might reach Saint John.

Back in the cabin, Peters was pouring each of the four compatriots a measure of Van der Baan's gin. Merriman took one himself and told Peters to do so too: the servant's efforts in cleaning up the deck had been noted and appreciated. Peters was also evidently happy to see Shrigley and he hurried away to cook up the roast pork he had earlier promised the captain. A few moments were then occupied by an inspection of Shrigley's head wound. The stitches were out and it seemed to be healing well. As for his own injury, Merriman had long since concluded that his ribs were only bruised, not broken.

'Rather spartan in here, isn't it, Alfred?'

Merriman sat on the lockers to the rear with Shrigley and Henderson. Eades and Brockle were on stools. The captain looked over his protégé; it truly filled him with pride to see Shrigley in captain's dress.

'Mine isn't very different, sir. I've yet to acquire much furniture. Is Mr. Webster at work?'

'He is. I fear for Hobbs but he could not be in better hands.'

Henderson raised his glass. 'To Mr. Hobbs. A fine officer and a fine man. I pray he pulls through.'

The others raised their glasses. Shrigley asked about Brockle's arm. The bosun claimed it was a minor break but was told by all that he must have Dr. Webster examine it.

Shrigley turned to Merriman. 'Captain, when I departed, I still did not know the result of the court martial. It was such a thrill to hear that you were here and with a new command.'

'Fortunately, the board saw sense,' said Merriman before gesturing towards the others. 'And I did have some welcome support from these fine fellows.'

Shrigley seemed mildly confused by this.

'Long story,' said Merriman. 'For later, perhaps.'

Shrigley continued: 'And I must congratulate you on your trip across. Twenty-three days. Despite all that's going on here, it is still much-discussed around the harbour. What a remarkable time.'

'We were very lucky. I gather you were not?'

'It certainly was not without incident. A clash with the French south of Ireland but this damned outbreak was just as difficult, if not worse. I thank the Lord for the presence of Mr. Webster.'

'How many men are on Partridge Island?'

'Just four. Two more died in the last few days of the trip but Webster thinks those four have a fair chance. The island has been used for quarantine before. They have food and water and John will return to check them if he's able.'

'This battle with the French? Many losses?'

'Six dead. We also offloaded some wounded upon arrival. The engagement was all over very quickly.'

'And the rest of the convoy?'

'Some are here, sir. Some went into Halifax along with our lead ship – the *Zeus*.'

'Halliwell?'

'That's right. As far as we know, he's still there.'

'You didn't stop?'

'Given our situation, I didn't dare enter the harbour but Halliwell's officers passed on a message. Admiral Sawyer's staff suggested we proceed here and make use of Partridge Island.'

'Very wise. If our encounter with the *President* is anything to go by, we are in for quite a fight.'

'Tom was telling me about your cargo, sir,' said Shrigley. 'Is there any news?'

'Nothing yet. Indeed, there may not be for some time. Hopefully Brook and Hokoloesqua have made good progress.'

'Hoko…?'

This drew a snigger from Eades, who partly recovered his situation by explaining fully to Shrigley. Merriman lightly admonished him and told him to go and fetch Adkins. The injured midshipman was sleeping but Merriman reckoned this meeting might improve his spirits As he took up the gin and refilled the glasses, the smell of roasting pork drifted into the great cabin.

Tom Henderson drank half his gin, made a noise of approval, then turned to Shrigley. 'Alfred, might we have some detail on your first engagement?'

'Of course. And then you must tell me more about this *President*.'

Ten minutes later, Eades returned with the limping Adkins, who seemed greatly cheered at seeing his former cabin-mate. As Shrigley continued his description of the clash with *Charmante* and *Gailliard*, Peters brought in some plates, each laden with cuts of pork, gravy and potatoes.

'Just the ticket, Peters,' said Merriman. By the time the attendant brought in the cutlery, he had some news from the deck.

'Prize-ship's in, sir,' said Peters. 'Hope she yields us a fortune.'

'Half a fortune at best,' countered the captain.

'Better than none,' muttered the servant.

'A toast then,' said Merriman, now on his third glass of gin.

'Ruination to the French *and* the Yankees?' suggested Bosun Brockle.

'Very apt,' said Merriman, 'but I've one better.' He raised his glass. 'To old friends and comrades. And to *Captain Shrigley*.'

Chapter Twenty

Ill Tidings

Nursing a moderately bad headache, Merriman was halfway through another breakfast of bacon when more news of the prize reached him courtesy of Midshipman Eades. Apparently, the overloaded ship was replete with sugar, coffee, hams and cotton; the crew were abuzz with more prize-talk.

Merriman told Eades to remind anyone he spoke to that the assessment and distribution of prizes was seldom quick, especially in time of war. As a general rule, once the value of a captured ship and its contents had been established, that sum was divided into eighths. The local commander (Admiral Sawyer in this instance) would receive one eighth, the captain would receive two-eighths, the officers would share another eighth, while the rest was divided between petty officers and crew. In this case, of course, they were also sharing everything with HMS *London*.

Eades also disclosed that Captain Perry's ship and the *Crocodile* had not been seen heading north; it was assumed that they would continue their patrolling duties.

With breakfast complete, Merriman hurried along to the officers' cabin, where he expected to find Mr. Webster, aware that he'd not returned to *Romulus* with Shrigley the previous night. There he found only Adkins, who struggled to get up before the captain told him to lay back and continue his recovery.

Merriman found Mr. Webster in the medical bay. He already felt somewhat guilty regarding the dinner and felt doubly so when he saw Mr. Askew and another hand standing solemnly beside the crewman who had been bandaged around the stomach. James Cripp was a member of the afterguard and had perished only an hour earlier.

Merriman stood with Webster while Cripp's messmates came to collect his body. It had already been agreed that the dead sailors would be buried on land and now another would join them. Merriman made a note to contact the helpful Stephen Humbert about the arrangements. When the sailors left with their fallen compatriot, the captain and the surgeon turned their attention to Ernest Hobbs.

'I'm no expert in such things,' said Merriman as they sat on two stools beside the lieutenant. 'But I do believe his colour is a little better.'

'A little, perhaps,' said Webster. 'The external bleeding is staunched and I was able to stay clear of the trachea but it's impossible to know fully what damage was done. Three hours ago, he awoke and croaked something inaudible. I told him to remain quiet: he will have to do so for many days.'

Merriman clapped a hand on Webster's shoulder. 'My sincere thanks, John. Are you happy to leave him in Mr. Askew's care for a few hours?'

'I am.'

'Then I insist that you eat a breakfast in the great cabin and take some rest there.'

Webster seemed to think about resisting but relented. 'That does sound appealing, captain, thank you. And then I must ask Captain Shrigley to convey me to Partridge Island – check on the infected crewmen.'

'I do hope you have some time for yourself before too long. I owe you a dinner or two.'

Webster checked Hobbs' pulse and then departed. Merriman remained behind and offered more praise and encouragement to Philip Askew, promising him a double share of their prize as he had acted as both sailor and physician with some skill. Though evidently exhausted, Askew proudly told the captain that Dr. Webster believed he had the "raw materials" for a medical career.

Later, with the doctor ensconced in the great cabin, Merriman made his way on deck to find the harbour-master's boat approaching once more. A new man was sitting between the oarsmen and he informed Merriman that there was now space for *Mercury* in the harbour.

'No idea what we're going to do with *her*,' added the man, pointing to *Blessings of the Bay*, which had just dropped anchor.

'I shall make the preparations,' said Merriman. 'Can you have us towed in?'

'As long as the wind stays low like this, sir, yes. I was also asked to pass on a message for you. From Mr. Humbert. He requests that you meet him at Fort Howe at your earliest convenience. His wife came to the office to inform us and was most insistent. Is there a reply, captain?'

'I shall come into the harbour with you myself.'

Lacking much choice in terms of a companion, Merriman asked Eades to accompany him. He also brought Tom Henderson along, who armed himself with a pistol. According to the locals, there was talk of spies abroad in Saint John and even sallies from American forces; few folk were leaving their houses without arms. Bosun Brockle was placed in command until the return of Van der Baan and charged with moving the *Mercury* into the harbour. Brockle greeted this news with enthusiasm: the repairs to the mizzen had been only temporary and access to a shipyard would be most helpful.

Fort Howe was protected by an impressive wooden palisade. Within the walls were two blockhouses and a large barracks. The blockhouses were at least thirty feet tall and featured windows on all sides to give a complete range of fire. Between the structures, two companies of infantry were being put through manoeuvres by a voluble officer.

Even before he'd reached the fourth building, where a Union Flag flew, Merriman was met by Stephen Humbert. The influential local greeted him warmly but his expression was grave. The reason for this became evident when Merriman, Eades and Henderson entered the office. Here, two clerks were working busily at desks. They stood to acknowledge the captain but he barely them noticed due to the identity of the remaining man.

Hokolesqua looked quite different from when they'd last seen him. There was dried blood on his hands, his clothes were filthy, his long hair unkempt. His exhaustion was evident as he got slowly to his feet.

'Captain.'

'What in God's name happened?'

'We were ambushed two days ago, close to the ruins of Fort Boishebert. I know not which tribe for it all happened so quickly. Mr. Brook thought we might pick up some time by taking a boat to Fredericton. I did try to tell him that we were being stalked. I…they must have seen the box.'

'Where is Brook?' asked Merriman, though the answer seemed obvious.

'Lost,' said Hokolesqua.

'By God. And they took the box, I suppose?'

'They did,' answered the tribesman. 'Mr. Brook had been hit by two arrows. He said that he would keep the strongbox so that they would go after him. I escaped. With this.'

Hokolesqua reached into his tunic and retrieved a leather pouch. 'The treaty is safe.'

Shaking his head in disbelief, Merriman turned away.

'That is something, captain,' offered Henderson.

'Mr. Brook was very brave,' added Hokolesqua. 'He fought long enough so that I could get away. They would have made him suffer for it.'

'Brave perhaps,' said Merriman, 'but not wise enough to heed you.'

'It was over the moment our path crossed theirs. We were unfortunate but the fault is mine.'

'How far did you get?' asked Eades.

'Thirty miles or so. We were actually making good time.'

'Ah,' said Mr. Humbert, turning towards the door.

In marched a broad, barrel-chested major, his crimson jacket in fine order, as was every other part of his uniform, including the tall, cylindrical black shako. This he removed upon entering the office. Ignoring the saluting clerks, he shook hands with Humbert then offered his gloved hand to Merriman.

'Major Rory Campbell, 104th Regiment of Foot,' announced Humbert.

Merriman swiftly introduced Henderson and Eades. He noted Campbell's derisive glance at Hokolesqua before the major questioned Mr. Humbert.

'Your note mentioned a matter of the utmost importance, Stephen,' said Campbell, his accent that of a distinguished Scotsman. 'I do hope I am not to be disappointed.'

'I think not, Rory.' Humbert gestured to Merriman.

'Major, it is perhaps easier if I show you.' Taking the treaty from Hokolesqua, Merriman passed it to Campbell. The major moved to better light by a window and – after only a few seconds – dismissed the clerks, who rapidly left.

'Trustworthy, I'm sure,' said Campbell, 'but we cannot be too careful with information such as this.'

He read the treaty again and examined the signatures. Holding the paper carefully in one hand, he pointed the other at Hokolesqua. 'I know your face but not your name. Some ally of Tecumseh, I suppose?'

'His cousin. Hokolesqua.'

Humbert then described Brook's failed attempt to reach Quebec. Major Campbell regarded Hokolesqua once more. 'The Treasury man dead. And yet you survived? Sure these tribesmen weren't fellow Shawnee?'

Hokolesqua clenched a fist but said nothing.

'With what end in mind?' countered Merriman. 'Why would he return here? To us?'

Campbell turned to him. His chin was striped by a horizontal scar.

'You've been in Upper Canada how long, captain?'

'A matter of days.'

'For me, it's the matter of *twelve* years. Believe me, there is no creature on two legs more venal, vicious and conniving than the Indian. They would love to scalp every last one of we Britons but they need our powder and guns to keep the Yankees at bay.'

Stephen Humbert stepped in. 'Rory, have we not discussed on many occasions the fact that we too depend on our native allies? Speaking plainly, without them, there would be no Upper Canada.'

Campbell took this with a raised eyebrow and perused the treaty once more. 'Governor-General Prevost must have this document. I have marched from here to Quebec on several occasions. Slow going but on horseback we might do it in two weeks. There is talk of Hull moving but I would guess I could be back before any major clashes take place.'

'Hull?' asked Merriman.

'William Hull. Governor of the Michigan Territory and a capable general. Old enough to have fought in the American rebellion thirty years ago.'

Campbell was still holding the treaty.

Merriman thought it best to intervene before Hokolesqua did.

'Major, I conducted Mr. Brook and the treaty here from Plymouth and I received my orders from Vice-Admiral Pertwee, who organised this operation in conjunction with the Treasury. I have no doubt that Governor Prevost will be glad to see it but the document is intended for Tecumseh: to guarantee the treaty in the name of His Majesty. And Hokolesqua here is to deliver it.'

Campbell passed the treaty back to him. 'Well, captain, if you feel you don't need my assistance, you are welcome to try again with your red friend here.'

'We *do* need your assistance, major. Very much so. But I'm afraid we cannot let the treaty out of our sight.'

Merriman handed the document to Hokolesqua.

Stephen Humbert stepped forward. 'Rory, if the governor was not incapacitated, he would ask for your cooperation in this.'

Merriman spoke up again: 'The Admiralty and the Treasury would also be most grateful, major. To be frank, given your experience of these lands and the route to Quebec, I do not see that anyone else is in a position to assist us as you can.'

Campbell seemed to appreciate the compliments.

Humbert once again showed himself to be a most adroit politician: 'I can imagine quite a scene, Rory. You and your soldiers conveying Captain Merriman and the treaty to the governor's residence in Quebec. He too will be most grateful, I'm sure of it.'

Campbell eyed Humbert for a moment before his face broke into a humourless smile. 'Have I not always said that you a very persuasive fellow? Flattery will get you nowhere but it seems to me that it is my duty to assist. I have only one condition.'

'Go on,' said Merriman.

'The decisions made between here and Quebec are mine and mine only. The Indian is not to address me at all.'

'As if to make the point, Campbell looked only at Merriman.

'We...will trust in your expertise,' said Merriman, feeling he had little choice. His relief at recruiting Campbell was tempered by the realisation that he was somehow now part of this expedition himself. The headache that had faded through the morning had now returned with added strength.

Campbell placed a hand on his sword-hilt. 'We shall depart from here at dawn. We have no spare horses so you'll have to find your own. Provisions too. Good day, captain. Good day, Stephen.'

Once the major had gone, Humbert forced a smile. 'We at least have the desired outcome. Well done, captain: you sensed the major's appreciation of the complimentary.'

As the clerks had returned to the office, Humbert lowered his voice. 'I should perhaps explain. His was not a purchased commission. He has worked his way up the ranks and understands the value of a prestigious assignment.'

'If he has achieved such progress, can I at least assume that he is a capable soldier?'

'I am no expert in military matters but he is well respected by all, even our native allies.'

Hokolesqua nodded. 'That is true.'

Merriman turned to the tribesman. 'Tell me, have you been aboard a naval vessel?'

'No, sir.'

'Well, come with me and Mr. Eades shall give you a tour of HMS *Mercury*. We can also offer you some hot water and a hot meal.'

While Hokolesqua was eating that meal, Merriman met with Van der Baan and Tom Henderson in the great cabin.

'Captain, I really must urge you to reconsider,' said the second lieutenant. 'Brook is dead. These are clearly very dangerous lands and in increasingly dangerous times.'

'There's no denying that, lieutenant, but I can hardly leave Hokolesqua to attempt it alone, nor am I overly keen on leaving him in the hands of the Major Campbell. I've already told you of his attitude.'

Merriman tugged at his ear and paced across the cabin. 'It's more than that. Admiral Pertwee charged me personally with this task.'

'But surely you discharged your responsibility by getting Brook to land, sir?'

'Our responsibility – our *duty* – is to defend Britain and her empire. It hardly matters if that is achieved on sea *or* on land. The bald facts of it are that this treaty must be conveyed to Quebec. Every hour might be crucial. All the time we saved coming across has been wasted.'

Tom Henderson was by nature a reserved fellow but he now weighed in: 'Captain Merriman, I think that Mr. Van der Baan simply fears for you. As do I.'

But Merriman had made up his mind. 'Fair enough, Tom. And it is appreciated. Now, you two are more than capable of guiding *Mercury*.' He shook Van der Baan's hand. 'Mr. Hobbs will not be capable of command for many weeks, if it all. So, until I return, you are captain. If asked to assist the fleet again, please do so.'

'Will you at least grant me one favour, sir?' asked the Dutchman.

'If I can.'

'One of the Irishman, Dwyer, was with the 87th Fusiliers. A fine soldier, by all accounts. If we were to reward him with a double prize-share, he can accompany you.'

'Dwyer? The tall chap?'

Though he hadn't known his name, Merriman had seen him around. Only a few inches shorter than Van der Baan, the Irishman possessed an impressive, pitch-black moustache.

'Knows his weaponry, sir. Could be most useful. Will you let me talk to him?'

'Certainly, I'll be glad to have him along.'

Peters was another one who shared his disapproval with the captain. Merriman ordered him to focus his energies on filling the pack he would take with him. He decided on a single change of clothes and was greatly relieved that he also had some comfortable shoes as well as his best pair. His bicorne hat would remain aboard; his boat-cloak would go with him.

Having concluded the tour of the ship, Midshipman Eades came to the great cabin with Hokolesqua and a request.

'Captain Merriman, I have read a great deal about these lands and the native peoples. Might I accompany you?'

Merriman had half-expected this.

'Eades, this is not some…adventure. It is a crucial mission and likely to be a perilous one.'

'But with Major Campbell, sir? Surely the presence of he and his soldiers reduces the risk?'

'I would hope so.'

Merriman admitted to himself that it would be pleasant to have the company of at least one familiar face.

'And fighting the Yankee ships is hardly without risk, sir' added Eades.

'Agreed. All right, you are now old enough to make your own decisions. I'd be glad to have your company but you must make a note in the logbook that you join me of your own volition.'

'Very well, sir.'

With that, the captain's rather disparate trio of travelling companions was completed. Eades and Hokolesqua were sent ashore to secure horses, thankfully assisted by Stephen Humbert and one of the governor's officials. Van der Baan brought Dwyer to the great cabin already in possession of three muskets and two pistols from the armoury. Merriman didn't like the thought of depriving his crew of armament; he liked the idea of depriving himself even less.

That evening, Merriman was visited by Alfred Shrigley. Weary of the great cabin, the captain suggested that they take a walk along the harbour. Shrigley remarked that Brockle seemed to be making good progress with the mizzen and Merriman confirmed that it was so. Better still, a ship had arrived with some replacement guns sent from Halifax. *Mercury* would soon possess a full complement.

'I've a suspicion Van der Baan will enjoy his time in command,' said Merriman. 'It seems I shall be away for at least five weeks or so.'

Aware of his plans, Shrigley had not yet expressed any opinion on them.

'You need not say anything, Alfred, I can tell your view well enough.'

Shrigley smothered a grin. 'Sir, I've seen you embark on enough shore missions to know that you enjoy it and that you see this as a matter of duty.'

'Both comments are fair.'

'I do, however, have a suggestion.'

'Go on.'

'From what I've heard, risking that trip in the present circumstances is …bold. To risk it twice seems, well…'

'Foolhardy?'

'Captain, though you received specific orders from Admiral Sawyer, I did not. In the absence of orders from any other senior officer, I am entitled to follow my own path. Or orders from a senior officer such as yourself.'

'A rendezvous in Quebec?'

'The weather is set fair for now. You may have to wait a few days for us but I can offer you a considerably safer path home.'

'A most kind offer, Alfred, but it seems rather selfish.'

'Sir, what you are doing is the opposite of that. Please allow me to assist. I am most concerned for you; as is Mr. Webster, as are your officers.'

'Very well then.' Merriman shook his hand. 'How fortunate I am to have you over here with me, Alfred. By the way, you do know that, as a fellow captain, you may now call me by my first name.'

'I don't think I could ever do that, sir. It simply wouldn't be right.'

Chapter Twenty-One

A Crossing By Land

No announcement was made to the crew. Seen off by Van der Baan, Henderson and Brockle, Merriman walked with his companions to a nearby stable. The horses – and a pack pony – were provided by a French-speaking man who seemed rather unhappy about the arrangement until Stephen Humbert arrived to smooth the way. He also accompanied them to Fort Howe and passed on two pieces of bad news. The first was that Governor Smith's condition had worsened. The second was that several sources indicated that American scout parties had crossed the border into Upper Canada.

Major Campbell and his party were ready at the fort gates. The officer now had his crimson sash at his belt and was accompanied by a Sergeant-Major named Fisk. Waiting nearby were a dozen infantrymen, all standing with their horses' reins in one hand, their muskets in the other. Though all wore their redcoats, several were so faded that they almost appeared brown. Their trousers were light blue but again of varying shades and quality. Some of the horses had saddlebags but many held only the familiar black knapsacks topped by a roll of bedding. If their gear was less than perfect, their muskets appeared exceptionally well maintained.

As for Merriman, he intended to keep his sword on him at all times. His pistol was in a case within one of the saddlebags on his mount, a tall grey.

'Good morning, major,' said Merriman. 'I didn't realise there were so many capable riders in our infantry regiments.'

'A few more than average in this part of the world, captain. Good to see you're on time. Who's this fellow?'

'Able seaman Dwyer, once of the 87th Fusiliers.'

'I trust you can ride, Dwyer?'

'Well enough, sir,' said the tall sailor, who had a musket over both shoulders.

'Shall I fetch the tents, major?' asked Sergeant-Major Fisk, another brawny fellow with silver chevrons on his tunic to mark his rank.

'Do so,' said Campbell. 'For your pack mule, captain – accommodation provided by the 104th.'

'Very kind.'

'What an interesting party you travel with, Captain Merriman – a youth, an Irishman and an Indian.'

'Midshipman Eades has served four years upon His Majesty's vessels, major.'

'Well, let us see how he fares on dry land. We shall depart immediately. My intention is to take the back road to Reversing Falls to avoid too much attention. We will cross on the ferry at slack water, and from there follow the river as far as Westfield and then strike north-west.'

'What's our first destination?'

'The town of Woodstock, some hundred and thirty miles away. Five or six days, I should think. From there, we will decide whether to cut across Maine, which will save us several days.'

'Understood.'

They began on foot, walking two abreast along narrow, dusty roads. Encountering only a four-man-patrol of local militia, the column was soon clear of Saint John's houses and passing large fields of corn and smaller patches of blueberries and raspberries. A few farmers were up and working and most shouted greetings and words of support to Major Campbell and his redcoats. Some of those farmers were free black folk, and Sergeant-Major Fisk explained that many had escaped slavery in the south to find freedom on this side of the border.

Major Campbell had two men out front with loaded muskets. Behind them, he strode along with Fisk. Then came the main body of men with their horses (including two spares) and four pack animals. Merriman's small party came next with a single soldier bringing up the rear, again armed with a loaded musket. The captain thought it a bit odd that they'd brought horses only to walk along but he supposed there was some reason for it.

He was alongside Hokolesqua, who had barely said a word all morning. Merriman was curious about the specifics of what had happened to Balthazar Brook but he thought it wise to leave those enquiries to another time.

'I hope your cousin appreciates this effort of yours,' he remarked.

'It is never easy to know his mind,' replied Hokolesqua. 'He always has so many things to think about it.'

'He is clearly very well-respected. How did he reach such a position?'

'He began as a war-chief. He was a good one but there are many war-chiefs, and plenty who wish to be one. I've heard it said that while some look over the next hill, Tecumseh looks over the next mountain.'

'A man of vision then?'

'A man who always wished to travel, gain knowledge of other tribes and of the whites.'

Hearing this term prompted Merriman to consider how the natives might view the "whites" as a single mass, not Frenchmen or Britons or Americans. He supposed that when their ships first arrived on these shores, it must have seemed thus. But now the natives had cause to distinguish – and indeed choose between – the "tribes" that had emanated from Europe.

'Hokolesqua, how is that your English is so good?'

'When I volunteered to work for my uncle, he insisted that I learn. I was taught by a retired English school teacher named Mrs. Basley. She came from Harrogate in Yorkshire.'

'Is that right? She was clearly a fine teacher.'

'She was very hard on me and I hated her as a young man. Now I realise she did me a great service.'

'And what is the issue with this fellow Harrison?' asked Merriman, who'd heard Hokolesqua speak of him to Eades.

'Governor William Henry Harrison!' declared the midshipman from behind them, immediately reddening when he realised his interruption was unnecessary.

Hokolesqua nodded. 'Harrison is the governor of the American state of Indiana. A crafty swine whose sole aim is to expand and promote his territory. He used a strategy that I believe you call "divide and conquer". He would make unfair deals and treaties with older leaders, smaller tribes – trying to take everything piece by piece. Tecumseh and others realised that this meant a slow death for us; that we need to unite if we're to have any chance of preserving our lands. He and Harrison have been enemies for many, many years.'

'I see.'

'The Americans would make us all farmers,' added Hokolesqua bitterly, 'make us like *them*.'

The road continued along the west side of the Saint John River. Now on horseback, they passed many small farms and more people at work in the fields. Some seemed to speak only French but they were friendly enough. Major Campbell deflected any questions about their mission, claiming they were just "on patrol". Due to the heat, Merriman had taken his jacket off and he now elected to keep it hidden, for the presence of a captain of the Royal Navy would surely raise yet more questions.

'No wigwams?' complained Eades as the day wore on and they'd still seen nothing of the natives.

'A hundred years ago you'd have seen them here,' replied Hokoloesqua. 'The Wolastoqiyik people have been here for centuries. There are a few still, but the whites have purchased the prime lands by the river.'

It seemed to Merriman a thorny issue. In general, he thought it a good thing that countries like Britain, France and Portugal had ventured out to the far places of the world and made them their own. He was very interested in native peoples but he thought it inevitable that they be civilised and become part of the modern world. And yet this process invariably involved great suffering and displacement. They did, after all, merely wish to live on their own lands.

'Mr. Eades, I think I can promise you wigwams before the day is out,' said Hokolesqua. 'And, if we are fortunate, the best salmon you have ever tasted.'

He was true to his word. The column made camp just short of Westfield before dusk. An hour previously, they had crested a ridge that offered a view of a small native encampment inland. Hokolesqua was in the middle of explaining to Eades how the structures were made when he was snapped at by Major Campbell, who was insistent that the column stay in formation.

Later that evening, once the small army tents had been put up, Hokolesqua and Eades returned from the river, each holding a salmon at least two feet long. The eyes of the gathered soldiers lit up, for they were about to dine on dried beef and bread. As Hokolesqua swiftly made his own fire and put the fish on wooden spits, Eades explained how the tribesman had spent ten minutes surveying the shore, then swum out and strung a net between two rocks. The salmon had been caught within minutes.

Unsurprisingly, the soldiers put their dried beef aside and welcomed the great hunks of pink flesh offered to them by Hokolesqua. It seemed to Merriman that the man possessed some of the reputed charisma and tact of his cousin, for he surely knew that – for the moment, at least – he and the redcoats depended on each other. Merriman thought the situation also reflected the wider relationship quite neatly.

Major Campbell made no objection to the men eating the salmon but, when it was offered to him, he refused it with a solemn shake of his head.

For four more days, the column continued north. Merriman learned that the short periods of walking were simply to spare the horses, who faced at least two weeks of near-constant work. This work was made harder when they passed beyond roads onto narrow, rutted tracks. Summer showers made the going even worse but they eventually reached the town of Woodstock.

Here they were welcomed, for the settlement had been founded only three decades earlier by men of De Lancey's Brigade, a loyalist provincial unit that had fought during the American rebellion. Many of their descendants remained and were now involved in the logging trade. With their party accommodated in an outhouse by the Saint John, Merriman and the others observed how timber was floated downriver, guided by flat-bottomed boats of a type he had seen used in France.

Major Campbell gained further intelligence regarding the movement of American troops. It seemed that more forays had been made across the border, though only one brief skirmish with redcoats was reported. On the morning of their departure from Woodstock, Campbell informed Merriman that they would probably take the risk of cutting across the north of Maine. He explained that this area of the American state was characterised by high ground and a myriad of waterways. It was sparsely inhabited, reducing the risk of running into enemy forces.

The column spent much of the next day on foot and Merriman was glad to be out of the saddle. His backside and thighs were extremely sore and both Eades and Dwyer complained of the same issue. Hokolesqua disclosed that he'd owned his mount for eight years. He rode with a casual elegance, sometimes with his arms crossed and apparently asleep.

In late afternoon, the column passed a partially built house; a canvas roof covering a log cabin, only three sides of which had been constructed. Two small boys chattering in French came out to greet them. Some of the soldiers had some French and spoke back to them in a friendly way. They were all set to continue when the boys' father appeared, his forearms stained with blood.

In accented but clear English, he explained that he had been slaughtering a pig and was yet to clean up. Informing them that his was the last farm for many miles, he offered them the use of his well and some food.

Major Campbell initially seemed wary but the Frenchman, who was named Allard, expressed his gratitude that the "patrol" was in the area. Only the previous day, he'd spoken to two trappers who claimed that a party of the dreaded Kentuckians had been spotted on the Aroostook River, barely thirty miles to the north-west.

'Honestly, I don't know how they could be sure,' remarked Allard, with a glint in his eye. 'They weren't close enough to see the size of their knives.'

The Frenchman was evidently a good-humoured fellow. Campbell took up his offer and issued a rare thank you when Allard guided the travellers to a fine patch of pasture and announced that they were welcome to stay the night. Though his dwelling was not yet complete, the settler had constructed two small outhouses. His pen of pigs was full, as was his chicken coop; and he also possessed a horse and a mule.

As the weary men lounged in the grass, they were served apples and beer by Allard's wife and daughter. Both were very pretty and Merriman belatedly realised that he was leering at them just like the soldiers. He admonished himself for such behaviour but later conceded to himself that it was only natural. Military men were so often away from the fairer sex that any sight of a pretty face or a well-formed figure was invariably enough to seize the attention.

'Monsieur Allard is a brave man,' said Eades. 'Out here alone with a young family and so much to lose.'

'More like mad, I'd say,' replied Dwyer, who was halfway through an apple. 'And all them Indians round here too.' The Irishman nodded to Hokolesqua. 'Not meaning any offence.'

'Not at all. There are warriors in other tribes who would raid this place, kill the man and take the others for slaves. But not the tribes that dwell here. And not *my* tribe.'

Due to the clear skies above, Major Campbell allowed the men to sleep without their tents. However, if they thought that meant an easy evening, they were mistaken. Before they cooked dinner, he put the redcoats though musket drill. Merriman was pleased to see that the soldiers were highly efficient, perhaps mainly due to the fierce supervision of both Campbell and Sergeant-Major Fisk.

At Dwyer's suggestion, captain and midshipman also did some practice. This involved retrieving a cartridge, biting it open, opening the pan, pouring some of the powder, shutting the pan, pouring the rest of the powder into the barrel, inserting the lead ball and finally inserting the cartridge paper. The Irishmen emitted a long sigh after their first attempt but, by the fifth, they were doing rather better. Merriman was far swifter with his pistol but felt the tuition was worthwhile. Dwyer encouraged him to make use of the bayonet attachment but Merriman declared that he would remain faithful to his dirk and Eades followed suit.

Hokolesqua did not take part in any of this. He sat alone, his jacket close by as usual. None of the men knew about the treaty and the tribesman did not take it from the jacket or ever speak of it. He sat there with a piece of wood, whittling away, while Allard's two boys observed him from the side of the pigsty. By the time the musket drill was over, he had whittled a basic but very clear little wooden duck. He stood and walked towards the children. They squealed at his approach and fled into the house. Aware that the others were watching him, Hokolesqua placed the carving on the top of a fence pole and walked out to the pasture to check on his horse.

Despite his tiredness, Merriman found it difficult to sleep that night. He wondered if it was this glimpse of family life because he found his thoughts dominated by Helen, Robert and Mary-Anne. The locale was very different but that sense of familial togetherness reminded him of idyllic times at Burton Manor. It seemed almost insane that a man should ever wish to leave.

Standing, he walked out of the meadow and stood in the open area between the outhouses, gazing up at the stars. He hadn't been there long when a light appeared within the incomplete cabin and Monsieur Allard stepped outside, a lantern in hand. Seeing the upright figure, he approached.

'Ah, Mister…'

'Merriman.'

'Ah, oui.'

'Sorry if I disturbed you.'

'You didn't, sir. I feel quite safe for once with the soldiers here. You are not a soldier, I think.'

Merriman had purposefully kept in the background to avoid an explanation.

Allard continued: 'Judging by your trousers, I would say you and two of your friends are naval men, is that correct?'

'It is.'

'And you, sir, have the bearing of an officer.'

'Well, I shan't deny it. I am here as a…liaison. For naval operations.'

'I see. I suppose some in our respective countries would consider this an unlikely moment of amity. You have faced my countrymen in combat?'

'I have.' Merriman found himself transported back to the bloody battlefield of the *Hercule*'s deck, recalling how the stubborn Captain Patrice Jourdan had refused to surrender.

'French we may be but we are also Canadians now,' said Allard. 'I would rather that, than be an American – though many see it differently.'

'It is a most complicated situation here.'

'Could we not say that for much of the world? And now Britain at war with America too.'

They heard the distant cry of a wolf. Allard had two dogs but they did not bark, merely grunting and grumbling at the noise.

'Monsieur Allard, you are very courageous – to settle out here with your family.'

'I suppose so. But is there not danger everywhere? I receive letters from home. So many men of my age are dead. My cousin lives in Paris. If La Petit Caporal does not get his way with Poland, he may invade Russia. Many more will die.'

'I think that would be ill-advised,' said Merriman. 'A country so vast.'

'I agree. But it might hasten the end of the war. I would like to see our nations at peace.'

'As would I, Monsieur Allard.'

The column left at dawn and covered another thirty miles that day, camping overnight in the village of Mars Hill, where they were again welcomed by friendly locals. Major Campbell questioned every person they passed and, as nothing more was heard of the Kentuckians, he elected that they would indeed turn west and cut across Maine. A great salient of the state divided New Brunswick, like a promontory surrounded by water. Hokolesqua had passed that way before – as had two of Campbell's men – but the vast expanse of waterways and marshy ground was notoriously difficult to navigate. Asking Merriman to accompany him, he raised this concern with Campbell. To be fair to the major, he did not deny that the trip might be awkward but he felt it essential to save time. Merriman didn't feel qualified to weigh in. He valued Hokolesqua's opinion but Campbell's leadership had served them well to date.

During the following afternoon, the captain was again approached by the tribesman. The column had been travelling due west all day and they were now riding, the mounts stepping across a waterlogged plain. This was not easy going for the horses and the whole place seemed infested with buzzing insects. Just to their north was a line of trees and it was towards this that Hokolesqua nodded when he spoke quietly to Merriman with their mounts side by side.

'Do not look, captain, for you won't see them, but we are being tracked.'

Merriman forced himself not to look. 'By whom?'

'I am not sure. Indians I would think, as they're very good.'

'Friendly? I suppose you don't know unless you see them.'

'They're probably just curious. And only a large band would attempt to take us on. But after what happened…'

'Of course.'

'What do you suggest, captain? I can tell the major but I would not want to provoke a confrontation.'

'Presumably if you approach them alone, there is less chance of conflict?'

'That depends on their intent but…yes.'

'Could you make some excuse, meet them in the trees?'

'I could. Perhaps you would smooth the way with major?'

'Certainly. The truth might be the best policy, in this case, but I suggest you go now, before someone else sees them.'

'I will,' said Hokolesqua, with a grin, 'but, believe me, no one else will see them. Most redcoats could step right over a native and not even know he was there.'

He guided his horse out of the column and set off towards the trees at a trot. Merriman took his grey along the other side of the column. By the time he reached the major, several of the soldiers were watching Hokolesqua make for the trees.

'Could I ask you to stop, major?'

Though he frowned, Campbell gave a signal and the soldiers came to a halt. Sergeant-Major Fisk alerted his superior to the movement behind them.

'What's going on?' demanded the major.

'He believes we're being tracked,' said Merriman. 'Thought it best to establish who we're dealing with.'

'Did he now?' Campbell gave a nod to Fisk, who immediately ordered the men to dismount and arm themselves. Campbell's horse shuffled backwards, prompting him to tug viciously on the reins.

'Then he should have notified *me* immediately. You don't seem to grasp, *captain*, that these red fellows must be kept in their place.'

217

He cast an angry glance towards Hokolesqua, who had just dismounted short of the trees. In seconds, the tribesman had disappeared.

Pulling his flintlock from his belt, Campbell moved clear of the horses and continued to observe. Along with Eades and Dwyer, Merriman dismounted too. Despite the boggy ground, the redcoats loaded and primed their muskets in short order. Merriman grimaced, aware that one trigger-happy fellow could endanger them all.

The sailors and the soldiers stood there for some time, every pair of eyes fixed on the trees, where no figure was visible. The first sign of progress came about ten minutes after Hokolesqua had disappeared: his horse, jerking its head around, clearly sensing its master.

When he did return, he was not alone. Behind him were four men in traditional clothing, bare-chested but with great headdresses of feathers. Hokolesqua raised a hand and called out.

'These are men of the Penobscot tribe. They would like to talk, major. Will you lower your guns?'

'Why do I need to talk to them?'

'I believe they can help us. It won't take long.'

Campbell muttered an oath but gave the order.

Five minutes later, Hokolesqua and the new arrivals stood facing Campbell, Fisk and Merriman. One of the four tribesmen was notably older but they all possessed similarly wiry frames and bore many battle scars. Though their skin was a similar dark hue to Hokolesqua, it seemed to Merriman that their features were more rounded, less angular. They were all armed with knives as well as fearsome wooden clubs that they carried on ropes over their shoulders.

'This is Sabattis,' said Hokolesqua, gesturing to the older man. 'The others are his three sons. He is offering one of them to us as a guide.'

'Why do we need another guide?' demanded Campbell.

'After the heavy rains of spring, the Aroostook has flooded in many places and the waters are high around Portage Lake and Eagle Lake. I asked these men about the westward route and this is what they told me.'

'You've no business telling them anything.'

'Major, it is eighty more miles to Canadian territory. We do not wish to tarry here on American lands, correct?'

At this, Sabattis questioned Hokolesqua – in French.

Fisk smiled at Merriman's confused expression. 'Some of the Indian dialects bear no relation to each other, captain. Another reason why they benefit from being civilised.'

Campbell spoke over the natives. 'You want me to accept help from the Penobscot? They fought with the French until they decided they needed us!'

'That was many years ago, major.'

'And what is to stop him leading us into some godforsaken place, letting us run out of water and food, then coming back with his friends to scalp us?'

Merriman thought it an inopportune moment to mention that Campbell had earlier claimed he didn't need navigational assistance.

'We not criminals. Or fools,' said Sabattis, using English for the first time.

Hokolesqua continued: 'In any case, these men are not aligned to any faction, not even my cousin's confederacy. They simply wish to make a deal.'

'What deal?' asked the exasperated Campbell.

'In return for the guide, he would like some powder.'

'Oh, would he now?'

Campbell spoke to Sabbatis in French, asking if the proposed guide, who seemed to the youngest son, also spoke the language. The young man was not as fluent as his father but – when questioned by the major about certain geographical features – seemed very knowledgeable.

'We not fools!' declared Sabattis once more.

'I heard you the first time!' snapped Campbell.

'They crossed northern Maine only a month ago,' said Hokolesqua. 'Major, I think this is a fair deal for four pounds of gunpowder.'

'Four pounds? Not a chance. Two at the most.'

They eventually settled on three. Sabbatis departed with his two others sons, leaving the young man named Tellus, who was apparently just eighteen.

'Well, sir,' said Eades, 'the older fellow was very determined that he not be considered a fool.'

'And with good reason,' said Hokolesqua.

Surprised that he had heard the comment, Merriman and Eades turned around. The tribesman glanced towards the departing trio before continuing.

'So much of their land has been taken. Most of the Penobscot now live on Indian Island near Old Town. They are ruled over by the government of Maine and the Indian agents. The Americans accuse them of "imbecility". That is how they make the Penobscot wards of court; how they take their lands and their wealth. And this is not the only place it has been done. But Sabbatis is no fool. None of us are.'

Chapter Twenty-Two

The Saint Lawrence

Ten days after she left Saint John, *HMS Romulus* passed between the mainland and the vast island of Anticosti, at last nearing the estuary of the Saint Lawrence, which was fifty miles across at its widest. Mr. Ives inspected Anticosti with his telescope, announcing that the only sign of human activity were two small deforested areas.

Commander Shrigley was more concerned about ships. All those he'd spoken to in New Brunswick seemed to think it unlikely that American naval vessels would be so far north but there were continuing rumours of a French warship lurking near Nova Scotia. Shrigley now had good reason to trust in both his vessel and his crew but *Romulus* was merely a brig-sloop and always vulnerable when alone.

Land had been in sight for the vast majority of their complicated route and he often found himself wondering about Captain Merriman, now journeying across such dangerous territory. Given that Sir James had not only survived the court-martial but made his remarkable crossing, the mission did indeed seem foolhardy. But Shrigley had often seen the captain make very quick, very clear decisions and – more often than not – he'd come out on top.

The first half of the trip had seen them fighting a thirty-knot easterly and some big, angry seas. Though no damage had been sustained, two sailors had been injured, which had at least given Mr. Peebles an opportunity to learn more from Dr. Webster. Conditions had thankfully improved since then, though the wind remained unreliable.

The surgeon was one of two men causing concern. John Webster had not attended any of the officers' dinners and had barely said a word, even to Shrigley. He had seemed in a rather disturbed state of mind on the day of their departure and there seemed to be no improvement since. Unless busy in the medical bay, Webster spent his time reading, invariably in the officers' cabin. Glanville and Ives reported that he didn't seem to be sleeping well and he had visibly lost weight.

Glanville was the other concern. Free of the ailing sailors and with their main mission now behind them, a rather lax attitude seemed to have settled upon the crew. Shrigley had told his two lieutenants to keep an eye on this but it seemed to him that only Ives had taken much action. Glanville had pledged to do so but there had been little tangible evidence. Shrigley wondered if the well-to-do officer had lost patience with being captained by a member of an inferior class.

Though he knew both men should be spoken to, Shrigley found himself putting it off. This was partly because he doubted himself and the decision to make for Quebec. Though glad to help Captain Merriman and be part of his mission, he wondered if this course of action might come back to haunt him, particularly if the early naval engagements went badly for Admiral Sawyer's force. Taking his vessel so far from the area of conflict could be seen as a neglect of his obligations to the war effort. If it came to that, at least he would have the captain on his side.

And when they returned? He would have no choice but to offer *Romulus* to the North Atlantic Station. Who knew how long this conflict would last or; when he might get back to England and see his family?

'You all right, sir?'

With him on the quarterdeck for the afternoon watch was Lieutenant Ives. He was still limping due to the wound he had suffered during the battle off the Irish coast but Mr. Webster seemed sure he was healing well.

'Yes, thank you, Ives.'

'Just that you're a tad quiet today, sir.'

Over time, Ives had revealed himself to be a very solid character. Though often overshadowed by Glanville, he went about his business with a committed attitude and struck a fine balance between keeping his captain informed of major issues while solving minor ones himself.

As Shrigley said nothing more, Ives continued: 'I was listening to Appleton and Rowley earlier today, sir. They were talking about those we left on Partridge Island – wondering who'll still be alive when we return.'

'Mr. Webster did seem quite confident about their condition,' said Shrigley, turning from the rail.

The two officers had retreated to the rear of the quarterdeck while sailors scrubbed away at the deck with their holystones.

'Their future though…,' replied Ives. 'Two of them have wives. Oatley has four children. Would they even recognise the poor fellow?'

'We shall have to assess the situation when we return. Can I ask you something? Just between us.'

Ives removed his hat and wiped his brow. Though there was a strong breeze, it was another warm summer day. Shrigley kept his hat on only for the sake of appearances.

'Lieutenant Glanville. I am sure I detect a change in him. He seems neglectful of his duties. I've also seen him fraternizing with the petty officers rather too much, and sometimes even with the men. It seemed to begin in Saint John.'

Ives chewed the inside of his mouth before speaking. 'It is difficult, sir. I've known Mr. Glanville for many years. I wouldn't wish to betray a confidence. Then again…'

'You needn't torment yourself, Ives. I know full well how important it is to keep relations within the officers' cabin on an even keel.'

'Appreciated, sir.'

'I shall address him directly.'

It seemed that the marine sergeant, Cathcote, shared Shrigley's concerns about the men becoming rather complacent. With the captain's permission, he had his soldiers out on the foredeck, completing musket drills. Due to the rather awkward swell, no weapons were to actually be discharged.

While Shrigley observed this, the lookout reported a small vessel coming their way. It turned out to be a fishing boat manned by half a dozen natives. They seemed to have a smattering of French but spoke mainly in their own tongue, gesticulating west towards the river, leaving the Englishmen utterly confused.

With the afternoon watch nearing its end, Shrigley asked Glanville to come along to his cabin before taking his turn on deck. The lieutenant's appearance also seemed to suggest a distracted state of mind: his breeches were in need of washing and his brass was very dull.

'Please, have a seat.'

'Thank you, sir.'

'It has come to my attention that you seem a little distracted from your work of late. Would you say that's fair?'

Shrigley had spoken to him three times since they left Saint John; twice about lateness, once about poor supervision of the petty officers.

'Ah…er…perhaps a little, sir. I haven't been feeling all that well?'

'I wasn't aware of that. Have you been to see Mr. Webster?'

'No, sir. Headaches – they come and go. Better now. I shall ensure my performance is up to scratch from this point on, sir.' Glanville nodded repeatedly and clapped his hands together but it all seemed a performance. 'New start.'

Shrigley was far from convinced. It was all rather odd.

'If there is something troubling you, I would rather know *now*. I depend on you.'

'And you can, captain. Most assuredly you can.'

Since his night of alcoholic indulgence, Shrigley had resolved not to touch a drop before they reached Quebec. He did, however, offer one to John Webster when the physician joined him for dinner in his cabin. The cook had roasted some duck purchased in Saint John and presented it with a fine, rich sauce.

Webster said little while they ate and refused the offer of a drink.

'John, I must confess I didn't ask you to the cabin purely for friendship's sake, though this matter is related in a way. I shall be frank: I am a little worried about you.'

The Welshman looked up, his delicate face now creased by a frown. 'Not in regard to my work?'

'No, no. In regard to yourself. You have been very quiet. Is something wrong?'

Webster sat back in his chair and flashed a joyless smile at Shrigley.

'It is, Alfred. I wonder if I can continue aboard ship.'

'The seasickness?'

'No, no, barely two days of that this time. Nor was it the smallpox. Such outbreaks are commonly dealt with by physicians.'

Webster gazed at darkness beyond the cabin windows. 'No, with this new conflict, it is the certainty that I will face so many more bodies torn to pieces. And what is it all for? Martial glory? Sometimes nothing more than monetary gain?'

'I understand. I think many of us entertain such thoughts. Even Captain Merriman, perhaps *especially* him because he has seen so many years of it.'

'Fear not, Alfred, I will stay with *Romulus* for the moment. But whether I can stand it for many more months – I am not sure.'

'This is only your second voyage, John. Such ruminations are normal. By the way, we will enter the river proper over the next few days. There should be some very picturesque views. Please do join us on deck when you can.'

'I shall. Thank you.'

A thought struck Shrigley. 'I'm not sure if it will make any difference to you but I know that Captain Merriman found it very difficult to undertake a voyage without a surgeon. He seemed quite envious that we had you here on *Romulus*. Please do always remember what it means to all of us – officers and men – to have a dependable physician out here with us. I hate to think how the last trip would have unfolded without you.'

Another forced smile. 'It is not that I don't take some satisfaction from the successes, Alfred. It is the failures. They do torment me.'

Around one o'clock in the morning, some sense or instinct told Shrigley to go on deck. Though all seemed well, he prowled from stern to bow, sure that something was amiss. And yet all that occurred out of the ordinary was an approach by Mr. Diggs. The bosun stood beside the captain at the bow as the *Romulus* reached north-west into the river, the black water illuminated only by the light of a half-moon. Ives and Haskell were back at the wheel, studying charts and keeping close attention on their location. There was thankfully also sufficient light to make out both banks of the Saint Lawrence.

'Can't sleep, sir?'

'Something like that, Diggs.'

'Captain, there are not many opportunities such as this so I shall keep it quick. If I disclose information to you, will you give me your word not to let anyone know I was the source?'

'I give you my word, Diggs.'

'Very well. To be clear, I'm doing so because I fear this problem will cause many more problems, and for several people. I heard that Mr. Glanville was called to your cabin today and I know that you have questioned his timekeeping. I also happened to overhear a discussion he had with Mr. Ives.'

Shrigley felt rather uncomfortable at this point but it was only Ives who had pledged to keep his counsel, not Diggs.

'You understand that gambling is involved?' added the bosun.

Of all the causes Shrigley had considered, this was not one.

'Go on.'

Diggs cleared his throat and glanced back to check they were alone. The closest sailors were twenty feet away.

'He's always liked the cards but previously kept his games confined to land. In Saint John, he played a couple of rounds with the armourer and some of the lads. From what I can gather, they meet up in the hold when there's no one about.'

'By God.'

'Not a good idea, sir – not for no one. And apparently, the lieutenant is bad at Brag and even worse at Faro. He owes them, sir. All of them. Don't know the exact amount but it's quite a bit.'

'I see. Thank you, Diggs.'

The bosun departed.

Shrigley made his way back towards the quarterdeck. He had just passed the mainmast when one of the lookouts gave a shout from the crosstrees.

'Obstacles in the water! Passing to starboard!'

Diggs and Shrigley were swiftly reunited and joined by Lieutenant Ives, who was already wiping sweat from his brow. Due to the danger of meeting outgoing vessels, *Romulus* was carrying lights at stern and bow. The three men looked down at the water. The lantern at the bow was one of the largest aboard but illuminated only a patch of the surface below. Diggs shuttered it so that they could see more with their eyes.

One minute passed. Two.

Ives hurried back to the mainmast and questioned the lookout, returning shortly afterward.

'He's not sure. Something large. A whale, perhaps.'

Midshipman Haskell came forward with another shuttered lantern. Shrigley went as far forward as he could, using the bowsprit to steady himself. Then he saw it: a dark cylindrical shape, moonlight glinting on the wet surface.

'There!'

'It will hit us!' declared Haskell.

'Not quite, I think,' said Mr. Diggs.

He was proved right as the shape passed the bow to starboard. Shrigley ran back along the rail, stopping close to the mainmast and leaning downward. A closer sight of it confirmed what he already suspected.

Timber. Huge logs half as long as the *Romulus* and easily large enough to put a hole in her. Even worse, they were fighting an ebb of three knots and making five of their own. At a combined eight knots, a solid contact might easily send the brig-sloop to the bottom.

'Logs!' he announced. 'Bloody great logs!'

'More of them!' came the shout from the crosstrees.

'Mr. Diggs, we will wear sail. I shall stay up here. Mr. Ives, give the order at the helm.'

'Aye, sir!' came the simultaneous replies.

The pair hurried backwards. Shrigley went to a spot halfway between the bow and the mainmast.

'At least now we know what those fishermen were trying to tell us.' Shrigley then raised his voice. 'Lookouts! Where are they?'

'One passing us to larboard now, sir. Too far to hit us.'

'Keep watching. Tell me as soon as you see them.'

As more orders were given, the sailors scaled the rigging and adjusted the sails. The bow turned to the north. Shrigley and Haskell stood still, eyes fixed on the gloom. The sea was not rough enough to create any white horses but Shrigley instead found himself fixating on any patches of dark.

'Another!' came the cry from the crosstrees. 'Larboard. Two points off the bow.'

The *Romulus* was side on to the timber, perhaps a hundred yards away. Though the speed of impact would be less than when she was heading towards it, the damage could still be fatal. Shrigley ran to the larboard rail, stumbling the last few feet. The dark shape loomed out of the darkness.

'Orders, sir?' snapped Haskell.

Shrigley had seen many such situations, usually adjudging the relative positions of ships.

'We're dead in the water,' said Haskell.

'All hands!' bellowed Shrigley. 'Make sail!'

'Captain, it's going to hit us!' said Haskell.

'We're slow but we're moving,' replied Shrigley, glad that they had not turned *through* the wind.

The sloop was already picking up speed. The sailors gave *Romulus* her best chance and the sails hauled her northward, out of the timber's path.

Shrigley lost sight of it in the darkness. Despite his confident tone, he closed his eyes, half-expecting the crash of an impact.

Several shouts did come, the last of them from Diggs, reporting with considerable joy that the log had missed the rudder "by a whisker".

Though greatly relieved, Shrigley allowed himself no time to enjoy the near miss. 'There may be more! We will continue our turn and head back out of the estuary.'

This was executed swiftly. With caution in mind, Shrigley then reduced sail as far as he could to retain steerage and let Romulus go out with the ebb. Though this made collision unlikely, he posted more lookouts and ensured that both helmsman and sailors were as ready as they could be for a swift change of direction.

As the hours passed with no further incidents, he felt more and more confident that they had avoided the danger. Several logs were spotted but *Romulus* stayed clear.

In keeping with his recent conduct, Lieutenant Glanville appeared on deck only when the crisis was over. Ives briefed him on what had occurred. Ignoring his apology, Shrigley instead conducted him to the stern so that they could speak in confidence.

'This matter of gambling. Is it true that you owe money to some aboard ship?'

Even in the gloom, the anger on Glanville's face was apparent. 'Who told you? I'll wring his bloody-'

'Answer the question, lieutenant. Do not dishonour yourself further.'

As if attempting to at least appear honourable, Glanville straightened his back and patted down his hair.

'It is true, sir.'

'How much?'

'Around…twenty pounds.'

'By God. How much *precisely*?'

'Twenty-six pounds. Owed to four men.'

'Some of them crew?'

'Yes.'

Alfred Shrigley had greatly enjoyed receiving his last packet of pay. As a commander, he now earned three times what he had as a lieutenant. Fiscally conservative by nature, he was always in possession of at least fifty pounds when at sea. He also had the advantage of previously witnessing Captain Merriman deal with such a situation.

'Here is what is going to happen. I will pay you and you will pay them at the earliest opportunity. You will compensate me as soon as you can.'

Glanville emitted a long breath. 'Thank you, sir.'

'I wouldn't thank me yet. If you ever gamble on this ship again, you will be struck from her books. That clear?'

'Very clear, sir.'

'Let us say no more about it then. You are now in command. Keep the four lookouts in place until further notice. When the light is sufficient, turn us back into the river – we will have the flood with us by then but we've still a long way to go.'

Chapter Twenty-Three

Allagash Falls

Tellus was evidently no fool. Along with Hokolesqua and Campbell's redcoat guides, the Penobscot tribesman charted a swift course across very difficult ground. They circumvented lakes, waded through streams, ploughed through dense forest, but were rarely deterred from a westward course. Halting overnight after two more days at the aforementioned Portage Lake, the column occupied a pleasant beach where again no shelters were required and the two natives obtained a remarkable haul of fish.

It was morning when the trouble came and Merriman could not possibly have imagined its form. As dawn spilled light onto the lake, he awoke from his slumber to the sound of a scream. Hauling his sword from the scabbard, he pushed his blankets aside and stood.

Not twenty feet away, two shapes were writhing on the sand close to the shore. In the dim light, Merriman could not work out what he was looking at, though one shape was considerable larger than the other. To his right, the sounds of movement. Then he saw a lantern swinging in the dark, held by the brawny arm of Sergeant-Major Fisk. The soldier halted ten feet away and the man beside him halted too. As this second man raised his musket and the pan flashed, Merriman glimpsed the grim visage of Major Campbell. As soon as he fired, Campbell snapped at the men coming behind him.

'Faster, damn you!'

'Help me!' came the cry from the shore.

His eyesight ruined by the flash, Merriman staggered backwards. Someone ran past him, also with musket raised. Three more balls were fired and only then did Merriman begin to realise what had occurred. Now accompanied by Eades, who had been sleeping next to him, he moved forward through the jabbering soldiers who had swiftly congregated. At the front of them were Campbell and Hokolesqua, smoking muskets still in their hands.

'Oh Jesus. Jesus Christ…' This came from a wounded man, who was rolling across the sand, clutching his right shin. Lying on its side next to him was a bear, its dark fur slick with blood in at least three places. The beast actually wasn't that large – perhaps only six feet long.

Hokolesqua picked up a half-eaten fish carcass that had been left on the shore and held it up.

'Did I not tell ask you all to bury this or throw it into the water? Did I not?'

Major Campbell clearly didn't much like this outburst but turned his ire on the injured man. 'You've only yourself to blame if that's yours, Dickens!'

The soldier ignored his superior completely. He was now sitting up, watching as Sergeant-Major Fisk hoisted his trouser leg. The teeth marks were quite visible on his shin and bleeding badly.

'Dear Lord!' he exclaimed before collapsing into the sand.

'Calm yourself, soldier,' said Fisk. 'They'll stitch up.'

Hokolesqua had walked away in disgust but Tellus came forward with a pouch from which he retrieved some herbs. These he put against the wounds.

'Stop it going bad,' he said. 'You lucky,' he added, pointing at the bear. 'Young one. Small.'

'Let's hope his parents aren't around,' said Dwyer, who had joined the crowd at the shore.

Campbell blazed at the men. 'Pack up now! We leave in a quarter-hour.' As he marched towards his horse, he aimed a finger at Hokolesqua. 'And you watch yourself, red man!'

Merriman sighed at this and stepped away.

232

'He has his reasons, sir.'

Sergeant-Major Fisk had moved away to let the soldiers help Dickens. While some of them prodded the lifeless bear, the Sergeant-Major joined Merriman at the shore and looked out at the placid water before continuing.

'The major has been here a very long time. When he was a young lieutenant, he was with a company travelling by boat along the St. Lawrence. They were attacked in the night by some tribe. The major only escaped death by jumping into the water. When he returned at dawn, he found every last man dead. They had been scalped and…worse. Much worse. The major buried every one of them before returning to his regiment alone.'

*

Major Campbell's meagre force soon lost another man. While they were constantly assailed by biting insects upon the low-lying land, a soldier acquired a bite on his neck that became inflamed and made him ill. Like the wounded Dickens, he was barely able to walk and was led along on his horse most of the time.

Though Dwyer was evidently a hardy soul – and the two native men seemed untroubled by the long, taxing journey – Merriman and Eades were also feeling the strain. After ten nights of walking on uneven ground, riding and sleeping on a very thin blanket, Merriman was desperate to hear from the guides that they were approaching Canadian territory. He knew that would mean only a few more days before they were safe in Quebec. Merriman was now spending much of day imagining a warm bath and a comfortable bed. As for Eades, he remained fascinated by the two native men but was struggling with blisters and sores.

Having passed Fish River Lake, where the column replenished its supplies of fresh water, trout and salmon, they pressed onward. Merriman often found himself speaking to Hokolesqua, who seemed glad to have Tellus with him. The pair took it in turns to stay "on guard", constantly scanning the territory around them and occasionally riding away on scouting forays.

'It seems odd that we've spent so many days on American land and barely seen a soul,' said Merriman as they traipsed on through a forest of tall spruce trees.

'These are not easy lands to farm,' said Hokolesqua. 'The waterways make planting and transport very difficult. What is it like for a sailor to be away from the sea for so long?'

Merriman almost mentioned his recent extended stay on land but didn't wish to explain the complications of the *Hercule* affair and ensuing court-martial.

'I've always said I'd rather be a sailor than a soldier.'

'I have seen your cabin, captain – so I understand that.'

'Ha! Don't be fooled by that, Hokolesqua. I started as a midshipman just like Mr. Eades – packed into the officers' cabin like everyone else.'

'I don't think I would like to be on a ship in a battle,' said Hokolesqua. 'On land, at least I have a chance to decide my own fate.'

'You might be right there.'

'What is your home like, captain?'

'Well, there are not so many mountains and lakes. Nor bears! I suppose England is quite a safe place, by comparison.'

'But you are at war. And have been for many years.'

'That is so.'

'Mr. Eades tells me that you have fought all over the world. Africa, South America, the Orient.'

'True.'

They rode on. Behind them, Eades issued the latest in a long series of yawns. Dwyer whistled a tune. At the front of the column, Campbell and Fisk led the redcoats through the trees. Fifty feet ahead of them, Tellus found the fastest way west.

'England has been at war with France for many years, yes, captain?'

'Yes. Though we sailors and soldiers must do our duty for the crown, I hope this new war won't last very long. I am getting old, and I don't want my son to have to fight as long as I have.'

'I don't have a son yet. I would wish the same for him but it is a pointless hope.'

'Why do you say that?'

'We have chosen a side but this is not really our war, captain. Our war is a different one.'

They were to cross the Allagash river just north of the Allagash Falls. Only a few miles short of it, the column camped out below the spruce trees. Tellus and Hokolesqua had caught yet more fish during the day. This was cooked by the soldiers and – as they were nearing their destination – Campbell also allowed the men some wine donated by Monsieur Allard.

After the dinner, they gathered around the fire beneath the tall, dark trees. Sergeant-Major Fisk drank his wine but announced his firm intention to return home at some point just to sample some "proper British ale". Evidently in better spirits himself, he enjoined Merriman and Eades to tell the men some nautical tales.

Despite his youth, Eades was well used to addressing men of all types and so fell easily into several tales involving whales and drinking and St. Elmo's Fire. Merriman still had no desire to relive the *Hercule* affair and so described their most recent engagement with the American frigate. Major Campbell joined the conversation at this point. He had heard of the powerful American ships and was impressed that they had survived their brief encounter with the mighty *President*. Overall, Campbell seemed a dour character to Merriman but the major now pressed him for more anecdotes. The captain had an ample store of such stories and he now reeled out quite a few, including unusual engagements and tales of excessive drinking, which he suspected the men would enjoy. He was close to the end of one story when a cry went up.

Campbell had two pickets out and the man to the north came charging into camp, announcing that someone was approaching. While Campbell kept half the force behind to load their muskets, Fisk had the others affix their bayonets and led them out into the darkness.

'Sir?'

The now familiar Irish brogue of Edwin Dwyer, who was always at the ready.

'Let's stay here for now.'

Dwyer gave Merriman reassurance but not as much as Hokolesqua. The tribesmen exchanged a few words with Tellus. Hokolesqua's hatchet was never far away and neither was Tellus' war club. Once they had their weapons, they departed in opposite directions, soon lost in the gloom.

'What's going on?' This came from the ill man, whose fever showed no sign of improving.

'Nothing,' Eades told him. 'Easy there.'

His musket loaded, Campbell led his five troops away from the camp. Soon, they too were lost amid the densely-packed trees. Merriman listened carefully but – other than the odd snap of a twig and hoot of an owl – everything was now quiet.

'Must have gone quite a way,' said Eades.

Merriman suddenly spun around, some feeling urging him to do so. He belatedly realised it was just the horses moving around.

'I'll watch that side,' said Dwyer, his own musket now loaded too.

Then came some shouts and dark shapes were soon converging on the camp.

'Just us, captain!' announced Major Campbell. Fisk was not far behind and with him were four troops carrying a wounded man.

'One of ours?' said Merriman, unable to see much of the new arrival.

'No. Found stumbling towards us. Saw the fire, it seems. Didn't say much before passing out.'

The injured man was laid out close to the fire. He had an awful wound on the back of his head and had been shot between the shoulders. After both Fisk and Hokolesqua examined him, they agreed that nothing more could be done other than easing his pain.

The incident had eradicated the relaxed calm of the earlier evening and prompted Campbell to put out four guards. In a sign that he at least respected the alertness of the natives, he also asked Hokolesqua and Tellus to take turns in joining his sentries.

Finishing off his allocation of the French wine, Merriman prepared his bed and laid out, eventually drifting off to sleep despite the ramblings and moans of the dying man.

By dawn, the poor fellow had expired. Fisk, who'd sat with him through the night, had ascertained a few details. The dead man had been a Canadian militiaman, part of a company who'd entered Maine much further to the south on a reconnaissance mission. He did not know where they had been attacked or how long he had wandered through the woods. However, the leader that killed the rest of the militiamen had proudly announced himself as a Kentuckian bent on the slaughter of any English or Canadian soldiers that crossed his path. His name was McLintock.

Emerging at last from the great forest of dark spruce and pale birch, the column struck the river in mid-morning. The Allagash was deep, narrow and rapid here and they turned north to find a crossing place. Great undulating slabs of grey rock edged the river, slowing the column's progress. Occasionally, they crossed these outcrops, more often they went around them.

Though none of them seemed surprised, Major Campbell, Hokolesqua and Tellus were concerned that the river was still so high, though they had various crossing points in mind. Merriman felt sure that, even if they found an area shallow enough, they would need many lines across the torrential water.

Allagash was not high like some waterfalls, but a long series of uneven steps, where white water crashed and hissed and broiled, producing a thin white spray. Leading his horse along, Merriman was gazing down at the water, somewhat entranced, when Eades called out to him and pointed up. In contrast to the chaotic torrent below, a golden eagle was gliding serenely above the river.

Merriman smiled as he watched it for a moment, reminded of all the many birds he had spotted back home with his children. He would have to find a picture of a golden eagle to show them.

The path grew even more narrow, with a thirty-foot drop to their left, dense forest to their right. Tellus was taking his turn at the front, meaning that Hokolesqua was towards the rear, close to Merriman. Up ahead, the path inclined sharply and the captain could see Campbell and the other redcoats following Tellus.

At the sound of two sharp whistles, Hokolesqua abruptly halted. Merriman narrowly avoided walking into the rump of his horse. Dropping the reins of his horse, Hokolesqua jumped neatly on to an outcrop of rock and spoke in French to Tellus, who had stopped halfway up the slope.

'What is it?' asked Merriman.

'Not sure,' replied Hokolesqua, brow furrowed. 'Something's-'

A shot rang out from above, startling many of the horses. It was followed by dozens more – and puffs of smoke – from the rocky outcrops at the top of the slope. It was a perfect spot for an ambush.

'Off the trail!' shouted Hokolesqua, grabbing his musket from his horse and running for the trees only yards away.

'Eades, leave your horse!' added the tribesman.

Merriman could hear Campbell yelling orders but the major was fifty feet ahead and he trusted in Hokolesqua.

As well as Eades and Dwyer, two redcoats left their mounts and followed their native ally into the trees. Merriman heard cries from the soldiers still on the trail.

'Captain!' Eades grabbed Merriman's arm and pulled him back a couple of feet.

The reason for this soon became clear as a panicked horse leapt over some undergrowth and charged past them, missing Merriman by inches. He nodded a thank you to Eades.

'We must get around behind them,' Hokolesqua told the four Englishmen and one Irishman. 'Stay low. Load as we move.'

'I'll do them both, sir,' said Dwyer, who had one musket in his hands, one over his shoulder.

This left Merriman having only to load his pistol as they moved. He was so intent on achieving this and keeping his footing that he had little idea of their location until Hokolesqua called a halt. His ears told him that the attackers were firing a lot more than what remained of Campbell's force.

With the flintlock loaded and primed, Merriman crouched down with the others in a patch of fern. They had come around in a wide arc, climbing a shallower incline, now facing back towards the river. Merriman glimpsed more puffs of smoke from the outcrops atop the ridge but saw not a single man. Hokolesqua evidently had.

'Kentuckians. Well hidden.'

'I see no blue or red,' said Eades.

'Militia,' explained one of the redcoats. 'Look more like trappers than soldiers. Damned good idea if you ask me.'

Hokolesqua turned to him.

'Smith, yes?'

'That's me.'

'I suggest you and Hawkins advance, fire when you have a target and keep it up. They'll think you're the danger but we'll try and give them another surprise from the rear.'

'Just us?'

'He knows what he's doing,' snapped Merriman. 'Do it.'

Hawkins and Smith looked at each other, shrugged, then did as they'd been told.

Hokolesqua moved more slowly now, adeptly using the trees for cover, bent over almost double. Merriman was glad that he, Eades and Dwyer had no red upon them and he could well understand the soldiers' concern. Still listening, he detected a change in the sporadic pattern of fire; whatever remained of Campbell's column had at least found cover themselves and were now exchanging shots with the Kentuckians.

Hokolesqua paused and crouched by a thick tree stump, the three sailors very close. Merriman peered over the tribesman's shoulder and caught his first sight of the Kentuckians. At the top of the ridge, two men were lying on dusty ground between rocks, looking down the barrels of their guns. They did indeed look more like trappers than soldiers, with their boots and clothes of hide and hats of black fur.

'Not this way,' said Hokolesqua. 'Not enough cover.'

He ran on until they could see more of the Kentuckians from the rear, visible at the far end of a narrow defile.

'This is better,' he said, dark eyes shining with intent. 'Follow me. When we're close enough, we mark our targets. Then we drop the muskets and attack with blades. We must hit fast and hard, use shock to our advantage.'

'How many are there, do you think?' asked Eades, voice wavering as he finally finished loading his musket.

'To fit in that area – no more than our force.'

Merriman wondered if he said this to ease their nerves. If so, it was ineffectual. Just when he needed to be at his most alert and sharp, he suddenly felt unaccountably weary. This feeling did not leave him as he followed Hokolesqua and Dwyer into the defile, now armed with the musket Dwyer gave him. The pistol he slid into his belt.

They all walked with weapons high, careful not to scrape the surrounding rock. With his view blocked, all Merriman could do was advance and wait for the engagement to begin. Though determined to make his shots count, he knew he'd feel better with his dirk in his hand. This was the weapon he had used most in engagements both at sea and on land.

With the continuing fire and the shouts from both sides, there was plenty of noise to cover them, especially when Smith and Hawkins joined the fight, prompting some of the Kentuckians to alter their aim. Even so, the last few feet before they stopped unfolded with agonising slowness. When they finally reached the far end of the defile, Dwyer moved slightly to the left and Hokolesqua to the right. There were now five Kentuckians in view, including a group of three closer to the river.

Hokolesqua and Dwyer dropped down on one knee and carefully aimed their muskets. Merriman saw what they intended and nodded for Eades to come up beside him. Hokolesqua then pointed to a target for each man. Merriman was to aim at the first man in the second group, who was no more than fifteen feet away.

The four attackers had just settled themselves when one of the nearer men turned away to reload. His head snapped up as he saw the enemy to the rear.

Merriman needed no order to fire. The muskets boomed. The two closer men were both hit in the back. Merriman hit his man on the side but the remaining two were already moving, with weapons loaded and ready. He dropped his musket and reached for his pistol.

Hokolesqua darted forward and snatched a musket from the hands of a dying man. Turning it on the advancing Kentuckian now aiming at him, he fired first and the enemy fell back, clutching at his face. But now all the militiamen realized they were being attacked from the rear. Two more appeared, with guns ready and aimed at the interlopers. Hokolesqua was trying to wrestle another musket from the other victim but this fellow was putting up more of a fight.

'Forward!' shouted Dwyer, clearly aware that if they stayed in the defile, they would die there. He inadvertently knocked Merriman's shoulder and the captain dropped the pistol he had just drawn: it fell and discharged harmlessly into the rock.

Merriman drew his sword and charged after the former soldier. Seeing the big Irishman bearing down on them, with bayonet at the ready, the militiamen seemed to panic. One never got his gun up in time while the other loosed a shot that did no more than pass through the sleeve of Dwyer's shirt. With a great swing of his bayonet, the Irishmen cut one man across the forearm and forced the others to retreat.

Vaguely aware that Eades was not with him, Merriman stayed clear of Dwyer and came in from the right side. Sidestepping a wild swing of an American bayonet, he drove in under the man's arm. Before his wounded foe could strike back, Merriman retracted his blade and chopped across his neck. It was a quick forceless blow, but a fatal cut to the throat didn't require much power. As blood seeped from the wound, the soldier staggered away, his hat falling from his head.

Dwyer swept again at his opponents. One militiaman threw himself backward and narrowly avoided the bayonet. The third man, however, had time to line up his attack, and his bayonet stuck poor Dwyer in the stomach. Before he could drive it in, the big Irishman launched a desperate swing, clubbing the American with the barrel of his gun.

'There!' came the shout of a deep voice.

Yet more Americans were now coming, led by a tall, broad fellow with a wild beard.

Though desperate to help Dwyer, Merriman was now heavily outnumbered and he fled towards the defile. Only then did he realise why neither Hokolesqua nor Eades had come forward: Eades was being led away by Hokolesqua, apparently injured.

Fully expecting to be shot in the back, Merriman reached the defile. He heard musket fire but nothing came anywhere near him. Turning, he saw a welcome flash of red as Major Campbell, Sergeant-Major Fisk and a third man scrambled at last to the top of the slope, forcing the Kentuckians to turn and engage them.

'What happened?' demanded Merriman when he reached the end of the defile.

'A flash,' said Hokolesqua. 'He's blind.'

Merriman now saw that Eades's throat and face had been burned by the detonation of his musket. He was blinking, his mouth hanging open as if still in shock.

'Please. Water.'

'This way,' said Hokolesqua.

He hurried around the edge of the rocky outcrop and they soon reached the path, which ran down the far side of the slope. It was narrower here, with a near-vertical forty-foot drop to the river. There were no more shots from the nearby battle: it was clearly a matter of blades now.

'This way, Silas,' said Merriman. Towards the base of the slope, the path passed a tiny cove, where he could get water for the injured midshipman.

'I shall reload and return,' said Hokolesqua, reaching for a new cartridge as he set off.

'Dwyer – help him if you can.'

'Captain!' Hokolesqua saw the Kentuckian first and was able to dive low.

Confused and panicked, poor Eades somehow got in front of Merriman. The ball struck him in the chest and he was blown onto the ground. Enraged, Merriman raised his sword but the American was already pulling a flintlock from his belt.

As he aimed it, Hokolesqua retrieved his hatchet. He closed with remarkable speed and swung down at the pistol barrel, knocking it out of the Kentuckian's grip. The weapon flew away into the trees.

It was the tall man. He was similar in size to van der Baan, much of his face obscured by a thick beard of fair hair. He had another weapon: an enormous hunting knife that he pulled smoothly from a leather scabbard. He looked his opponent over.

'You Shawnee?'

Hokolesqua was in a fighting crouch, hatchet at the ready. He nodded.

'Good work back there – flanking us. If not for you, every one of these English dogs would have been scalped. Still got time for you though.'

'McLintock, is it?'

'Heard of me have you, Shawnee?'

'My name is Hokolesqua.'

'Ain't heard of *you*,' said the Kentuckian.

'Captain, are you there?'

As the two warriors closed on each other, Merriman went to Eades. Blinking and wheezing, the unfortunate midshipman was lying on his back. His shirt was still smoking where the ball had struck and blood was spreading out from the wound, which had hit centrally upon his breastbone. Merriman had seen enough injuries in his time to know that only immediate surgery could help the lad, and there was no chance of that. Eades' blinking eyes now looked to the sky as his wheezing worsened and air hissed from the wound.

'Hold on there, Silas. I'm with you.'

As he knelt by Eades on the narrow path, dust struck them both, displaced by Hokolesqua.

Despite his size, McLintock was remarkably agile and skilled with his knife, darting and sweeping at Hokolesqua, who also had to consider the sharp drop to his right. Even if he'd been able to leave Eades, Merriman would have been unable to offer much help from his position.

Eades let out an awful cry, his hand going to the wound then recoiling as he touched it.

'Ha!'

McLintock's latest attack almost sent Hokolesqua over the edge. The Kentuckian swept at his head but the tribesman ducked low and rolled back across the path. Back on his feet in an instant, he swung his hatchet at McLintock's stomach, only for the bigger man to somehow grab the weapon's shaft. Turning away, he ripped it from Hokolesqua's grasp, leaving him defenceless.

Merriman looked around for his sword but could not see where it had fallen.

'You first, Shawnee, then them two,' said McLintock, brandishing the huge knife. 'Like all Englishman, they can't fight worth a damn.'

'Aye, well I'm Scottish.'

The left half of his face stained with blood, Major Campbell walked calmly along the path towards them, sword in hand. His sash had been torn from his coat, and one sleeve had a great rent in it. His eyes raged at McLintock.

'You've killed a lot of my men today, Yankee.'

'Likewise, major,' growled the Kentuckian.

Campbell had evidently had enough of talking. He charged at McLintock, sweeping his sword at him, only to find the blow blocked by the big knife. As the blades clanged together, Merriman scrabbled around in the nearby grass, looking for his sword. But he still could not find it.

Showing his usual bravery, Hokolesqua entered the fray without a weapon, closing in on McLintock's back. But the Kentuckian knew he was there and – though trapped on the narrow path – he turned and deterred Hokolesqua with a thrust of his knife.

The man seemed to have a sixth sense for combat because he then used the hatchet to block a thrust from Major Campbell. But Hokolesqua took his chance, darting around McLintock's back and throwing both hands at his knife hand. As he held it high, Campbell drove again at their enemy's throat.

The Kentuckian got his arm up and let his limb take the blow, not making a sound as the sword blade pierced his skin. Bucking his back to get rid of Hokolesqua, he was not ready for the left-handed punch from Campbell that rocked even his giant frame. Hokolesqua let go with one hand in order to smash a fist into McLintock's ear.

The big militiaman was dazed, unable to do much as Campbell swept two-handed at his stomach. As the wound opened up, blood splattered the dusty ground between the Kentuckian's feet.

'Damn,' growled McLintock. 'Damn you all.'

Neither the soldier nor the tribesman had to do anything more. The militiaman staggered forward and back, holding his ruined stomach, fingers covered in blood.

He tripped over his own feet and pitched over the edge of the path, smashing into the rocks before rolling into the water. Merriman saw the great, limp body borne away by the Allagash.

He turned back to Silas Eades. The midshipman's eyes had at last closed. Merriman took his hand again; it was already turning cold.

Chapter Twenty-Four

A Shallow Grave

Merriman had never seen so deadly a skirmish. Of the redcoat soldiers, only three were still alive, including Private Hawkins, who'd joined the flanking manoeuvre that had helped turn the course of the battle. He was the most seriously wounded of the three and had suffered a nasty wound to his thigh. Sergeant-Major Fisk had downed two militiamen before being shot directly in the heart. Even the two ailing redcoats had joined the battle and lost their lives. The brave Dwyer had also succumbed to his injuries, as had Tellus.

As for the Kentuckians, eight had been killed and a group of perhaps five or six had fled.

The dead were now placed in a line close to the defile, including Midshipman Eades. Major Campbell had instructed one of his remaining men to gather useful items and personal effects from the bodies. The other two were out in the woods, attempting to track down more horses. Merriman was very surprised that four mounts had already returned.

Major Campbell now stood with one hand resting on the hilt of his sword, the tip planted in the ground. After the killing of McLintock, he had made his way alone down to the cove to wash the blood from his face. His gaze moved from one dead man to the next until they alighted on Silas Eades.

'Sorry, captain. We walked straight into that ambush.'

'Not at all, major. You and your men fought bravely.'

'They covered their movements very well,' said Hokolesqua.

Merriman said nothing but he had not taken his eyes off Eades. He knew better than most how mistakes were seen more clearly when looking back but it now seemed madness to have brought the midshipman along. He had met the boy's parents once. They had seemed so proud of the lad.

It would be a very difficult letter to write. And of course they would not know for weeks. He always found it rather sickening to be in possession of that knowledge; that power.

Major Campbell examined his torn cuff for a moment before pulling the whole thing off. He then used it to clean his sword and replaced the blade in the black scabbard. He then marched up to Hokolesqua and offered his hand.

'Quick thinking, Hokolesqua. Without your intervention, it would have been even worse.'

'I am only sorry I did not detect them. I thank you for coming to my aid, Major Campbell. I've seldom faced a warrior such as that man. It seems the reputation of the Kentuckians is well deserved.'

One of the redcoats came around the side of the defile, leading two more horses.

'Found these too, sir.'

'Good.'

'Hawkins is asking about the enemy dead, sir. Should we gather them, bury them?'

Campbell frowned at the man. 'Have you seen the state of us, soldier? We must make for the border and hope to God we few make it. We will bury our dead and that is all. The enemy stay where they lay.'

Every man present was evidently exhausted and yet the grave had to be dug. Hokolesqua was desperately concerned about the Kentuckians who had escaped returning with reinforcements. Having brought Tellus' body to join the others, he set off on his horse to conduct a circular patrol.

There was no time for the privilege of rank. In an enervating late afternoon heat, Merriman and Campbell laboured with the three remaining redcoats. They at least had their shovels but with so many to bury, the shallow grave had to be large.

By the time they finished, the sun was low, the trees where they worked cloaked by gloom. Eades's body was the last to go in. Merriman had already taken some effects from his coat, including a pocket watch and a letter from his mother.

He found that he could not watch as the soil was shovelled back on to the row of bodies. It seemed very harsh compared to the naval way but he supposed it wasn't so different. As he stood facing the river, the falls still rumbling away, Hokolesqua returned towing two horses.

'Ah, well done,' said Merriman. One was his mount and both saddlebags were still attached.

While the three redcoats finished the grave, Major Campbell spent his time gathering muskets, powder and shot. He handed a loaded weapon to each of his soldiers before they mounted up. Finally, he put his own red coat on again. Hawkins handed him his shako but the major stuffed it straight into a saddlebag.

Campbell turned to Hokolesqua. 'What do you think?'

'Would you agree that we are too tired to attempt a crossing tonight, even if we could reach one?'

'Agreed.'

'Then my suggestion is that we stay clear of the river for now – it makes us too easy to find. But we can continue north, then cut west and find somewhere tomorrow. We should be back in New Brunswick by nightfall.'

'By God I hope so,' said Campbell, wearily hauling himself up on to the horse.

As it turned out, they needed to travel only three miles downstream before finding a crossing point. Hokolesqua seemed surprised when they came upon it, suggesting to Merriman that even the calm, tough tribesman had been affected by the brutal battle at the Falls.

This stretch of river was still fast-moving but – crucially – it was much wider and appeared to be no more than four or five feet deep. Better still, there was an islet in the middle that would make the crossing easier. With barely an hour of daylight left, Hokolesqua presented his companions with a choice. They could risk a swift crossing or remain on the near bank (still not far from the site of the battle) and make a more careful attempt the following morning.

Merriman's body wanted nothing more than to lie down and sleep. His mind, however, wanted to get as far from the battle – and the enemy – as possible. Major Campbell concurred and they were soon leading their horses into the water. Hokolesqua's pony seemed used to such travails and the pair reached the islet with ease. Campbell offered to bring up the rear and so the first of the redcoats crossed next.

This soldier was a short fellow named Illingworth. He advanced slowly, his horse following obediently, until the water was close to his shoulder. With the water splashing his face, progress slowed until he was barely moving at all.

'Push on, man!' shouted Campbell.

'The water is strong, sir!' replied the infantryman.

His uncertainty seemed to spread to his mount, which began to resist. Hokolesqua entered the water once more. He took the horse's reins but waited long enough for Illingworth to get moving again. When the soldier reached the islet, he bent over and vomited.

The next to cross was a Private Dawson. Though he had sustained several nasty cuts to his forearms, he removed his bandages, placed them on his saddle to keep them dry, and set off across the river. Despite the protests of his horse, Dawson kept moving, even when assailed by several clumps of branches floating along.

'Damned fine soldier,' said Major Campbell as he stood and observed with Merriman. 'Never a word of complaint.'

Despite his injury, Private Hawkins also got across, though he required help from his compatriots on the far side.

Next came the turn of the captain and, though he had his height on his side, Merriman was surprised by the force of the water, which threatened to take his legs away with every step. He had never felt his age so much in those moments and was grateful – if mildly ashamed – that Hokolesqua felt obliged to come and help him.

Campbell needed no assistance and the five were soon reunited. The undergrowth at the island's centre was so thick that they had to go around the sandy shore. Merriman and Illingworth requested a few minutes to gather their strength, during which time Hokolesqua took three of the horses across. Though the water was no stronger or deeper on this side, Merriman found himself struggling and he again required assistance, this time to negotiate the muddy ground on the far bank.

He staggered to a log and sat there, not entirely sure he would ever get up again. Every part of his body ached and his mind seemed to be blanketed under a black fog.

'Come, captain,' said Hokolesqua, offering his hand. 'We shall get you on your saddle and I promise to find us a good place for the night before dusk.'

Merriman could not refuse the man and so was soon on his feet, and then on his horse.

*

Not for the first time, Hokolesqua was true to his word. He guided the small party directly west, rounding several bogs, before finding a pleasant leafy glade, well-hidden but with sufficient space for the horses. On several occasions, Merriman noted the others looking around for their compatriots, as if unable to believe that over half their number were gone. No fire was needed for warmth, nor did they wish to offer any clue to their location.

Private Dawson showed good sense, offering to stand sentry and telling Hokolesqua to get some much-needed rest. The tribesman settled down and went to sleep immediately, one hand on his musket.

Major Campbell was using their only lantern to sort through their ammunition and shot, having told Illingworth and Hawkins to also rest.

'Some help, major?' asked Merriman, though he'd barely the energy to stand.

'No, captain. You should rest too.'

'I am very sorry about your men.'

'Not the first I've lost; won't be the last.'

Merriman believed the losses had affected him more than that but the tough Scot evidently wasn't going to say so.

'Hope he still has that treaty,' added Campbell.

'He has it,' said Merriman, who had double-checked with Hokolesqua only a few minutes earlier.

Campbell didn't look up as he continued to collect cartridges.

'It must reach Tecumseh. It *must*. Or all this was for naught.'

Grateful to still have his blankets and spare clothing with him, Merriman lay down and swiftly fell asleep himself.

Later, he heard voices and woke. He sat up but was relieved to be told by Campbell that it was merely Hokolesqua taking over guard duties. When he tried to go back to sleep, Merriman could think only of the battle. And when he ceased thinking of that, it was Silas Eades and the shallow grave: clumps of dark soil falling on his pale, peaceful face.

*

They rose at dawn and struck west once more. It was obvious to all that Hokolesqua was not quite sure of his bearings until they reached a rocky ridge with a fine view to the south and west. They spied a cluster of smoking fires many miles to the south and Campbell agreed that this could well be an American force of some size. This sight spurred them on and – once they'd found a safe path down from the ridge – they eventually came across an overgrown but clear trail that ran south-west, which suited their purposes. Stopping only to rest the horses and eat a little, the weary party pressed on.

Merriman found himself possessed by a profound feeling of dread. The near-miraculous Atlantic crossing and delivery of Hokolesqua and the treaty to Upper Canada had immediately given way to disaster. Brook had been killed. This second effort had led them to a brutal confrontation with the Kentuckians. And even though Quebec was no more than two or three days away, Merriman felt convinced that some further disastrous turn would befall them.

The events of late afternoon did little to improve his mood. Hokolesqua came across a set of footprints that he seemed to think were very recent. And when he found a cartridge paper and a discarded apple core nearby, it seemed clear that soldiers of some variety were in the area.

An hour before dusk, they reached a deserted log cabin that been emptied of anything of value. All were disappointed because even Hokolesqua was unsure if they were in Maine or New Brunswick.

Yet the discovery of the cabin did help them. A barely discernible trail led north from it and – half a mile later – emerged onto one side of a wheatfield. On the other side of the field was a much larger cabin and the glow of light.

Those inside alerted by barking dogs, the cabin door opened as the six men approached, towing their horses. Campbell boldly took the lead, walking with their lantern and his spare hand raised.

At the door, a large, round-faced woman perused the new arrival before stepping aside. Three soldiers came outside. All were holding muskets and dressed in a grey uniform that Merriman had not seen before.

'Hello,' said Campbell. 'English?'

'French, Monsieur,' said the oldest of the three soldiers. 'But I see that you are a redcoat.'

'I am. And you?'

'Corporal La Sarre-Smith of the Voltiguers Militia under Lieutenant Colonel Charles de Salaberry.'

'Voltiguers? Never heard of such a unit.'

'We were formed only last week.'

'Salaberry I do know – he fought with the 44th Regiment. Tell me – are we in New Brunswick?'

'You are, sir. Yes.'

The soldiers turned to each other and grinned.

'Might I ask what you're doing here, corporal?'

'Certainly. Madame Laurier here has just cooked us a fine dinner. Most welcome after a day on patrol. We were assigned to this area to watch for American incursions.'

'I see. We have come from Saint John and require swift passage to Quebec. How far is it from here?'

'No more than thirty miles.'

'Can you guide us?'

'No but I will find you a guide.'

'My thanks.'

At that Campbell's shoulders sagged and his head dropped. He gave the lantern to Merriman and walked away alone, into the darkness.

The militiaman looked the captain over. 'You have seen action, I think.'

'Yes. Yes, we have.'

Chapter Twenty-Five

Two Leaders

Viewed from the south bank of the Saint Lawrence River, Quebec glittered in the July sunshine. Merriman was at first confused about what he was looking at, before being told that many roofs in the city were covered with tin, to avoid the fires that had previously ripped through the predominantly wooden housing.

It had taken the French militiamen some time to find a guide for the soldiers but they'd eventually hired a shepherd who got them close to the city for a fee of one pound. The remaining horses were now in very poor shape and were placed in the first stables they came to on the south side. Placing their essentials inside a single saddlebag each, they hurried onwards, Merriman taking a moment to affectionately pat the mount that had served him well. He, Hokolesqua and the four soldiers crossed the Saint Lawrence in a flat-bottomed ferry.

Major Campbell knew Quebec quite well and led the way. The main part of the city was built on a bluff topped by stone walls. Many more defensive earthworks were under construction with hundreds of labourers toiling in the summer sun. Merriman was relieved to see no less than five separate columns of marching soldiers. Campbell saluted the officers leading them but was evidently in no mood to tarry.

When they reached the steep road that led to the top of the bluff, he swiftly commandeered a nearby horse and cart and ordered the driver to take them up. When the man protested, Campbell raised a fist and swore at him, leading the local to cower and then grab a box so that the six men might step up into his cart more easily.

As the cart rumbled up the steep street, Merriman saw Hokolesqua place his hand inside his coat for perhaps the tenth time since they'd crossed the river. Like Campbell, like the soldiers, like Merriman himself, he'd spoken very little since the battle at the falls. Merriman supposed that they were occupied by thoughts of it, trying to recover in their own way.

As they wearily disembarked from the cart, the captain threw a shilling to the driver. They had stopped beside a high, barred gate in the middle of a high stone wall. The building beyond was largely obscured by tall trees. Two redcoats were on duty behind the gate. Before Major Campbell could even announce himself, a young lieutenant appeared.

'Good day, sir. Lieutenant Barings, 41st Regiment of Foot.'

Merriman noted him taking them in. All six of them had torn, muddy, bloodstained clothing. Hokolesqua was the only clean shaven one among them.

'Campbell, 104th.' The major gestured to the men either side of him. 'Captain Sir James Merriman of the HMS…the…'

'HMS *Mercury*.'

'Yes. And Hokolesqua – cousin of Tecumseh. Is he in Quebec?'

'No,' said Lieutenant Barings, causing the heads of all six men to drop. 'He left this morning for Montreal. I take it this is an urgent matter?'

'What time this morning?' asked Hokolesqua.

'At dawn, I believe.'

'By horse?'

'Yes, with his party.'

'I can catch him,' said Hokolesqua. 'I know which route he will take. Lieutenant, I need a horse.'

Merriman reached out and grabbed his arm. 'Hokolesqua, listen to me. They can send someone else. You are as exhausted as the rest of us.'

'No!' The moment of anger was brief. 'No, captain. I know the route. I will be quicker. Please, Lieutenant.'

Barings shifted his gaze to Major Campbell, who swiftly delivered his verdict:

'This fellow is an exceptional rider and possesses reserves of endurance the like of which I've never seen. Get him the finest horse you have.'

Merriman knew better than to waste more time trying to persuade Hokolesqua but he urged him to be careful, even though he was now in friendly territory. The tribesman was about to mount up when he reached inside his coat and handed Merriman the leather wallet containing the treaty. 'Captain, there's no sense me taking it. The governor-general must see it too. It's safer here.'

Merriman reckoned he had never held an object of such importance and he pledged to Hokolesqua that he would hand it over personally. As the tribesman was escorted to a nearby army stable by one of the guards, Lieutenant Barings led the four soldiers and one sailor inside.

The governor-general's residence was a chateau in the French style, a grand building with towers at each corner, topped by green tiles. Barings collared a footman and sent him to fetch one the governor-general's private secretaries. This fellow met them at a side door, and seemed rather confused by the sight that greeted him.

Merriman took the lead, introducing himself and showing the private secretary the treaty. As the administrator examined the document, Campbell and the soldiers also took a look.

'That the king's signature, sir?' asked Private Hawkins.
'It is,' said Merriman.
'Remarkable,' said the secretary. 'Shall I take it?'
'I promised to deliver it personally.'
'As you wish. I'm afraid Governor-General Prevost is in a meeting with the legislative council. He won't be available for at least an hour. Lieutenant, might I suggest that you take the…new arrivals to the guards' quarters where they can refresh themselves.'

Though desperate for their costly mission to be resolved, Merriman was grateful for this moment of respite. The bathhouse of the guards' quarter was extremely well-appointed. Hot water was provided for all five men to bathe and they also took the opportunity to shave. Dirty clothes were handed over for cleaning and some spares given to two of the soldiers, who had lost their gear.

Outside the guards' quarters was a well-shaded bench where Merriman later sat, barefoot and in breeches and shirt. It was a remarkably peaceful spot and he soon dozed off.

When he awoke, Major Campbell was beside him. The army officer had laid his tunic over the end of the bench and was now polishing the brass. Merriman saw that he had done a remarkable job of cleaning up the red and white.

'Apologies if I woke you, captain. When I get to bed tonight, I do not plan to rise for two days.'

'Not at all, major. I feel the same. Rather hungry too.'

Neither of them spoke for a while. Merriman watched two women emerge from the chateau and set about plucking flowers from a well-maintained bed.

'I have a second mission,' said Campbell. 'I am not often in Quebec these days. This is a rare chance to plead the case of the New Brunswick Regiment. We need muskets, cannon and provisions. If the governor-general doesn't heed me, I shall work my way down the chain. And then I have some letters to write.'

'I too. You have some standard phrases, I suppose?'

'King and country and all that. A line or two of a more personal nature usually suffices. I've a feeling I'll be writing many more in the coming months.' Campbell ceased his work for a moment, the oily cloth in his hand. 'Still, I daresay you've written hundreds.'

'I daresay I have.'

They both looked up as Lieutenant Barings marched out of the guards' quarters.

'Captain Merriman, sir, please follow me.'

Governor-General George Prevost was a ruddy-faced fellow with wavy brown hair and thick sideburns. At the conclusion of his meeting, he had sent for Merriman and the pair met in the gardens at the rear of the chateau. Merriman had his spare uniform on but felt obliged to apologise for the state of it, and indeed his shoes.

'Not at all, captain. I am simply grateful that you reached Quebec. You had done your duty by reaching Saint John with such alacrity; this added effort is greatly appreciated.'

This seemed the moment to hand over the treaty. Prevost took it and examined it.

'I was present when Tecumseh signed this. Seems like years ago. Do you know the latest on the king?'

'There are so many rumours, sir. I do not know the truth of it. They say he never leaves Windsor Castle now and has contact with only a few. Governor, how are relations with Tecumseh?'

Still holding the treaty, Prevost began walking and gave a grim smile. 'Well, they will be considerably easier now. Tecumseh is a very stubborn fellow and, despite my entreaties, he would not commit to the alliance without seeing the king's signature. I'm afraid we had both begun to assume that the treaty had not arrived on these shores or had since been lost. We departed on reasonable terms but he would offer no firm commitment. As you can imagine, I was therefore most relieved to hear of your arrival. What can you tell me about his cousin? I've not met the fellow.'

'Hokolesqua is very capable. We would not have reached Quebec without him. Great credit must also go to Major Campbell. I'm afraid to say he lost more than half his men.'

'I was told. The Kentuckians. Colonel Blackstock of the 41st has also been informed. He will wish to discuss intelligence with Major Campbell.'

'I will write a full account. The major demonstrated great bravery.'

'It sounds as if you feel a decoration is due?'

'That will be up to his superiors.'

'Quite so. You know Tecumseh has a chief's medal. Silver. Another symbol of our alliance. They were commissioned under His Majesty some years ago. He hasn't worn it for some time.'

As they halted by a blooming red rose bush, another of the governor's personal secretaries appeared.

'Sir, Monsieur Sella would like to reconvene regarding points nine and eleven.'

Prevost sighed. 'There are times, captain, when I miss the simplicities of military command. Politics is a most complex business. My predecessors did not even allow a French contingent on the Legislative Council. In doing so, I seem to have created a rod for my own back. Still, we need them as much we need the Indians.'

Once the governor left, Merriman returned to the guards' quarters. Here he was met by Lieutenant Barings, who informed him that Major Campbell was now deep in discussion with two local officers. Barings then had a corporal named Seaton escort him to the second floor. Here, two rooms had been put aside for the new arrivals: one for the men, one for Merriman and Campbell.

In the first room, Hawkins, Illingworth and Dawson were sound asleep, all with bandaged wounds. Merriman moved on to the second room. He closed the door, disrobed and laid down.

*

Later that evening, he was awoken by Major Campbell. At first, he thought the major had just come in. He then realised that Campbell had slept for many hours like himself and was now getting up and dressing for dinner. Lieutenant Barings had invited them to eat with the officers stationed at the chateau.

Merriman's hunger trumped his fatigue and he joined Campbell and three others in the mess. The food was quite excellent and the major was eating heartily, and drinking wine at a rate that would put any sailor to shame. Merriman thought of Shrigley, who'd always been able to consume large amounts, despite his slender frame. Merriman was not in the mood.

Thanking his hosts and feeling somewhat melancholic, he went for a walk.

Having wandered down into the town, he made his way to the port. Once at the wharves, he encountered a group of jovial merchant officers smoking cigars and engaged them in conversation. There was no report of *HMS Romulus* and he began to consider what he would do if – for some reason – Shrigley did not arrive. The thought of returning to Saint John across land was a terrible one. He also learned that securing passage via the sea route might be a long, complicated affair. Merriman was struck by guilt once more: stranding himself in Quebec and leaving *Mercury* without her captain now seemed somewhat less than a masterstroke.

As he trudged back up the hill towards the chateau, he was trailed by a couple of young lads. Seeing his uniform, they threw dozens of questions at him: about ships and sailing and cannons and the French navy and the American navy. Merriman enjoyed the distraction and gave them a penny each at the chateau gate.

Dawn brought most welcome news: the return to Quebec of Tecumseh and Hokolesqua. Merriman did not see them until both he and Major Campbell were summoned to a meeting in the chateau's state room at ten o'clock.

Both spent yet more time working on their uniforms before being escorted to their destination on the second floor by Lieutenant Barings. They entered to find Governor-General Prevost accompanied by two private secretaries and Major-General Henry Procter, commander of the 41st Regiment. Merriman and Campbell were introduced to Procter and then followed Prevost to a table beside a large window.

Standing over the treaty beside Hokolesqua was Tecumseh. Tall and slender, with a prominent, rather noble nose, the chief wore a fine blue jacket and was clutching a red hat. With his other hand, he greeted the two officers. He was also wearing the silver chief's medal around his neck, which Merriman imagined Prevost had been relieved to see.

Tecumseh was one of those fellows who possessed a certain charismatic presence and he spoke deliberately and with great earnestness. 'Captain Merriman, Major Campbell, my cousin tells me that we owe you a great debt.'

'Simply following orders,' said Campbell.

'An honour to deliver this document,' replied Merriman. 'It is my great pleasure to meet you at last.'

Tecumseh turned his gaze to the treaty. 'It has travelled so very far.'

Hokolesqua spoke up. 'The captain's ship crossed the ocean with tremendous speed.'

'Three thousand miles of water,' said Tecumseh. 'I cannot even imagine it.'

'We were fortunate.'

The chief now addressed Prevost and Procter, who had joined them at the table. 'When I left yesterday, I did not hold out much hope. But with this, I can go to our brothers the Ottawa, the Wyandot, the Delaware, the Sauk, the Meskwaki, and the Ojibe. All can now be certain of British support and offer their support in return.'

Tecumseh and Prevost moved to another large table and a map showing the entirety of Upper Canada. Major Campbell was not slow to take his opportunity to engage Major-General Procter on the subject of weaponry and supplies for New Brunswick.

Hokolesqua moved to the window and, after a time, glanced back at Merriman. 'Captain, I do not know much about ships but that one bears a red ensign like your own. Could it be your friend?'

Merriman hurried to the window and saw the British brig-sloop easing its way along the Saint Lawrence, ghosting along under only her topsails. There was, to his knowledge, no other vessel of that size anywhere near Quebec.

'I do believe that is HMS *Romulus*. Yes, that's her.'

For the first time in what seemed many, many days, Merriman felt himself smile. He not only looked forward to seeing Alfred Shrigley, John Webster and the crew; he would soon be back aboard a ship of His Majesty's Navy, and back on the water once more.

THE END

Author Biography

Robin Burnage

Robin Burnage continues the adventures with fresh eyes on the horizon!

He has taken over the helm of The Merriman Chronicles, a naval adventure series begun by his late father, Roger Burnage, and is determined to see it through to the end.

Before turning to writing, Robin worked in financial sales, horticultural wholesale and then property management, but was always more drawn to boats than boardrooms. In 2012, he sold up, bought a yacht, and spent five years sailing full-time. That was followed by a long road trip through Europe in a battered old Land Rover, and later a motorhome.

These days, he's back on dry land in Wales, looking out over the Irish Sea—and quietly plotting the next leg of Merriman's journey.

A short note about reviews:

In short – if you enjoyed the book, please let others know!

Book reviews truly are the lifeblood of independent publishing. Whether it's a few simple words, a full paragraph or more, your review helps new readers discover The Merriman Chronicles and keeps the series alive.

Ratings matter too, but it's reviews - even the briefest ones—that truly make a difference to authors.

Thank you for your support and helping the stories reach a new audience.

For more background information, book details and announcements of upcoming novels, check the website at:

www.merriman-chronicles.com

You can also follow us on social media:-

https://twitter.com/Merriman1792

https://www.facebook.com/MerrimanChronicles

https://www.instagram.com/merriman1792/

Follow the Author on Amazon

Desktop, Mobile & Tablet:

Search for the author, click the author's name on any of the book pages to jump to the Amazon author page, click the follow button at the bottom.